T0342459

A Research Agenda for Event Impacts

Elgar Research Agendas outline the future of research in a given area. Leading scholars are given the space to explore their subject in provocative ways, and map out the potential directions of travel. They are relevant but also visionary.

Forward-looking and innovative, Elgar Research Agendas are an essential resource for PhD students, scholars and anybody who wants to be at the forefront of research.

Titles in the series include:

A Research Agenda for International Business and Management
Edited by Ödül Bozkurt and Mike Geppert

A Research Agenda for Political Demography
Edited by Jennifer D. Sciubba

A Research Agenda for Heritage Planning
Perspectives from Europe
Edited by Eva Stegmeijer and Loes Veldpaus

A Research Agenda for Workplace Stress and Wellbeing
Edited by E. Kevin Kelloway and Sir Cary Cooper

A Research Agenda for Social Innovation
Edited by Jürgen Howaldt Christoph Kaletka and Antonius Schröder

A Research Agenda for Multi-Level Governance
Edited by Arthur Benz, Jörg Broschek and Markus Lederer

A Research Agenda for Space Policy
Edited by Kai-Uwe Schrogl, Christina Giannopapa and Ntorina Antoni

A Research Agenda for Event Impacts
Edited by Nicholas Wise and Kelly Maguire

A Research Agenda for Event Impacts

Edited by

NICHOLAS WISE

Assistant Professor of Tourism Planning and Development, School of Community Resources and Development, Arizona State University, USA

KELLY MAGUIRE

Lecturer in Tourism Management, Department of Hospitality, Tourism and Leisure, Technological University of the Shannon: Midlands Midwest, Ireland

Elgar Research Agendas

Edward Elgar PUBLISHING

Cheltenham, UK • Northampton, MA, USA

Published by
Edward Elgar Publishing Limited
The Lypiatts
15 Lansdown Road
Cheltenham
Glos GL50 2JA
UK

Edward Elgar Publishing, Inc.
William Pratt House
9 Dewey Court
Northampton
Massachusetts 01060
USA

Paperback edition 2023

A catalogue record for this book
is available from the British Library

Library of Congress Control Number: 2021943469

This book is available electronically in the **Elgar**online
Geography, Planning and Tourism subject collection
http://dx.doi.org/10.4337/9781839109256

ISBN 978 1 83910 924 9 (cased)
ISBN 978 1 83910 925 6 (eBook)
ISBN 978 1 0353 2209 1 (paperback)

Printed and bound by CPI Group (UK) Ltd, Croydon, CR0 4YY

Contents

Figures

Tables

Contributors

Lucia Aquilino is a passionate researcher in tourism and events. She has worked for British universities as a lecturer in tourism and event management. She is now focusing her research efforts on Italian tourism and event activities and how these contribute to develop communities and reshape the image of rural areas.

Alexander Bond is Senior Lecturer in Sport Management at Leeds Beckett University's Carnegie School of Sport. Alex's research focuses on economic sociology, how social and economic networks structure society, inequalities and the economics of professional sport. He leads the Management and Governance Theme for the Research Centre of Social Justice in Sport and Society at Leeds Beckett University and serves as Associate Editor of the *Managing Sport and Leisure* journal.

Waldemar Cudny is a geographer, working as Associate Professor at the University of Lodz, Faculty of Geographical Sciences, Poland. He specializes in event studies, post-socialist cities and car tourism. He is the author of over 70 publications including articles and several books, among others about city branding, festivalization and tourism.

Jelena Đurkin Badurina is Assistant Professor in the Faculty of Tourism and Hospitality Management at the University of Rijeka. Her current research focuses on social enterprises, cooperatives, community entrepreneurship and community-based tourism. She conducts interdisciplinary focused research and has authored and co-authored over 20 papers focusing on Croatia and the greater region surrounding Rijeka, Croatia.

Larry Dwyer publishes widely in the areas of tourism economics, management, policy and planning. Larry is a Fellow and past president of the International Academy for Study of Tourism. He is past president of the International

Association for Tourism Economics, and currently serves on its International Advisory Board.

Angela Fileno da Silva earned a PhD in history from the University of São Paulo and also has a degree in tourism from Unibero. Angela currently works as a researcher at Instituto Çarê and has taught in private universities in São Paulo since 2002. Recent research and publications have focused on Afro-Brazilian festivals, Brazilians in Nigeria and Caiçaras' traditions.

Rafaela Neiva Ganga is Senior Research Fellow and Guest Senior Lecturer in Evaluation at Liverpool John Moores University, researching the value of culture at an individual level (health and wellbeing) and at a societal level (participation and culture-led regeneration). From February 2020, Rafaela Nieva Ganga has led the commissioned evaluation of the Liverpool Borough of Culture programme, building upon her work as lead researcher on the Impacts 18 participation and engagement study.

Susanne Gellweiler is Professor for International Events Management at the Dresden School of Management, part of SHR Berlin University of Applied Sciences. Susanne completed her PhD at Bournemouth University (2011) and worked at Liverpool John Moores University before returning to Germany in 2018. Her research in events focuses on impacts, volunteering, experiences and stakeholder management.

Tara Fitzgerald completed her PhD at the University of KwaZulu-Natal, Durban, South Africa, which focused on the role of mega-projects in displacing the urban poor and their livelihood challenges after forcibly relocating in the periphery. Her research interests include urban challenges, human rights, displacement and social justice.

Jeeyeon Jeannie Hahm is Associate Professor at the Rosen College of Hospitality Management at the University of Central Florida. She teaches various undergraduate and graduate courses in event management. Her research areas include destination image, mega-events, consumer behaviour in tourism and events and film-induced tourism.

Takamitsu Jimura is Programme Manager for the MSc in International Tourism Management and Senior Lecturer in Tourism at Liverpool John Moores University. His research interests include tourism and local communities at World Heritage sites, cultural heritage and tourism in Japan, tourism and destination marketing and sustainability management in tourism and heritage.

Jada Lindblom recently completed a PhD in community resources and development from Arizona State University. She is a community and economic development field specialist with the University of New Hampshire Cooperative Extension and an adjunct instructor of tourism and events management at New York University's School of Professional Studies.

Landy Di Lu is Assistant Professor in the School of Kinesiology at University of Minnesota – Twin Cities. Her research focuses on examining institutional and organizational change in sport and the governance of interorganizational relationships and collaboration in event planning and management.

Jan Andre Lee Ludvigsen is Senior Lecturer in the School of Humanities and Social Science at Liverpool John Moores University. His main research interests are located within the sociology of sports and include sport mega-events, mega-event security governance and football fandom.

Kelly Maguire is Lecturer in Tourism Management at the Technological University of the Shannon: Midlands Midwest. She previously held the position of Senior Lecturer in International Tourism Management and Events Management at Liverpool John Moores University. Her research interests include sustainable planning for events, tourism and event impacts and Local Authority planning.

Brij Maharaj is Professor at the University of KwaZulu-Natal, Durban, South Africa. He is an urban political geographer who has received widespread recognition for his work which focuses on displacement, human rights, segregation, economic development and the socio-economic impacts of mega-events.

Judith Mair is Discipline Leader of the Tourism Discipline Group at the UQ Business School, University of Queensland, Australia. Her research interests include the impacts of tourism and events on community and society, and consumer behaviour in tourism and events. She is the author of over 50 academic papers in international peer-reviewed journals and four books, and is the editor of *The Routledge Handbook of Festivals*.

Laura Misener is Professor in the School of Kinesiology at Western University, Canada. Her research focuses on how sport and events can be used as instruments of social change, with an emphasis on how sport for persons with a disability can positively impact community accessibility and social inclusion.

Daniel Parnell is Associate Professor in Sport Business at the University of Liverpool Management School. Dan's research interests lie in business management, policy and social and economic networks in sport. He serves as Editor-in-Chief of the journal *Managing Sport and Leisure* and is the co-founder of The Football Collective, a global network of football scholars. He is also a co-editor of the book series Critical Research in Football. On top of this, Dan maintains extensive links within professional sport clubs, is trustee of Sport Leaders UK and is the chief executive officer of the Association of Sporting Directors.

Erin Pearson is a PhD student in the School of Kinesiology at Western University, Canada. Her research interests include sport events and their impacts, disability, access and inclusion in event spaces, knowledge management and transfer processes for events, and media representation of athletes.

Marko Perić is Associate Professor in Strategic Management, Project Management, and Sport Management in Tourism in the Faculty of Tourism and Hospitality Management at the University of Rijeka. His recent research has been published in *Small Business Economics*, *Tourism Management Perspectives*, *Local Economy*, *Event Management*, *The Service Industries Journal* and *Journal of Sport and Tourism*.

Enqing Tian is Associate Professor at East China Normal University. His scholarly interests include the social issues in sport and physical education and sports geography with an emphasis on sense of place. His recent publications appear in *International Review for the Sociology of Sport*, *Sport in Society* and *International Journal of the History of Sport*.

Flávia Ulian earned a PhD in geography from the University of São Paulo. Currently Professor and Coordinator of the Land Transport Technology Course at FATEC TATUAPÉ, Tatuapé Technology College, São Paulo, Brazil, Flavia has also taught tourism courses and researches and publishes on accessibility, environmental impacts and urban mobility.

Kylie Wasser completed her PhD in 2019 with a focus on organizational governance and event legacy. Kylie has lectured at Western University, Australia and presented her research at international conferences. Her research interests include sport policy, globalization, sport for development, organizational studies and using a critical lens to dissect sport and recreation.

Nicholas Wise is Assistant Professor, School of Community Resources and Development, Arizona State University. He has recently published work on events and community/social impacts in *Event Management*, *International Journal of Contemporary Hospitality Management*, *Journal of Community*

Psychology and *International Journal of Events and Festival Management,* and has co-edited nine books.

Preface

The events industry has seen rapid growth in the past few decades and while the industry has a promising future, disruptions caused by the Covid-19 pandemic have challenged those in the industry and those researching events to rethink future directions. Types, size and scale of events and the setting or venue for which they are held are vast, with creativity as a key initiative and the use of new technologies an important driving force. Planning, producing and hosting events are important and strategic for destinations, as they can help with place branding and image, lead to increased opportunities and contribute new opportunities locally for communities. Despite the size or type of event, may it be an afternoon or weekend community celebration held in a local park, an international conference held in a large city or a mega-sporting event, all events have an impact on the people, places and environments in which they take place. This book recognizes the importance of addressing, understanding and evaluating event impacts. All of the contributors teach and research in the areas of events, and therefore recognize the importance of contributing to a research agenda for event impacts. The concept of this book was inspired by the growth of research evaluating the range of impacts that events create and cause in places around the world. The book includes 19 chapters with 25 contributors from around the world. While the examples included in this book are snapshots and offer a range of insights and examples, the purpose of the book is to show avenues for research, written for students, practitioners and scholars who are interested in research or concerned with issues facing the contemporary events industry. We also believe that this book can be used as both a key or supplementary reading source in a range of event management or event studies classes, but is not limited to these classes as the insights relate to a range of social science disciplines and management fields.

Nicholas Wise and Kelly Maguire

1. An introduction to *A Research Agenda for Event Impacts*

Nicholas Wise

Researchers who focus on event studies or event management seek ways to explore how events impact on places, communities, and the environment (Armbrecht et al., 2019; Getz and Page, 2020; Maguire, 2020; Mair, 2019; Preuss, 2007b; Rojek, 2013; Wise and Harris, 2017, 2019). Events research draws inspiration from and builds on a wide range of interdisciplinary approaches across the social sciences, physical sciences, arts and humanities, and business and management literatures (see Andrews and Leopold, 2013; Van Niekerk, 2017). Events today play a key role in planning and development decisions, and they contribute to image formation and place brands, because in many cases when an event is hosted, people recognize the event and use it to associate it with places (Cudny, 2020; Hahm et al., 2019). All events have or create an impact, which leaves an impression on people, places, and/or environments. The timeliness of this book is a chance to reflect on how different experiences are measured and managed (Biaett and Richards, 2020).

Scales of events and types of events are vast, and no matter the size or purpose of an event, the aim is to unite people through mutual interests to share an experience (see Kim and Dombrosky, 2016; Wise, 2020a). Given events is a vast industry, some argue that a one-size-fits-all approach is not appropriate in events studies and thus each event must be evaluated based on the specific impacts that it creates: on the local environment, for the local community, and what it contributes to the local economy. Given this local consideration, both internal and external forces create impacts that challenge researchers to look at wider trends and patterns that refer us to local–global, local–national, or local–regional trends, issues, and considerations. This is also why it is essential that researchers avoid generalizations and seek ways to assess event impacts from various theoretical lenses, management perspectives, or planning principles, so that various perspectives are recognized and realized and impacts are explored and evaluated holistically.

1

This book, as part of *Elgar Research Agendas*, contributes insight into contemporary scholarship on ways of exploring and approaching event impacts. A key intention of this book is to show the links between theory and practice by pointing scholars, practitioners, and students to research directions and critical considerations that need to be addressed when studying events and the impacts that events create. A widely used quote by Allen et al. (2010, 60) just over a decade ago now still points us to the fact that "events do not take place in a vacuum [and] they touch almost every aspect of our lives". These aspects involve social, cultural, economic, environmental, and political considerations and directives that can influence decisions and policies in various ways (Fredline et al., 2003; Holmes et al., 2015). Researchers have sought ways to explore relationships across these impacts, but this can and still does represent challenges given directives and interests need to be agreed among various stakeholders (see Maguire and McLoughlin, 2019). Critically, many decisions are based on the economic value that an event can bring to a place, and these values can in many cases be speculative. Therefore, what is essential when events are being planned and organized is to ensure an event is monitored and managed in a way that considers these overlapping considerations so that true and wider impacts are identified.

Whether an event is worth staging will depend on who and what is being impacted. Similar to Musgrave and Raj (2009), Allen et al. (2010) point to social, environmental, and economic concerns as the three pillars of event impacts. Bladen et al. (2018) point to who is affected by events, and categorize based on personal impacts, organizational impacts, and external impacts to showcase that events can impact individuals, influence decisions and directions for organizations, and contribute to external dimensions that direct change and collaborations. People who attend events or live in a place hosting an event will have different experiences, and these may be positive or negative; this can also shape event legacies (Agha et al., 2012). This will depend on one's ability to attend, participate, or engage in the experience of an event, but ways of planning and critical scholars point researchers to issues concerning inclusion and exclusion (Cowan, 2016; Duignan et al., 2019). Organizations are involved in organizing and/or hosting events or invest in events because they are seeking reputation and profit. Then there are the external impacts that Musgrave and Raj (2009) speak to based on interactions between those engaged in the events industry and what events contribute to the economy, what events do to the environment, or how events embrace people, cultures, and society.

The scale and duration of an event will more or less show the extent of an event's impact, and depending on how successful an event was or how it was received will either extend event impacts or limit impacts going forward. With any event lifecycle there are the pre-, during, and post-event phases (Gellweiler et al., 2018; Holmes and Ali-Knight, 2017), or initiation, planning, implementation, event, and closure phases as highlighted in Bladen et al. (2018). A lot of research has addressed these different phases independently, so calls for more longitudinal approaches will allow researchers to understand the different extents of impacts at these different stages. Studies that focus on the bidding stage seek to gain insight into support, awareness, and attitudes towards hosting an event (see Richards and Marques, 2016; van der Steen and Richards, 2019). A lot of pre-event studies conducted just prior to an event being held are about understanding the vision of event impacts and how well managing authorities are planning and preparing (e.g. Wise et al., 2021). Studies conducted during an event tend to focus on delivery, and because the focus is placed on operations and the spectacle of the event itself, this can distract from underlying social problems or environmental issues that an event is causing (see Mooney et al., 2015). Post-event is another crucial time to explore not just the aftermath of an event but also whether promises were kept and to begin analyzing legacies to understand if the costs and benefits of hosting are resulting in new opportunities locally and financially secure futures for the host destination (Maharaj, 2017; Wise, 2019). Bladen et al. (2018) break this down from short- to long-term impacts, noting the immediate post-event period (0–2 years), intermediate post-event period (2–5 years), and legacy period (5 years and longer). A challenge with post-event research is it cannot be rushed and many studies need to reflect on events over a decade after they were held to fully understand the impact of an event (see García, 2005).

Important to note is that longitudinal research is not just concerned with a single event lifecycle, but can explore trends and happenings each year for events that are held annually (see Wise et al., 2015). Event impacts can and will differ based on the timing of an event (time of day or year, season), duration (a short-term event that lasts a few hours or a long-term event which takes place over several weeks or across a calendar year), visibility (exposure in the media or projects that brought about tangible change to the landscape), and the type of event (weddings or local celebrations, cultural events, music festivals, or sporting events). The stakeholders involved also have very different experiences and their reactions require consideration over time. Those involved with policy decisions, strategy, investing, and the supply side bring influence from the top, and position change in a way that they see as being beneficial based on the visions and objectives that will result in desired outcomes that are also sustainable (Ziakas, 2019). There are also consumers, and the ability to keep up with and meet consumer demand will ensure that they are satisfied with an event product. A key consideration here is that top-down actors who work to deliver visions and visitors to the event often only play temporary roles, but it is the local community and residents who see and experience the full lifecycle of an event or see how an event changes and grows year after year. Local residents, then, are the stakeholders who are continually impacted over time. The local and surrounding environment may take/suffer the burden of events, but finances may be a lot more fluid and flow in and out of the host destination.

Important to any event is community participation and support among all stakeholders. Improving access and promoting equitable futures requires the input and involvement of the local population. Event planners will look to use different techniques, promotion strategies, or methods to encourage participation, but they need local residents to want to get involved. According to Wise et al. (2021, 54), "when people are not satisfied with urban planning agendas there is a chance they may disengage, and therefore not be aware of future events/activities". To overcome this issue and to help engage residents, Richards (2017, p. 9) mentions the need for "more proactive use of events in order to drive a wide range of different policy agendas". Waitt (2003) found that seeking ways to also unite locals through events helps create a new or renewed sense of belonging, and Zhao and Wise (2019) add that a key consideration is how enthusiastic locals feel when they are at an event. Concerning involvement and enthusiasm, researchers have found links between the quality of information provided and levels of enthusiasm towards an event or attraction (see Camacho et al., 2019). This also can involve how satisfied people are with how an event is impacting the environment. Some argue that events and environmental sustainability may be a contradiction in terms; for planners who want to maximize the financial success of an event a key focus still requires recognizing and dedicating efforts to minimize negative environmental impacts. Hanrahan and Maguire (2016) present provisions to ensure the environment is protected. Protecting the environment and ensuring the community is involved is an attempt to work towards financially secure and eventful futures.

The point at the end of the last paragraph directs readers to three key areas concerning event impacts: legacy, sustainability, and regeneration. Legacy, according to Preuss (2007a), involves a number of dimensions, planned or unplanned, negative or positive, and tangible or intangible. Scholars who have classified legacies address economics, social, and environmental legacies, but also infrastructure, changes to public life, politics, and culture, and symbols, memories, and history (Cashman, 2005). From a legacy standpoint, places seek to sustain gains from investments put into an event, use the event to market destinations, sustain positive aspects of an event's image, and understand how an event changed or improved the local quality of life (Karakadis and Kaplanidou,

2012). Moreover, event impacts and legacies look at ways of increasing capital, whether this be economic (assets, investments, profits), social (social networks to encourage action and activity), physical (infrastructural, landscape change), symbolic (prestige, new recognition), cultural (knowledge, skills, education), or human (improvements to people's livelihoods, new skills or expertise).

Pertinent and related to discussions of legacy is sustaining impacts over time, through policies that work towards more inclusive and equitable futures (Finkel, 2015), increasing place competitiveness (Aquilino et al., 2019), or putting in place protective measures for the environment (Hanrahan and Maguire, 2016). The key focus is on maximizing benefits and minimizing negative impacts, all the while putting emphasis on supporting communities and protecting resources (Getz, 2013). Academics, policy makers, and planners addressing critical directions and issues related to sustainability are often influenced by the 2030 United Nations Sustainable Development Goals. Recent work in tourism has provided some directions (Boluk et al., 2019), and these are also relevant in event studies and management research. A number of chapters in this book focus on legacy from various standpoints; informing stakeholders of these and ensuring they are aware of legacy initiatives is essential.

The regeneration or redevelopment of spaces and places is a key contributor of event impacts, especially in terms of how impacts are understood and envisioned (Wise and Harris, 2017), as new developments focus on expanding event portfolios in a destination (Ziakas and Costa, 2011). Changing and altering spaces for events can have social, economic, and environmental consequences, especially when it comes to tangible developments. Moreover, regeneration initiatives are part of wider regional and urban policy agendas to "upgrade" places and create eventful futures (Smith, 2012), whether this is linked to place images or changing economic bases (Wise and Harris, 2017). However, Roberts (2017, 9) adds that "regeneration is not solely a reaction to changed circumstances. In some instances regeneration is proactive and seeks either to avoid an emerging problem, such as the consequences of decline of a basic industry, or to improve the prospects of a particular neighborhood." Scholars have addressed three recognized types of event-influenced regeneration strategy: event-led regeneration, event-themed regeneration, and event-added regeneration (Bladen et al., 2018; Evans, 2019; Sadd, 2010; Smith and Fox, 2007). Looking at these considerations, event-led regeneration puts events at the center of regeneration efforts, with events and the venues built acting as catalysts for development and branding, which can also be considered a flagship approach (Wise and Harris, 2017). Event-led regeneration includes reusing brownfields or industrial lands and repurposing these areas for events (Holmes et al., 2015). Considering event-themed regeneration, this is where events are just a part of a wider strategy (or a lever approach), whereby events contribute to policy and intentions to host events (Bladen et al., 2018). Event-added regeneration is when events are not fully leveraged for regeneration purposes, which can be a showcase approach to define the changes made (Bladen et al., 2018).

This book includes 19 chapters, organized into three parts. In events research, a lot of consideration is placed on sport, and while this book includes cases and insights on sport, it also looks to include examples from a range of different event types. Part I includes three chapters that outline the theory and concepts that align with economic, environmental, and social impacts of events. Part II includes 12 chapters that present a range of research themes and examples. Each chapter starts by introducing a research area and reviews work and conceptual directions concerning an area of research. The chapters then move on to present a case example to show and discuss the work in this area, before finishing with a discussion of future directions of research, which helps position both theoretical and practical avenues that need consideration. Part III includes three chapters that focus on going forward in event impacts research, pointing to legacy and sustainability and the need for continued assessment so that event impacts are not just descriptively overviewed but also critically evaluated.

Part I addresses the three impacts recognized in triple-bottom-line considerations of sustainability (Dwyer, 2005; Hede, 2007; Wise, 2020b). This part begins with Larry Dwyer's chapter, "Economic impacts of events". Dwyer overviews approaches that researchers consider, focusing on standard economic impact analysis, computable general equilibrium modeling, and cost–benefit analysis. Dwyer has published extensively on the economic impacts of events and tourism (see Dwyer, 2019; Dwyer et al., 2004, 2005). In this chapter, Dwyer addresses how different stakeholders benefit from these analysis techniques and how policy makers use data to inform decisions. Evaluating economic impacts results in understanding economic returns and where to invest in the future. This approach is persuasive and guides future decision making based on tangible results and secured outcomes. In Chapter 3, Kelly Maguire considers the growth of the events industry and how this puts additional stress and pressure on the environment. Some of the approaches that Maguire outlines are environmental impact assessments, strategic environmental assessment, models for sustainable event management, global criteria, and indicator systems. Taking a planning focus, Maguire categorizes environmental impacts and critically overviews responses and management approaches. This chapter builds on and is informed by her work on environmental impacts and local authority planning (see Hanrahan and Maguire, 2015; Maguire, 2020; Maguire and McLoughlin, 2019). Chapter 4 by Nicholas Wise, Susanne Gellweiler, and Enqing Tian moves on to discuss events and social impacts, challenging scholars to consider intangible approaches and critical directions concerning research in and with local communities. Wise et al. present a range of perspectives from the literature and address key questions and social conditions that researchers can take forward in social impact studies. The authors of this chapter assess the social impacts of events across numerous cases and discuss a number of conceptual directions (see Gellweiler et al., 2018, 2019; Tian, 2017; Tian and Wise, 2020; Wise, 2019).

Part II, "Research themes and case examples", focuses on a range of contemporary topics and issues with cases to put each research area into perspective. In Chapter 5, Jeeyeon Jeannie Hahm focuses on convention events. Conventions and business events are the most common types of events and destinations that regularly host events in their venues are looking to expand operations and host capacities in modern venue complexes. Hahm provides insight from Orlando, discussing the importance of the Orange County Convention Center and how this venue has not only expanded but adapted to host safe events during the Covid-19 pandemic. Hahm has also published research on convention attendees (Hahm et al., 2016).

Another popular type of events and an area that is rapidly expanding is sports tourism. Marko Perić, Jelena Đurkin Badurina, and Nicholas Wise focus on sports tourism and event impacts in Chapter 6. Sports events tourism is experiencing growth and leading to competition between destinations to attract and host such events. Perić et al. look at the Risnjak Trail running events in Gorski kotar, Croatia as an example of how sports tourism is being developed to expand event opportunities and experiences in this part of the country. Building on their prior work on events and sports tourism, an important impact here is developing the region and helping overcome seasonality (see Wise et al., 2019).

Chapter 7 focuses on religious events and commercialization. Flávia Ulian and Angela Fileno are concerned with cultural and religious events and the importance of embedded histories. In this chapter Ulian and Fileno focus on the Lavagem do Bonfim and a devotion to which there has been a festival dedicated since the nineteenth century in Salvador, the capital city of Bahia in Brazil. The authors provide a number of directions on aspects of heritage and pilgrimage surrounding how events create wider social and cultural impacts. While this chapter is based on a new project on which the authors are collaborating, their published work has addressed related insight on how events impact on communities. Ulian has looked at how events impact on people locally (see Ulian and da Silva, 2020), looking at these impacts from a different event context, while Fileno has looked at history and heritage and how colonialism impacts on communities (see Fileno, 2019).

Chapter 8 by Takamitsu Jimura builds on conceptual insights from Chapter 7 and looks at more contemporary events based on intangible cultural heritage. Jimura's chapter provides directions on the impact of heritage and builds on developments from a recent monograph (see Jimura, 2018). This chapter discusses UNESCO principles to guide the importance of research, first focusing on the intangible cultural heritage convention before presenting a case example of fireworks (*hanabi*) and fireworks displays (*hanabi-taikai*) in Japan which have been a tradition and form of entertainment in the country since the seventeenth century. The event impact considerations refer to social and economic impacts, but do point to the need to focus on environmental sustainability as well.

Jada Lindblom presents "Transformational atmospheres of international sporting events" in Chapter 9. The focus on "atmospheres" and events is influenced by scholarship from cultural geography to attract people to experience activities that connect people with a place. After discussing conceptual directions on affective atmospheres, Lindblom moves on to present initial findings from the Red Bull Cliff Diving World Series, a popular event held in the city of Mostar, Bosnia and Herzegovina. A range of community impacts are discussed and the chapter includes insights from a resident survey and subsequent interviews with those attending the event. Lindblom addresses the need to focus on co-production as this can enhance experiences of those attending and participating in events. This chapter was developed alongside Lindblom's dissertation work on tourism in Mostar, Bosnia and Herzegovina (see Lindblom et al., 2020).

Research on sporting events often focuses on the context of development in urban areas. In Chapter 10, Lucia Aquilino focuses on rural events and social development to provide a perspective on events in rural locales. This study offers some critical directions that build on and relate to prior research focusing on the World Alternative Games, an event that takes place in Britain's smallest town, Llanwrtyd Wells. The event is known for its wacky approach and was developed to promote rural tourism in this remote part of Wales (see Aquilino et al., 2020, 2021). While Chapter 9 addressed a sense of community, placemaking, and rural destination marketing, this chapter is concerned with social development and how events contribute to new community identities which are embraced and contested. A key takeaway from this chapter is the need to focus not only on community development, but also on fostering and encouraging participation.

In Chapter 11, "Local authority planning, sustainability, and event governance", Kelly Maguire discusses how local authorities play an important role when it comes to overseeing all aspects of events, and must work with communities to ensure that events are socially, economically, and environmentally sustainable. Maguire provides directions in this area, which is important at the local authority level to ensure event planning is sustainable and meets the needs of those impacted (see Maguire, 2019), and is also critical of shortcomings when it comes to planning and managing events locally. This chapter presents insights from Ireland and addresses approaches locally while acknowledging national directions that are shaping new policies to put in place so that impacts are maximized and move towards securing sustainable futures.

Chapter 12 on the impact of events on place branding by Waldemar Cudny presents geographical insights building on theoretical perspectives of space and place. Events are playing an increasingly important role when it comes to marketing places at different scales, from the nation or region to local destinations. The growth of events has also resulted in increased competition and this is challenging planners to devise unique brands that reflect the identity of places and create recognition so that tourism opportunities will build following the hosting of events. In this chapter, Cudny presents the case of Euro 2012, where one of the host cities for this event was Gdansk, Poland. The author looks at different dimensions, paying attention to media messages (referring to image spaces) and event experiences, each contributing to an impression of a place. Cudny presents directions and relates to a number of recent findings from a book he recently edited (see Cudny 2020).

"Mega-event trends and impacts" by Tara Fitzgerald and Brij Maharaj, Chapter 13, focuses on event hosting in emerging economy nations, with specific emphasis on the BRICS (Brazil, Russia, India, China, and South Africa) as these countries are seeing increased attention within mega-event hosting trends (see Maharaj, 2015; Wise, 2020a). The authors begin the chapter by overviewing insights on mega-events and looking at recent hosts among the BRICS nations. They then look at critical perspectives and different political structures and refer to issues that emerged during the bidding process and time of hosting, which saw funds poured into infrastructures and directed away from social programs, addressing not only general challenges and points of critique and protest, but also concerns around human rights violations, types of resistance tactics, and future concerns.

The postponement of events is the focus of Chapter 14 by Alexander Bond, Daniel Parnell, and Jan Andre Lee Ludvigsen. This chapter reflects the current state of events directly impacted by the Covid-19 pandemic. Numerous events and mass gatherings at all scales have been impacted, with many being cancelled or postponed. While sporting events are directly impacted, other types of events have since moved operations online until gatherings are once again considered safe. For instance, the postponement of the Tokyo Olympics 2020 to 2021 had major economic and financial implications, as did the postponement of UEFA Euro 2020 to 2021. This chapter on postponement relates to their recently published work on events and the Covid-19 pandemic that considers directions for sport event planners and managers (see Ludvigsen and Hayton, 2020; Parnell et al., 2020). The authors address the need for flexibility, while acknowledging that postponement represents a range of knock-on challenges and issues when it comes to financial commitments, securing investments, and logistical issues surrounding planning and organizing.

Chapter 15, "Disability, access, and inclusion" by Erin Pearson and Laura Misener uses the example of parasport events and the growth of these events, where there are a number of tensions surrounding access and inclusion. Pearson and Misener begin by outlining guidelines around accessibility and inclusion at events with a focus on social legacies, addressing insights from recent research on parasport (see Misener et al., 2020). Event legacy and leveraging is a conceptual focus that the authors build on, and the examples referred to in this chapter are the Ontario Parasport Legacy Group and the 2015 Pan/Parapan American Games. In the Canadian province of Ontario, objectives were set to increase the participation of persons with disability, the number of parasport coaches, awareness of parasport, and work towards increasing the implementation of accessibility standards in sport/recreation facilities. Pearson and Misener address the approaches, strategies, and challenges that emerged and point to a number of informed recommendations going forward.

Chapter 16 by Judith Mair discusses events and climate change. Climate change is a pressing issue, with climate action being one of the 17 United Nations Sustainable Development Goals, and nations and organizations are working to find solutions to combat climate change as this will have implications that can negatively impact our economy and society. Mair considers recent developments and explores this critical and contemporary topic, building on insights published a decade ago (see Mair, 2011). Some critical directions that Mair points to in this chapter are resilience, mitigation, and adaptation. Mair presents and discusses different types of events that are most affected by climate change impacts and points to a number of critical research directions, addressing links across policy and practice by discussing important policy and stakeholder implications.

The final three chapters of the book present some directions going forward with event impact research. Chapter 17, "Evaluating cultural legacy: From policy to engaged research" by Rafaela Neiva Ganga, focuses on reconciling policy and evaluating events, focusing attention on the evaluation of Liverpool as the European Capital of Culture in 2008 and 2018. Ganga also considers events and different scales, discussing boroughs of culture events held in Liverpool and London. This chapter provides insight on how legacy is maximized through evaluation and the need to address a wide range of event impacts. Chapter 18 by Kylie Wasser, Landy Di Lu, and Laura Misener addresses legacy and lasting impacts through a systematic review of evidence on different types of organizational forms used for legacy delivery. This work provides directions on this topic from sport development and governance standpoints (see Misener and Lu, 2020; Misener and Wasser, 2016). The directions offered are written for a number of stakeholders in the hope that collaboration opportunities can be recognized so as to maximize future impacts. "Concluding remarks and event impacts going forward" by Kelly Maguire provides a brief conclusion that summarizes critical points from the book and puts future event impacts research into perspective.

Key considerations involve exploring, interpreting, and realizing impacts and require researchers to keep an open mind and be critical of who benefits from hosting events. A focus on event impacts and the wider benefits that events create see researchers focus on issues surrounding sustainability, the need to define legacies, and the extent that regeneration efforts focus on events as places seek to change to gain a competitive advantage, secure economic futures, work towards protecting the environment, and ensure socially sustainable futures.

References

Agha, N., Fairley, S., and Gibson, H. (2012), Considering legacy as a multi-dimensional construct: The legacy of the Olympic Games, *Sport Management Review* 15(1), 125–139.

Allen, J., O'Toole, W., Harris, R. and McDonnell, I. (2010), *Festival and Special Event Management*, Wiley, Oxford.

Andrews, H. and Leopold, T. (2013), *Events and the Social Sciences*, Routledge, London.

Aquilino, L., Armenski, T. and Wise, N. (2019), Assessing the competitiveness of Matera and the Basilicata Region (Italy) ahead of the 2019 European Capital of Culture, *Tourism and Hospitality Research* 19(4), 503–517.

Aquilino, L., Harris, J., and Wise, N. (2021), A sense of rurality: Events, placemaking and community participation in a small Welsh town, *Journal of Rural Studies* 83, 138–145.

Aquilino, L., Wise, N., and Harris, J. (2020), Wackiness and event management: The case of the World Alternative Games, *Event Management* 24(5), 567–577.

Armbrecht, J., Lundberg, E., and Andersson, T.D. (eds) (2019), *A Research Agenda for Event Management*, Edward Elgar, Cheltenham, UK and Northampton, MA, USA.

Biaett, V. and Richards, G. (2020), Event experiences: Measurement and meaning, *Journal of Policy Research in Tourism, Leisure and Events* 12(3), 277–292.

Bladen, C., Kennell, J., Absom, E., and Wilde, N. (2018), *Events Management: An Introduction*, Routledge, London.

Boluk, K.A., Cavaliere, C.T., and Higgins-Desbiolles, F. (2019), A critical framework for interrogating the United Nations Sustainable Development Goals 2030 Agenda in tourism, *Journal of Sustainable Tourism* 27(7), 847–864.

Camacho, D.P., Alonso Dos Santos, M., and Duclos Bastias, D. (2019), The relationship between factors that contribute to support and future intentions in relation to a major sporting event, *Academia Revista Latinoamericana de Administración* 32(4), 442–454.

Cashman, R. (2005), *The Bitter-Sweet Awakening: The Legacy of the Sydney 2000 Olympic Games*, Walla Walla Press, Sydney.

Cowan, A. (2016), *A Nice Place to Visit: Tourism and Urban Revitalization in the Postwar Rustbelt*, Temple University Press, Philadelphia, PA.

Cudny, W. (ed.) (2020), *Urban Events, Place Branding and Promotion*, Routledge, London.

Duignan, M.B., Pappalepore, I., and Everett, S. (2019), The "summer of discontent": Exclusion and communal resistance at the London 2012 Olympics, *Tourism Management* 70, 355–367.

Dwyer, L. (2005), Relevance of triple bottom line reporting to achievement of sustainable tourism: A scoping study, *Tourism Review International* 9(1), 79–93.

Dwyer, L. (2019), Economic assessment of special events: A perspective article, *Tourism Review* 75(1), 191–193.

Dwyer, L., Forsyth, P., and Spurr, R. (2004), Evaluating tourism's economic effects: New and old approaches, *Tourism Management* 25(3), 307–317.

Dwyer, L., Forsyth, P., and Spurr, R. (2005), Estimating the impacts of special events on an economy, *Journal of Travel Research* 43(4), 351–359.

Evans, G. (ed.) (2019), *Mega-Events: Placemaking, Regeneration and City-Regional Development*, Routledge, London.

Fileno, A. (2019), A terceira geração de brasileiros em Lagos. Moisés da Rocha e as fissuras da dominação colonial, *Anos 90* 26, 1–20.

Finkel, R. (2015), Introduction to special issue on social justice and events-related policy, *Journal of Policy Research in Tourism, Leisure and Events* 7(3), 217–219.

Fredline, L., Jago, L., and Deery, M. (2003), The development of a generic scale to measure social impacts of events, *Event Management* 8, 23–37.

García, B. (2005), Deconstructing the city of culture: The long-term cultural legacies of Glasgow 1990, *Urban Studies* 42(5/6), 841–868.

Gellweiler, S., Fletcher, T., and Wise, N. (2019), Exploring experiences and emotions sport event volunteers associate with "role exit", *International Review for the Sociology of Sport*, 54(4), 495–511.

Getz, D. (2013), *Event Tourism: Concepts, International Case Studies, and Research*, Cognizant Communication Corporation, Putnam Valley, NY.

Gellweiler, S., Wise, N., and Fletcher, T. (2018), Understanding the "lived experience" of sport event volunteers: Using the hermeneutic circle as a guiding conceptual framework, *Event Management* 22(4), 629–642.

Getz, D. and Page, S. (2020), *Event Studies: Theory, Research and Policy for Planned Events*, Routledge, London.

Hahm, J., Breiter, D., Severt, K., Wang, Y., and Fjelstula, J. (2016), The relationship between sense of community and satisfaction on future intentions to attend an association's annual meeting, *Tourism Management* 52, 151–160.

Hahm, J., Tasci, A.D.A., and Breiter Terry, D. (2019), The Olympic Games' impact on South Korea's image, *Journal of Destination Marketing and Management* 14, 100373.

Hanrahan, J. and Maguire, K. (2015), Local authority planning provision of policies and guidelines for event management: An Irish perspective, *International Journal for Responsible Tourism* 4(2).

Hanrahan, J. and Maguire, K. (2016), Local authority provision of environmental planning guidelines for event management in Ireland, *European Journal of Tourism Research* 12, 54–81.

Hede, A.-M. (2007), Managing special events in the new era of the triple bottom line, *Event Management* 11(1/2), 13–22.

Holmes, K. and Ali-Knight, J. (2017), The event and festival life cycle-developing a new model for a new context, *International Journal of Contemporary Hospitality Management* 29(3), 986–1004.

Holmes, K., Hughes, M., Mair, J., and Carlsen, J. (2015), *Events and Sustainability*, Routledge, London.

Jimura, T. (2018), *World Heritage Sites: Tourism, Local Communities and Conservation Activities*, Wallingford, CABI.

Karakadis, K. and Kaplanidou, K. (2012), Legacy perceptions among host and non-host Olympic Games residents: A longitudinal study of the 2010 Vancouver Olympic Games, *European Sport Management Quarterly* 12(3), 243–264.

Kim, S. and Dombrosky, J. (2016), Economic impact of small scale event to the local economy: Case of Canfield Fair, *Journal of Tourism Insights* 7(1), 1–10.

Lindblom, J., Vogt, C., and Andereck, K. (2020), Construal level theory as a framework for navigating community contexts in tourism planning, *Tourism Planning and Development*, www.tandfonline.com/doi/abs/10.1080/21568316.2020.18552381-19

Ludvigsen, J.A.L. and Hayton, J.W. (2020), Toward Covid-19 secure events: Considerations for organizing the safe resumption of major sporting events, *Managing Sport and Leisure*, https://doi.org/10.1080/23750472.2020.1782252

Maguire, K. (2019), Examining the power role of local authorities in planning for socio-economic event impacts, *Local Economy* 34(7), 657–679.

Maguire, K. (2020), An examination of the level of local authority sustainable planning for event management: A case study of Ireland, *Journal of Sustainable Tourism*, https://doi.org/10.1080/09669582.2020.1828431

Maguire, K. and McLoughlin, E. (2019), An evidence informed approach to planning for event management in Ireland, *Journal of Place Management and Development* 13(1), 47–72.

Maharaj, B. (2015), The turn of the south? Social and economic impacts of mega-events in India, Brazil and South Africa, *Local Economy* 30(8), 983–999.

Maharaj, B. (2017), Contesting displacement and the struggle for survival: The case of subsistence fisher folk in Durban, South Africa, *Local Economy* 32(7), 744–762.

Mair, J. (2011), Events and climate change: An Australian perspective, *International Journal of Event and Festival Management* 2(3), 245–253.

Mair, J. (ed.) (2019). *The Routledge Handbook of Festivals*, Routledge, London.

Misener, L. and Lu, L.D. (2020), Changing parasport landscape and the evolution of the International Paralympic Committee governance, in Yamamoto, M.Y., Seguin, B., Garcia, B., and Chatziefstathiou, D. (eds), *Routledge Handbook on the Olympic and Paralympic Games*, Routledge, London, 217–228.

Misener, L. and Wasser, K. (2016), International sport development, in Sherry, E., Schulenkorf, N., and Phillips, P. (eds), *Managing Sport Development: An International Approach*, Routledge, London, 31–41.

Misener, L., Lu, L.D., and Carlisi, R. (2020), Leveraging events to develop collaborative partnerships: Examining the formation and collaborative dynamics of the Ontario Parasport Legacy Group, *Journal of Sport Management* 34(5), 447–461.

Mooney, G., McCall, V., and Paton, K. (2015), Exploring the use of large sporting events in the post-crash, post-welfare city: A "legacy" of increasing insecurity?, *Local Economy* 30(8), 910–924.

Musgrave, J. and Raj, R. (2009), Introduction to a conceptual framework for sustainable events, in Raj, R. and Musgrave, J. (eds), *Event Management and Sustainability*, CABI, Cambridge, MA, 1–12.

Parnell, D., Widdop, P., Bond, A., and Wilson, R. (2020), Covid-19, networks and sport, *Managing Sport and Leisure*, https://doi.org/10.1080/23750472.2020.1750100

Preuss, H. (2007a), The conceptualisation and measurement of mega sport event legacies, *Journal of Sport and Tourism*, 12(3/4), 207–228.

Preuss, H. (2007b), *The Impact and Evaluation of Major Sporting Events*, Routledge, London.

Richards, G. (2017), From place branding to placemaking: The role of events, *International Journal of Event and Festival Management* 8(1), 8–23.

Richards, G. and Marques, L. (2016), Bidding for success? Impacts of the European Capital of Culture bid, *Scandinavian Journal of Hospitality and Tourism* 16(2), 180–195.

Roberts, P. (2017), The evolution, definition and purpose of urban regeneration, in Roberts, P., Sykes, H., and Granger, R. (eds), *Urban Regeneration* (2nd Edition), SAGE, London, 9–43.

Rojek, C. (2013), *Event Power: How Global Events Manage and Manipulate*, SAGE, London.

Sadd, D. (2010), What is event-led regeneration? Are we confusing terminology or will London 2012 be the first games to truly benefit the local existing population?, *Event Management* 13(4), 265–275.

Smith, A. (2012), *Events and Urban Regeneration: The Strategic Use of Events to Revitalise Cities*, Routledge, London.

Smith, A. and Fox, T. (2007), From "event-led" to "event-themed" regeneration: The 2002 Commonwealth Games legacy programme, *Urban Studies* 44(5/6), 1125–1143.

Tian, E. (2017), China's "G-7 revolution" in soccer, *International Journal of the History of Sport* 34(17/18), 1915–1932.

Tian, E. and Wise, N. (2020), An Atlantic divide? Mapping the knowledge domain of European and North American-based sociology of sport, 2008–2018, *International Review for the Sociology of Sport* 55(8), 1029–1055.

Ulian, F. and da Silva, R.B. (2020), Using mobile methods to analyze physical activity in the District of Itaquera, São Paulo, Brazil, *Sport in Society* 23(1), 24–39.

van der Steen, T. and Richards, G. (2019), Factors affecting resident support for a hallmark cultural event: The 2018 European Capital of Culture in Valletta, Malta, *Journal of Policy Research in Tourism, Leisure and Events*, https://doi.org/10.1080/19407963.2019.1696352

Van Niekerk, M. (2017), Contemporary issues in events, festivals and destination management, *International Journal of Contemporary Hospitality Management* 29(3), 842–847.

Waitt, G. (2003), Social impacts of the Sydney Olympics, *Annals of Tourism Research* 30(1), 194–215.

Wise, N. (2019), Towards a more enabling representation: Framing an emergent conceptual approach to measure social conditions following mega-event transformation in Manaus, Brazil, *Bulletin of Latin American Research* 38(3), 300–316.

Wise, N. (2020a), Eventful futures and triple bottom line impacts: BRICS, image regeneration and competitiveness, *Journal of Place Management and Development* 13(1), 89–100.

Wise, N. (2020b), Urban and rural event tourism and sustainability: Exploring economic, social and environmental impacts, *Sustainability* 12(14), 5712.

Wise, N. and Harris, J. (eds) (2017), *Sport, Events, Tourism and Regeneration*, Routledge, London.

Wise, N. and Harris, J. (eds) (2019), *Events, Places and Societies*, Routledge, London.

Wise, N., Flinn, J., and Mulec, I. (2015), Exit festival: Contesting political pasts, impacts on youth culture and regenerating the image of Serbia and Novi Sad, in Moufakkir, O. and Pernecky, T. (eds), Wallingford, CABI, 60–73.

Wise, N., Đurkin Badurina, J., and Perić, M. (2021), Assessing residents' perceptions of urban placemaking prior to hosting a major cultural event, *International Journal of Event and Festival Management* 12(1), 51–69.

Wise, N., Perić, M., and Đurkin, J. (2019), Benchmarking service delivery for sports tourism and events: Lessons for Gorski Kotar, Croatia from Pokljuka, Slovenia, *European Journal of Tourism Research* 22, 107–128.

Zhao, Y. and Wise, N. (2019), Evaluating the intersection between "green events" and sense of community at Liverpool's Lark Lane Farmers Market, *Journal of Community Psychology* 47(5), 1118–1130.

Ziakas, V. (2019), Issues, patterns and strategies in the development of event portfolios: Configuring models, design and policy, *Journal of Policy Research in Tourism, Leisure and Events* 11(9), 121–158.

Ziakas, V. and Costa, C. (2011), The use of an event portfolio in regional community and tourism development: Creating synergy between sport and cultural events, *Journal of Sport and Tourism* 16(2), 149–175.

PART I

Assessing event impacts

2. Economic impacts of events

Larry Dwyer

Introduction

In recent years, there has been a substantial increase in the number and type of special events (Getz and Page, 2016). For present purposes, special events may be defined as 'major one-time or recurring events of limited duration, developed primarily to enhance the awareness, appeal and profitability of a tourism destination' (Getz, 2008). The very largest special events are often referred to as 'mega-events'.

Special events are widely recognized to have a range of impacts – economic, social and environmental. Commonly agreed positive outcomes are that special events have the capacity to increase the opportunities for new expenditure within a host region by attracting visitors to the region; stimulate business activity; create income and jobs; support business development and related investment (Prayag et al., 2013); create intangible benefits for local residents who attend the event (Yolal et al., 2016); produce wider economic and/or socio-cultural benefits for the destination, including enhancement of the image of a city or region, facilitating business networking and civic pride, providing for continuing education and training, facilitating technology transfer and the like (Duffy and Mair, 2018); and develop or enhance community values, foster social bonding, 'sense of place' and resident well-being (Moscardo et al., 2017). In many destinations, they form a fundamental component of the destination's tourism, marketing and wider development strategy (Lundberg et al., 2017).

Some negative effects of special events must be acknowledged: events can generate adverse environmental impacts such as various forms of pollution and environmental degradation, and adverse social impacts such as congestion, crowding, resident displacement from certain areas, disruption to local businesses and community backlash (Andersson et al., 2012); and both domestic and international events are invariably associated with a large carbon footprint, particularly involving travel to and from the event destination (Andersson et al., 2017).

The success or otherwise of a particular event should not be measured only by its direct financial contribution to organizers. By their nature, events are associated with impacts on the community that go beyond financial considerations. An event may incur a financial loss to organizers but produce net benefits for the community. Since the individual firms (transport companies, hotels, restaurants, tour operators and so on) that provide services to event attendees are unable to capture all of the benefits of funding the special event, they will be unwilling or unable to fund the event individually. Free riding will occur as the very firms that benefit from the event seek to avoid providing the funding for it to be held. If a large enough number of firms attempt to 'free ride', the event will not be held, and any benefits of staging the event will be lost to all stakeholders. As a consequence, events will tend to be provided to societies at a level below that which is optimum or desirable.

The benefits of holding an event are at times regarded as substantial enough for governments to provide funding or in-kind support to help develop particular events. Governments are often asked to provide financial support for special events, including the allocation of large expenditure to upgrade the required facilities. There are sometimes good economic and non-economic reasons why a government may provide support for a special event on behalf of the broader public. Public spending is justified if the benefits to the host community are greater than the costs. Increasingly governments and event organizers require credible estimates of the event impacts and net benefits to justify the extent of support for particular events. The main problem facing any government for any given event is determining what degree of support, if any, is warranted. Increasingly, event evaluation techniques are used by policy evaluators such as government finance departments to inform policy makers whether allocating resources in support of some event is appropriate and, if so, to what extent. A rational events strategy for government involves funding events at a level which is appropriate given the benefits they create, and which reflects the benefits that could be obtained by allocating the funds elsewhere.

Three main approaches to the economic evaluation of special events may be distinguished. These are:

- standard economic impact analysis (EIA);
- computable general equilibrium (CGE) modelling; and
- cost–benefit analysis (CBA).

For many years, economic event evaluation has been dominated by 'standard' EIA. More recently, this technique has been severely criticized, and the other two evaluation techniques have been developed in response. CGE and CBA techniques each promise much more reliable estimates of the economic value of events.

Economic impact analysis of an event

The fundamental ingredient needed to conduct an EIA of an event is an estimate of the 'new injected expenditure' that is generated by the event. This refers to expenditure that would not have occurred in the host region had the event not taken place.

Prior to assessing the economic impact of a special event, it is necessary to define the geographical boundary of the host region. This boundary will determine whether the estimated expenditure is new to the host region or is sourced from within. Three main levels of jurisdiction of an event may be identified:

- A *local authority* will be interested primarily in the economic activity and jobs created within its area.
- The *state (regional, provincial) government* primarily will be interested in the impact on the region and, perhaps, on the local area (especially if it is a depressed area or keeping voters happy is important).
- The *national government* will be interested in the impact of events on the national economy as a whole, but it also may be interested in the state and local impacts for regional policy reasons.

In evaluating the economic impact of the Melbourne Formula One Grand Prix, for example, there may be interest in assessing its impact not only on the city of Melbourne but on the state of Victoria. To complicate matters, some events, such as football World Cups, may cover more than one country.

Once set, the geographical boundaries of an event provide the basis for distinguishing between 'local residents' and 'visitors' to the event. Clearly, the smaller the host region geographically, the greater the number of attendees that will be *visitors* to the region. The geographical boundary also determines whether income received and expenditure made by event organizers and sponsors come from within the region or outside. In our Melbourne Grand Prix example, an attendee from Bendigo, a city in Victoria, would be classified as a *visitor* to Melbourne. However, the same person would be classified as a *local* when the impact of the event on the economy of the state of Victoria is being assessed. If the event organizer purchased some equipment for the event from a supplier in Geelong, also in Victoria, this expenditure would be classified as a *leakage* if the assessment focuses on Melbourne, but regarded as sourced from within the state of Victoria. If the focus is national, then only injections and leakages of expenditure into and from Australia are relevant.

A clear definition of event jurisdiction is important in event EIA, both to estimate 'new money' associated with an event and the area defining the scope of event impacts. To make informed decisions about events policy, governments and event organizers will also need to assess the extent to which the economic impacts of the event in the host region come at a cost to other regions. In addition to local effects, public-sector funding agencies need to know the state- or region-wide impacts as well as any nation-wide effects. Positive economic impacts on the host region may be substantially offset by losses in other regions comprising the national economy (Blake, 2005). Thus, local impact studies will not provide public-sector decision makers with sufficient guidance as to whether they should support local events financially or otherwise, since they will also need to know the overall region- and nation-wide impacts. Regarding environmental impacts, global pollution due to increased carbon emissions from international transportation associated with event attendance is typically ignored in event evaluation since it falls outside the event 'jurisdiction'. This is a serious omission as a narrow perspective of the event jurisdiction can result in substantial underestimation of the environmental costs associated with larger events.

The 'new' expenditure of visitors, accompanying persons, organizers, delegates, sponsors, media and others that occurs as a result of an event is allocated to different industry sectors (accommodation, restaurants, tours, entertainments, etc.) and used as the input to an economic model to estimate the economic impacts on a destination. The economic model identifies and quantifies the linkages between different sectors of the local economy and linkages with other regions (Briassoulis, 1991). The injected expenditure stimulates economic activity and creates additional business turnover, employment, value added, household income and government revenue in the host community. The type of model employed will determine the size of the multipliers and the estimates of changes in economic activity resulting from holding the event (Dwyer et al., 2004).

The standard model used for economic impact estimation of special events has been the input–output (I–O) model (Crompton, 2006). Over the past two decades I–O models have been heavily criticized for their unrealistic assumptions, narrow focus and exaggerated multipliers and estimates of economic impacts, and for their lack of a welfare measure to inform public policy (economic impacts are gross measures, not net benefit measures) (Briassoulis, 1991; Dwyer et al., 2004, 2005, 2006). It is unrealistic to use models to estimate the economic impacts of events that assume no capacity constraints and consequently no impact of the event on wages or prices or the outputs of other industries. The assumption of constant prices alone makes I–O models unsuitable for event assessment, particularly for larger-scale events (Jago et al., 2010). Compounding this problem is the propensity of consultants to deliver the biggest possible impact estimates for clients eager to develop events, by applying inappropriate multipliers (Crompton, 2006; Jeong et al., 2016).

Estimating economic impacts of special events using computable general equilibrium modelling

Critics claim that I–O modelling typically does not provide an accurate picture of the economic impacts of events and is thus incapable of informing event organizers, funding agencies or governments of the 'return on investment' estimated from event funding (Blake 2005; Dwyer et al., 2005, 2006; Madden 2006). These critics argue that the economic assessment models used for estimating the economic impacts of major events should reflect contemporary developments in economic analysis, particularly regarding the use of CGE modelling (Allan et al., 2017a). Increasingly, event researchers now use CGE models to estimate economic impacts, particularly for larger events (Jago at al., 2010). CGE models represent best practice in assessing the economy-wide impacts of changes in visitor expenditure. CGE analysis captures the complex pattern of feedback effects and resource constraints that characterize actual economies. Like standard EIA models, CGE models simulate the effects of an event-related expenditure shock on economic variables, such as gross domestic product (GDP), prices, wages, income, employment and investment in the event destination. However, CGE models include more specifications of the behaviour of consumers, producers and investors, thus permitting specific models to be calibrated to actual conditions for a particular event in a particular economy (Blake, 2005; Dwyer, 2015; Allan et al., 2017a). They are designed to capture the complex pattern of price changes, feedback effects and resource constraints which exist in all economies following a demand-side shock such as that occasioned by the holding of a special event.

In contrast to I–O analysis, which always produces a positive gain to the economy however disastrous the event, CGE models recognize that the greater resource requirements associated with event-related expenditure are likely to result in lower resource use and output in other industrial sectors. The impact of major events varies significantly across different sectors of the destination. CGE modelling of major events such as the Olympic Games and World Cup football reveal that positive economic impacts on the host region are substantially offset by losses in other regions in the national economy (Blake, 2005). A study of the impacts of the Melbourne Formula One Grand Prix found that the economic gains to the state of Victoria were almost entirely offset by losses to other states of Australia (Victorian Auditor General Office, 2007). Sectors that expand typically include construction, passenger land transport, business services, hotels and restaurants. Sectors that contract typically include manufacturing, agriculture, fishing and other services (Dwyer and Forsyth, 2019).

Factor constraints result in higher input prices, including wages, discouraging production of other goods and services. In open economies with flexible exchange rates, increased event-related spending by foreign visitors puts upward pressure on the exchange rate, discouraging export- and import-competing sectors. These 'inter-industry' effects, with implications for income distribution in the wider economy, must be accounted for in an overall assessment of event impacts (Dwyer et al., 2004).

The assumptions of a CGE model can be varied and the sensitivity to them tested to assess the economic impacts of an event. These include assumptions about factor constraints, workings of the labour market, changes in real wage rates and prices, exchange rate changes and government taxing and spending policies. The fact that CGE simulations can be undertaken using different assumptions, the realism of which can be discussed and debated, provides a transparency to the event assessment process that rarely exists in I–O modelling. This can provide very useful information in predicting the economic impacts of particular types of events in different macroeconomic contexts.

There is increasing use of CGE modelling in the assessment of special events. Important studies include the Sydney Olympics 2000 (Madden, 2006), London Olympics 2012 (Blake, 2005), Melbourne Formula One Grand Prix 2005 (Victorian Auditor General Office, 2007), Beijing Olympics (Li et al., 2011, 2013); World Cup football 2010 (Bohlmann and van Heerden, 2008);

Glasgow 2014 Commonwealth Games (Allan et al., 2017b); and the 2018 Commonwealth Games, Gold Coast, Australia (Pham et al., 2018).

Challenges to common practice event economic impact assessment

Best practice event assessment using standard EIA requires that the relevance of a number of issues be understood and taken into account in the analysis of results. Some issues are addressed here.

Factor constraints

Resource constraints on land, labour and capital that are generally present in an economy can limit changes in economic activity resulting from an event-related increase in the final demand for goods and services. Many special events are staged in communities that are already popular tourist destinations. If hotels, restaurants and other attractions in a host city normally tend to be at or near capacity, throughout the event period, event-related expenditure may simply replace rather than add to regular visitor expenditure (Blake, 2005; Madden, 2006).

Given capacity constraints, the more likely effect is that a special event leads to wage increases that will attract local workers from other activities, or possibly unemployed and underemployed people from other regions. When the host economy is at or near full employment, the labour necessary to prepare for the event might reside in other communities with a labour surplus, and so must be 'imported', thus limiting the potential multiplier effect (Dwyer et al., 2006). Staffing levels in many firms may be relatively insensitive to changes in turnover. Many firms may better utilize their current staff through provision of overtime, part time or weekend work. The relatively short duration of most events makes it unrealistic for employers to hire and train new employees. An increase in labour demand that comes about because of an event will typically lead to some combination of reduction in unemployment within the region and an increase in wage rates in event-related sectors. The increased prices and wages choke off some of the potential increase in economic activity. A recent overview of the *ex-post* literature on the multiplier effects of mega-events shows that *ex-ante* estimates of the effects on employment (and income) are significantly overestimated and that in practice these effects are not distinctly different from zero (Barrios et al., 2016).

Treatment of construction expenditure

Special events often generate investment in direct infrastructure (e.g. stadia) and general infrastructure (e.g. roadways, transport systems, accommodations). Additional investment in tourism/recreation infrastructure can increase the attractions available in an area for use by locals as well as visitors. Facility construction associated with events can be a source of economic and urban development and bid documents for cities wishing to host an Olympic Games or Paralympics emphasize this (Jago et al., 2010).

As a lead up to a special event, additional investments may occur in areas such as airport and transportation improvements, and in attractions such as museums and heritage precincts. Construction of new facilities and venues can be used by locals for other purposes after the festival, and the regeneration of urban areas and infrastructure can help to justify the investment required for organizing these festivals (Barrios et al., 2016; Yolal et al., 2016). However, it is only investment that would not have been generated except for the special event that represents the injection of 'new money' into the destination. If the construction activity would have proceeded irrespective of the event, then it is not counted in economic impact assessment.

There is a widely held but mistaken view that construction expenditures associated with events always have a positive effect on the economy. However, the economic resources required to stage the event are correctly modelled as a cost (Blake, 2005). While the investment generated by events, privately or publicly sourced, has multiplier effects on income, value added and employment, so also would the alternative forms of investment that it replaces. Where the investment expenditure is based on a special grant from an external source, for example, a central government grant to a region, or an internationally sourced grant or donation to a developing country for investment in event-related facilities, the expenditure represents 'new money' for the host destination. However, if a central government reallocated funds originally earmarked for, say, hospital construction in one region to build an event facility in another, this switching would be a net gain to the second region and a net loss to the first. The issues here are not straightforward since they involve hypothetical issues of what would have occurred had the particular type of investment not taken place (Dwyer et al., 2006).

Treatment of taxes and subsidies

The hosting of a special event will have implications for government revenues and outlays.

Taxes

An event that stimulates economic activity may generate an increase in tax receipts. In a federal system, some of these will accrue to the host-region government and some to the national government. While tourism-related industries may expand due to the special event and thus pay more taxes, other industries may experience reduced output and sales revenues and thus pay less taxation. The net effect on government tax revenue cannot be known prior to the modelling exercise. Where taxation revenues are used by government to fund facilities construction, this reduces the net disposable income of residents and hence their consumption of goods and services within the destination. Since government spending on construction is usually financed from taxation, the net effect of the construction projects may be negative (Blake, 2005).

Subsidies

Events often are subsidized by governments. In addition to direct subsidization, including tax concessions, this can take various indirect forms, for example, public expenditure on the construction of facilities and supporting infrastructure such as roadworks, provision of additional police, ambulance officers and so on. The government has several funding options regarding an event-related subsidy: it could cut expenditure in other areas, leading to reduced economic activity in these areas. Alternatively, it may increase taxes. For example, it might raise business taxes in the destination. This could have a significant negative impact on the regional economy because it would make the region less competitive and economic activity would shift elsewhere (Allan et al., 2017b). The extent to which government subsidizes (funds) events from taxation or borrowings can affect the economic activity generated. It is possible that the overall net impact on economic activity of an event that relies very heavily on subsidies could be negative, as host city debts must be accounted for. A common legacy of many past mega-events worldwide has been a huge debt and much underutilized infrastructure. Operating losses subsequently incurred by facilities constructed for a specific event, combined with interest repayments on debt, are economic costs over the longer run. To the extent that these losses are met from tax revenues, residents subsidize the events sector.

Cost-benefit analysis

For many decades, GDP as the key performance variable in EIA event assessment has been the preferred measure for assessing progress in human development, although it was never created for that purpose (Stiglitz et al., 2009a). While this measure is a critical indicator of a country's macroeconomic condition and the opportunity afforded to meet material needs, its inadequacy to measure people's lives and well-being has become increasingly acknowledged (Bleys, 2012; Radermachier, 2015). A growing number of researchers argue that event assessment which focuses only on economic impacts is too narrow in scope to provide sufficient information to policy makers and government funding agencies and that, where practical, a more comprehensive approach should be employed to embrace the importance of social and environmental impacts in addition to economic impacts. These critics highlight the potential importance of CBA in event evaluation (Victorian Auditor General Office, 2007; Abelson, 2011; Dwyer et al., 2016; Dwyer and Forsyth, 2019).

CBA is a comprehensive economic appraisal technique that compares all the benefits associated with an event, project, policy or activity, with the associated costs – those present and those expected in the future. The objective of CBA in event assessment is to determine whether a destination is better or worse off because of hosting the event, estimating the community welfare effects in monetary (e.g. dollar) units. A welfare effect is simply any cost or benefit experienced by a member of the relevant community whether occurring in markets or as implicit values. In event assessment using CBA, costs and benefits, including social and environmental aspects, are assigned a monetary value, allowing the calculation of the net benefits from holding the event. CBA takes serious account of resident benefits and costs in event assessment, in contrast to EIA and most CGE approaches which typically treat resident expenditure as simply 'transferred money' having no economic effect.

Benefits are measured by willingness to pay – what people are willing to pay (or give up) to get what an event provides – and are estimated by measuring the additional consumer surplus and producer surplus of a given option over the 'do nothing' or 'no event' case (Boardman et al., 2011).

Costs are measured by 'opportunity cost' which is the value of the marginal benefits foregone from the same resources in alternative uses – holding a special event requires the use of resources (or inputs) that could be used elsewhere. For example, the host destination may suffer a loss of sales revenue that would otherwise have accrued to local businesses from other tourism market segments.

For a special event to be socially acceptable, the sum of the (social and private) benefits must exceed the sum of the (private and social) costs to society, and represent the best use of limited funds, when alternative calls on these funds exist. Since CBA estimates 'net benefits' to a destination generated by an event it possesses a policy significance lacking in standard EIA assessment of special events.

It seems useful to elaborate a little on the types of benefits and costs that comprise CBA of a special event (Victorian Auditor General Office, 2007; Abelson, 2011; Dwyer and Forsyth, 2019). A list of potential benefits could include the following:

- *Visitor and sponsor payments to the event organizer.* The ticket sales and sponsor revenue received by the event local organizer indicate people's willingness to pay to attend the event. They also benefit the resident taxpayer in that they offset the costs incurred in staging the event and reduce the size of any government subsidy.
- *Consumer surpluses to households.* Market prices typically do not adequately reflect the true value of a good to society. For many events, the price that patrons are willing to pay to attend the event exceeds what they are required to pay to attend and thus there is a net gain to the patrons from the event being available over and above ticket prices.
- *Other consumer benefits.* Indirect participation at related (off-site) activities such as satellite events, public screenings and off-site parties indicates that residents also derive benefits from these activities. Since they would not exist in the absence of the event, they are counted as benefits to residents in addition to the consumer surpluses from event attendance itself.
- Benefits also accrue to residents who value the positive experiences that an event brings to others, whether users or non-users. Many residents experience a sense of pride irrespective of any direct or indirect participatory benefits, simply because their destination plays host to the special event (Mair and Duffy, 2018). Since festivals and events provide a number of opportunities for enhancing social interactions and relationships (Yolal et al., 2016), they are likely to play a unique role in improving residents' well-being and quality of life. These values can, in principle, include

a substantial range including symbolic, educational, aesthetic, political, spiritual, lifestyle, prestige, community pride and social cohesion, all of which enhance social capital (Moscardo et al., 2017).

- *Business (producer) surplus (loss)* comprises the net returns to locally owned capital associated with the event. Producer surplus is the difference between the value of output and the cost of the factors of production (land, labour and capital), where their cost reflects their value in alternative uses.
- *Labour surplus* refers to the net benefits to local workers (after compensation for work effort and tax) associated with the event. It is the difference between the wage received and the so-called 'transfer payment' that they would receive in alternative employment. Labour surpluses occur when workers are employed at a wage higher than what they would have been prepared to accept to enter into employment.
- *Legacy effects.* Economic, social, environmental, cultural and political factors influence the economic, physical and psychological well-being at both individual and community levels in the long term. Legacy benefits of special events to a destination include attributes such as favourable media exposure, improved destination image, better branding, increased future tourism, improved management practices, better destination coordination among government agencies, education and public health benefits, improved inclusion of handicapped persons, cultural preservation, youth and sport development and greater social inclusion (Thomson et al., 2013). Event and festival attendance activities and mixing in public spaces can play an important role in both preserving and building social capital (Mair and Duffy, 2018). On the other hand, destination image and reputation can be harmed if event-related management, facilities and services are regarded as inadequate.

In event assessment the costs that are compared with benefits typically include such variables as:

- Capital expenditures on event-related infrastructure including payments of interest on debt.
- Operating expenditures associated with the event (e.g. event management and staging, marketing/promotion and catering, administration).
- Other event-related costs incurred by government agencies such as road agencies, ambulance, fire brigade, police and emergency services.
- Volunteers, who generally take leave from their employment to provide services at the event, are typically not included in these costs. While there would be a cost to the community through their involvement in the event

in terms of lost production, it is generally not possible to provide any reliable cost estimates on this in most situations.

- Social and environmental costs such as disruption to business and resident lifestyles, traffic congestion, road accidents, crime, litter, noise, crowding, property damage, environmental degradation, vandalism, congestion, air/water pollution, event carbon footprint (including event-related transport). Events are associated with increased energy consumption and water use and waste generation, which can put strain on the limited resources of some locations.

Compared to EIA studies of special events, the literature on event assessment comprises relatively few studies employing CBA. Prominent among these are the evaluation of the Eurovision Song Contest held in Israel (Fleischer and Felsenstein, 2002), the V8 car races held in Canberra (ACT Auditor-General, 2002), the Vancouver Winter Olympics 2010 (Shaffer et al., 2003) and the CBA of a Formula One Grand Prix (Victorian Auditor General Office, 2007).

Some outcomes of an event on a destination are not sufficiently well accepted or measurable to be included either in a CGE or CBA. These are often referred to as 'intangible' outcomes which vary from one event to another, depending on size and type. *Intangible benefits* include such items as increased business confidence, increased trade and business development, enhancement of business management skills, enhanced 'sense of place', enhanced destination image and emergent values such as increased community interest in the issues relevant to the event 'theme'. Increased convention business is often generated by major events. Businesses and governments use corporate entertainment facilities at events that can serve as networking opportunities to result in new sales/trade and new investment. Yolal et al. (2016) found that community benefits and cultural/educational benefits are positive predictors of subjective well-being of residents. There is however a significant lack of research into what specifically drives well-being and, in particular, how event attendance can contribute to subjective well-being in a positive or negative way (Moscardo et al., 2017).

Intangible costs include the perception that events generate crowding, with inflated prices, causing a loss of other tourism and business to the host destination. A potential cost that is often emphasized by researchers is loss of local business trade and income due to event-created congestion and crowding out. However, in most cases, these switches are income distributional effects rather than efficiency effects, since consumers simply change the timing of their purchases or transfer their purchases to another location in the short run.

This may create local winners and losers but the net effect on businesses from switches in local purchases is generally small (Abelson, 2011).

Since for some types of costs and benefits there are no observable financial transactions that could be used to measure their magnitudes, these types of effects are often ignored. They represent, nonetheless, very real effects of events on a destination and must be recognized in the overall assessment of the costs and benefits of hosting special events. Techniques are improving in respect of valuation of social and environmental impacts (Boardman et al., 2011). Standard environmental valuation techniques such as those based on stated preference, revealed preference and imputed valuation can be employed to estimate costs of event environmental effects. Recent event evaluation research has estimated both user and non-user values expressed by event visitors and residents employing concepts related to total economic value (Andersson et al., 2012, 2017). Stated preference techniques such as contingency valuation can be used to assign monetary values to social impacts by requesting residents to estimate the degree to which they are willing to pay to secure or avoid a major event. There is, however, no agreed standard for social impact measurement. In certain cases, it may be useful to study the perceptions that residents of the host community have of event-related phenomena such as traffic congestion, noise, pollution and parking availability (as presented in Deery et al., 2012). Since informed policy making, however, requires that these intangibles be taken into account, incorporating these costs and benefits into event assessment highlights an important research agenda for the future.

Computable general equilibrium modelling or cost–benefit analysis?

Since neither technique is completely comprehensive, when deciding which to employ in event assessment both have a role to play.

CGE can be used to estimate the economic impacts of special events including inter-industry effects, employment changes and income redistribution (Dwyer et al., 2005, Dwyer and Forsyth, 2019). CGE modelling, in principle, captures all the event-related economic effects, direct and indirect. This informs stakeholders regarding the effects of alternative resource allocation, policy, management or tourism development strategies. For some tasks in event evaluation, particularly measuring the impacts of injected expenditure, there seems to be no appropriate alternative other than using a CGE approach. CGE models can be and are used to analyse distributional effects of an event. They will measure both initial and ultimate incidence of event-related expenditure, while CBA can only handle the initial incidence (Dwyer et al., 2016). However, CGE modelling, like standard EIA, normally treats resident expenditure as merely 'transferred expenditure' excluding resident values from the assessment process. Destinations that neglect the importance of special events to their own residents cannot be expected to make informed decisions regarding either an appropriate 'events budget' or appropriate levels of funding for particular events.

A CBA picks up a whole range of benefits and costs to the host destination from the event that would not be picked up in an economic impact model. These include non-priced effects that do not get included in the markets which are modelled – noise from an event, the consumer surplus of home patrons, loss of park amenity and traffic congestion associated with the event and so on. In CBA, estimation of resident benefits is central to the assessment exercise. CBA estimates the surpluses to event consumers, residents, producers and labour that are essential to event assessment (Abelson, 2011). For special events, judgement can be made as to whether the economic benefits are greater than the costs, and also as to whether the event would represent the best use of the funds, when funds are limited and alternative calls on funds exist. EIA cannot do this. In bringing residents' values back into the assessment, CBA thus improves the information base for public-sector decision making. However, since there is no accepted way of handling injected expenditure within a CBA, it does not measure event-related economic impacts including effects on GDP, household incomes or employment creation, either direct or indirect. This is a serious limitation of CBA, since many events are targeted towards visitors to a region generating economic impacts, requiring an economic impact study. On the other hand, EIA omits valuation of the event's environmental and social effects.

The upshot of this discussion is that *both* CGE and CBA are essential to the evaluation of special events since they focus on different aspects of the evaluation problem. Given that government funding agencies are now demanding that event evaluation be undertaken using state-of-the-art techniques (Victorian Auditor General Office, 2007), it can be expected that evaluation of special events will increasingly incorporate CGE modelling of the economic impacts and CBA of the wider economic, social and environmental effects. Methods of integrating the two approaches are under development (Dwyer et al., 2016; Dwyer and Forsyth, 2019).

Going forward in economic impacts of events

The issues addressed above call forth several areas for further research on the topic of evaluation of special events.

One obvious focus for research is to reconcile economic impact models such as CGE and wider evaluation approaches such as CBA. Given the common theoretical constructs for welfare measurement used in both partial and general equilibrium models today and the evolution in computation, CGE is likely to improve relative to CBA (Dwyer and Forsyth, 2019). CGE models are evolving in analytic power and accuracy and are now able to capture more and more effects of expenditure shocks. As they become more disaggregated, they support more accurate measures of benefits and costs. CGE modelling of events may be expected to improve with advances in software and the ability to readily disaggregate industries and households (Dwyer, 2015). There is greater scope to use welfare measures in CGE modelling of tourism impacts for enhanced policy relevance, and event assessment is one such area. Given that government funding agencies are now demanding that event evaluation be undertaken using state-of-the-art techniques (Victorian Auditor General Office, 2007), it can be expected that evaluation of special events will increasingly incorporate CGE modelling of the economic impacts and CBA of the wider economic, social and environmental effects. While promising substantial gains in the process of event evaluation, 'holistic' models, combining CGE and CBA, must be rigorously tested on valuing real-world events. An expected outcome of the use of hybrid models is a narrowing of the divide between practitioners and theorists regarding best practice event evaluation to the benefit of all stakeholders.

A second focus for future research involves an improved effort to articulate the specific community goals and wider economic development goals associated with special events (Holmes et al., 2015). If these goals are not purely economic, this implies that economic estimates *per se* are too narrow to support policy in respect of special event development. A holistic approach to event assessment, embracing economic, social and environmental measures and outcomes, fits nicely with the Beyond GDP approach to development which is gaining widespread support from policy makers and researchers worldwide. Recognizing the inadequacy of standard economic measures such as GDP for capturing critical dimensions of people's well-being, the Beyond GDP research agenda is concerned with developing measures of progress that capture broader aspects of people's living conditions and of the quality of their lives (Stiglitz et al.,

2009a, 2009b; Bleys, 2012). To date, a substantial body of research and statistical work providing alternative or complementary metrics of human progress has been developed (Durand, 2015; Stigliz et al., 2018). There is now a solid and well-established case for looking 'beyond GDP', using well-being metrics in the policy process and assessing policy outcomes in terms of its impact on people's well-being as well as on societies' standard of living (Fuchs et al., 2020). While not formulated specifically for tourism activity, the approach serves as a guide to measuring the current and future well-being of destination residents associated with tourism development, including the development of special events (Dwyer, 2021). With human well-being regarded as the overarching objective of event development, researchers should acknowledge the crucial relevance of the wider economic, social and environmental impacts essential to an overall 'holistic' event assessment. Estimation tools required to measure well-being effects associated with special events need more detailed attention from researchers.

The Beyond GDP approach has relevance also for valuing the legacy effects of events over time. From an intergenerational perspective, sustainable development is development that ensures for future generations a level of human well-being at least equal to that prevailing today. The so-called 'capitals approach' to measurement of sustainability, consistent with the Beyond GDP approach, examines the evolution over time of the different stocks of capital that sustain the various dimensions of well-being, and in particular at how decisions taken today affect future levels of these stocks (Arrow et al., 2012). Four types of capital stocks – economic, human, social and natural – are essential to sustain well-being outcomes over time (OECD, 2009; Stiglitz et al., 2018). The different capital stocks are interdependent and work together to support or reduce well-being into the future. While some event research has recognized the importance of maintaining quantity and quality capital stocks to embed sustainability into event development, the focus has been on either natural capital (Boggia et al., 2018) or social capital (Moscardo et al., 2017), with little effort to analyse the fundamental trade-offs between the different capital stocks essential to measuring the sustainability of event development. Event researchers need to better appreciate the essential dynamic dimension of sustainable development, and the importance of changing capital stocks, unable to be captured within static models (Dwyer, 2021). Contrary to what many event researchers have been saying, it is the changing quantity and quality of capital stocks that will determine the legacy effects of special events. The capitals approach has the potential to provide the conceptually appropriate basis for analysis of the legacy effects of events and future research should acknowledge this.

While the literature continues to focus on evaluating single events, growth in the events sector combined with global competition means that most destinations attempt to develop a suite of events with long-term and synergistic effects (Getz and Page, 2016). This requires comparison of the relative value of permanent (e.g. annual) versus one-time events. Overall, the broader question for policy makers is whether special events are the most appropriate and cost-effective channel to pursue these qualitative and social goals. Making the special event fit the regional development strategy makes more sense than making the regional strategy fit the event (Getz and Page, 2016). The recommended approach to event evaluation using both CGE modelling and CBA needs to be embedded within a wider framework that recognizes the new emphasis on developing and managing a portfolio of events to best enhance human well-being. This requires that well-being assessment be employed proactively as an adaptive management tool to achieve better development outcomes from holding special events, not just the identification or amelioration of negative or unintended outcomes. This strategy also calls for significant trade-offs between different types of events with associated value judgements on the part of decision makers. At the same time questions also arise as to how power and politics influence the types of events held within a destination and the distribution of resultant costs and benefits. The issues involved comprise a fertile research field in event assessment.

Conclusion

Estimates of event impacts such as contribution to GDP, value added and employment will depend both on the type of model used and on the particular assumptions that underlie that model. It was argued that standard EIA, based on I–O modelling, exaggerates the economic impacts of special events. The deficiencies in I–O analysis have given rise to the development of CGE models to assess special events, particularly larger events. However, estimation of the economic impacts is only part of the evaluation story. Since many wider effects of special events exist, beyond economic impacts, these must be accounted for in a comprehensive event assessment. Event assessments need to be broadened to take, where practicable, a more comprehensive approach embracing not only economic, but social and environmental factors. The assessment method must recognize the relevance and importance of resident values. This flags a role for CBA alongside CGE modelling. An important topic for future research should be the issue of reconciling EIA and CBA.

To date, much event evaluation still falls well short of 'best practice'. Long-term evaluation of leveraging and legacy effects is needed, together with an examination of the extent to which special events foster community and wider economic development goals associated with human well-being. Several implications for the research agenda in event evaluation were identified. These include an improved effort to articulate the specific community goals and wider economic development goals associated with special events, and an effort to link event assessment with the Beyond GDP approach that emphasizes human well-being as the key performance indicator. To address sustainability issues including legacy effects the analytical framework can be informed by the capitals approach that is receiving greater attention in the wider sustainability literature. The 'hybrid' approach proposed in this chapter, combining CGE modelling with CBA, should now be tested in studies of real-world events. An important expected outcome of the proposed research is a narrowing of the divide between practitioners and theorists regarding best practice event evaluation to the benefit of all stakeholders.

References

Abelson P. (2011) 'Evaluating major events and avoiding the mercantilist fallacy', *Economic Papers*, 30(1): 48–59.

ACT Auditor-General (2002) 'Performance audit report V8 car races in Canberra: Costs and benefits', Canberra, July.

Allan, G., Lecca, P., McGregor, P., McIntyre, S. and Swales, J. (2017a) 'Computable general equilibrium modelling in regional science'. In *Regional Research Frontiers*, Vol. 2, eds. Jackson, R. and Schaeffer, P. (pp. 59–78). Cham: Springer.

Allan, G., Lecca, P. and Swales, K. (2017b) 'The impacts of temporary but anticipated tourism spending: An application to the Glasgow 2014 Commonwealth Games', *Tourism Management*, 59: 325–337.

Andersson, T.D., Armbrecht, J. and Lundberg, E. (2012) 'Estimating use and non-use values of a music festival', *Scandinavian Journal of Hospitality and Tourism*, 12(3): 215–231.

Andersson, T.D., Armbrecht, J. and Lundberg, E. (2017) 'The use and non-use values of events'. In *The Value of Events*, eds. Lundberg, E., Armbrecht, J., Andersson, T.D. and Getz, D. (pp. 89–104). Abingdon: Routledge.

Arrow, K.J., Dasgupta, P., Goulder, L.H., Mumford, K.J. and Oleson, K. (2012) 'Sustainability and the measurement of wealth', *Environment and Development Economics*, 17(3): 317–353.

Barrios, D.S. Russell and Andrews, M. (2016) 'Bringing home the gold? A review of the economic impact of hosting mega-events', No. 320, Center for International Development at Harvard University.

Blake, A. (2005) 'The economic impact of the London 2012 Olympics', Research report 2005/5, Christel DeHaan Tourism and Travel Research Institute, Nottingham University.

Bleys, B. (2012) 'Beyond GDP: Classifying alternative measures for progress', *Social Indicators Research*, 109(3): 355–376.

Boardman, A.E., Greenberg, D.H., Vining, A.R. and Weimer, D.L. (2011) *Cost–Benefit Analysis: Concepts and Practice*, 4th edn. Boston, MA: Prentice Hall.

Boggia, A., Massei, G., Paolotti, L., Rocchi, L. and Schiavi, F. (2018) 'A model for measuring the environmental sustainability of events', *Journal of Environmental Management*, 206: 836–845.

Bohlmann, H.R. and van Heerden, J.H. (2008) 'Predicting the economic impact of the 2010 FIFA World Cup on South Africa', *International Journal of Sport Management and Marketing*, 3(4):, 383–396.

Briassoulis, H. (1991) 'Methodological issues: Tourism input–output analysis', *Annals of Tourism Research*, 18: 435–449.

Crompton, J.L. (2006) 'Economic impact studies: Instruments for political shenanigans?', *Journal of Travel Research*, 45: 67–82.

Deery, M., Jago, L. and Fredline, L. (2012) 'Rethinking social impacts of tourism research: A new research agenda', *Tourism Management*, 33(1): 64–73.

Duffy, M. and Mair, J. (2018) 'Engaging the senses to explore community events', *Event Management*, 22(1): 49–63.

Durand, M. (2015) 'The OECD better life initiative: How's life? and the measurement of well-being', *Review of Income and Wealth*, 61(1): 4–17.

Dwyer, L. (2015) 'Computable general equilibrium modelling: An important tool for tourism policy analysis', *Tourism and Hospitality Management*, 21(2): 111–126.

Dwyer L. (2021) 'Tourism development and sustainable well-being: A Beyond GDP perspective', *Journal of Sustainable Tourism*, www-tandfonline-om.ezproxy.lib.uts .edu.au/doi/full/10.1080/09669582.2020.1825457

Dwyer, L. and Forsyth, P. (2019) 'Evaluating special events: Merging two essential approaches', *Event Management*, 23(6): 897–911.

Dwyer, L., Forsyth, P. and Spurr, R. (2004) 'Evaluating tourism's economic effects: New and old approaches', *Tourism Management*, 25(3): 307–317.

Dwyer, L., Forsyth, P. and Spurr, R. (2005) 'Estimating the impacts of special events on an economy', *Journal of Travel Research*, 43(4): 351–359.

Dwyer, L., Forsyth, P. and Spurr, R. (2006) 'Assessing the economic impacts of events: A computable general equilibrium approach', *Journal of Travel Research*, 45(1): 59–66.

Dwyer, L., Jago, L. and Forsyth, P. (2016) 'Economic evaluation of special events: Reconciling economic impact and cost–benefit analysis', *Scandinavian Journal of Hospitality and Tourism*, 16(2): 115–129.

Fleischer, A. and Felsenstein, D. (2002) 'Cost-benefit analysis using economic surpluses: A case study of a televised event', *Journal of Cultural Economics*, 26(2): 139–156.

Fuchs, D., Schlipphak, B., Treib, O., Long, L.A.N. and Lederer, M. (2020) 'Which way forward in measuring the quality of life? A critical analysis of sustainability and well-being indicator sets', *Global Environmental Politics*, 20(2): 12–36.

Getz, D. (2008) 'Event tourism: Definition, evolution and research', *Tourism Management*, 29(3): 403–428.

Getz, D. and Page, S.J. (2016) 'Progress and prospects for event tourism research', *Tourism Management*, 52: 593–631.

Holmes, K., Hughes, M., Mair, J. and Carlsen, J. (2015) *Events and Sustainability*. Abingdon: Routledge.

Jago, L., Dwyer, L., Lipman, G., van Lill, D. and Vorster, S. (2010) 'Optimising the potential of mega-events: An overview', *International Journal of Event and Festival Management*, 1(3): 220–237.

Jeong, J.Y., Crompton, J.L. and Dudensing, R.M. (2016) 'The potential influence of researchers' hidden' procedure decisions on estimates of visitor spending and economic impact', *Journal of Travel Research*, 55(7): 874–888.

Li, S., Blake, A. and Cooper, C. (2011) 'Modelling the economic impact of international tourism on the Chinese economy: A CGE analysis of the Beijing 2008 Olympics', *Tourism Economics*, 17(2): 279–303.

Li, S., Blake, A. and Thomas, R. (2013) 'Modelling the economic impact of sports events: The case of the Beijing Olympics', *Economic Modelling*, 30: 235–244.

Lundberg, E., Armbrecht, J., Andersson, T.D. and Getz, D. (eds) (2017) *The Value of Events*. London: Taylor & Francis.

Madden J. (2006) 'Economic and fiscal impacts of mega sporting events: A general equilibrium assessment', *Public Finance and Management*, 6(3): 346–394.

Mair, J. and Duffy, M. (2018) 'The role of festivals in strengthening social capital in rural communities', *Event Management*, 22(6): 875–889.

Moscardo, G., Konovalov, E., Murphy, L., McGehee, N. and Schurmann, A. (2017) 'Linking tourism to social capital in destination communities', *Journal of Destination Marketing and Management*, 6(4): 286–295.

OECD (2009) *Measuring Capital*, 2nd edn. Paris: OECD.

Pham, T., Becken, S. and Powell, M. (2018) 'The economic impacts of the Gold Coast 2018 Commonwealth Games 2018: Post-Games report', Griffith Institute for Tourism, Griffith University, www.publications.qld.gov.au/dataset/economic-impacts-of-the-gold-coast-2018-commonwealth-games-2018-post-games-report

Prayag, G., Hosany, S., Nunkoo, R. and Alders, T. (2013) 'London residents' support for the 2012 Olympic Games: The mediating effect of overall attitude', *Tourism Management*, 36: 629–640.

Radermachier, W.J. (2015) 'Recent and future developments related to "GDP and Beyond"', *Review of Income and Wealth*, 61(1): 18–24.

Shaffer M., Greer, A. and Mauboules, C. (2003) 'Olympic costs and benefits, *Canadian Centre for Policy Alternatives Publication*, February.

Stiglitz, J.E., Sen, A. and Fitoussi, J.-P. (2009a) 'The measurement of economic performance and social progress revisited: Reflections and overview', Paris: Commission on the Measurement of Economic Performance and Social Progress, www.stiglitz-sen-fitoussi.fr/documents/rapport_anglais.pdf

Stiglitz, J.E., Sen, A. and Fitoussi, J.-P. (2009b) *Mismeasuring Our Lives: Why GDP Doesn't Add Up*. New York: New Press.

Stiglitz, J., Fitoussi, J.-P. and Durand, M. (2018) *Beyond GDP: Measuring What Counts for Economic and Social Performance*. Paris: OECD.

Thomson, A., Schlenker, K. and Schulenkorf, N. (2013) 'Conceptualizing sport event legacy', *Event Management*, 17(2): 111–122.

Victorian Auditor General Office (2007) *State Investment in Major Events*. Melbourne: Victorian Government Printer.

Yolal, M., Gursoy, D., Uysal, M., Kim, H.L. and Karacaoğlu, S. (2016) 'Impacts of festivals and events on residents' well-being', *Annals of Tourism Research*, 61: 1–18.

3. Environmental impacts of events

Kelly Maguire

Introduction

The events industry worldwide has experienced phenomenal growth in recent years in respect of number, diversity and popularity (Maguire, 2019). So much so that the growth of events has subsequently been recognised as critically important to the economic health of destinations. Building on the insight and directions discussed in Chapter 2, the event industry has established a reputation as a major direct and indirect contributor of economic growth and a driver of social change and development. Around the world, planners at national, regional or local authority scale have begun to recognise the advantages host destinations derive from event activities. As such, event planners and managers strive to continually use events to achieve a diverse range of tourism, place marketing, economic and social objectives in an attempt to drive and sustain economic growth (Wood, 2005; Getz and Page, 2016). Because of this, events now appear as prominent fixtures in many destination development and management plans worldwide. While onus is placed vastly on the strategic use of events by governments, a question that is regularly raised and the challenge facing local planners is how best to manage and sustain event growth while at the same time safeguarding the environmental resource base. This aligns with the exponential growth of the events industry around the world, and increasing demand will continue to put strain on the environmental resources necessary to sustain events going forward.

Focusing on environmental impacts, Maguire (2020) discusses how the visual and physical impacts created by events to the environment and indeed to host societies have begun to draw attention to the way events are planned and managed. Given the legal responsibility of many local managing authorities to license events and facilitate and regulate the process of planning for large-scale outdoor public events, Maguire (2019) noted that managing authorities have the power to organise events in a way that is safe and effectively more sustainable. This is to ensure that the host community and the surrounding environments are protected from the direct impacts of events. However, a number of scholars have alluded to the need to rethink event governance and place environmental sustainability firmly at the forefront of event planning processes and practices (Dredge and Whitford, 2011; Mair and Laing, 2013; Whitford et al., 2014; Maguire, 2019, 2020). As Maguire (2019) disclosed it is now simply not enough to merely tick regulatory boxes; instead, actionable and measurable efforts must be taken and must be placed centre stage in event management planning practices by all stakeholders – and is especially the responsibility of managing authorities and event organisations (at all levels). Thus, a key regulatory focus of many countries is achieving sustainable development at the local level so that resources are not burdened by hosting events. This transition towards environmental sustainability should be a fluid shift since such legal frameworks underpin the remit of local destination planners to manage future growth and development in a sustainable way.

This chapter will begin by placing a focus on the need to plan for environmental sustainability at events and will outline five adaptable approaches that may potentially aid the transition towards greater levels of sustainability in the process of planning for environmental impacts of events:

- environmental impact assessment (EIA);
- strategic environmental assessment (SEA);
- the DIT ACHIEV Model of Sustainable Event Management;
- the Global Sustainable Tourism Criteria for Destinations (GSTC-D); and
- the European Tourism Indicator System (ETIS).

Such approaches may permit an easy, cost-effective and viable solution to facilitate an evidence-informed approach to planning for event management and to manage environmental event impacts more effectively moving forward.

Planning for environmental sustainability at events

The events industry has registered continuous exponential growth in the past decade, creating significant benefits in terms of socio-economic development and employment, which are now at stake following the current global pandemic destinations are experiencing. At the same time, such growth has represented important challenges relating to the carrying capacity of host destinations, consumption of natural resources, impacts on the environmental resource base and contribution to climate change. The importance of this research is therefore paramount at a time when the event sector on a global scale is proliferating in terms of event type, size and scale and in light of calls being made to transition the industry towards more sustainable thresholds (Maguire, 2020). The positive benefits derived from events have been well recognised in event management literature (Sharpley and Stone, 2011; Fredline et al., 2013) but it is experience that has shown that event activities can generate many negative impacts that can often outweigh the positive outputs of events that need to be addressed (Case, 2013; Mair and Whitford, 2013; Liu and Wilson, 2014; Maguire, 2019). The need to plan for event management is therefore becoming an increasingly important and yet more complex task for event organisers, managing authorities and policy makers. A sustainable approach to planning for event management according to Maguire (2020) will be essential to better managing, controlling and monitoring the potential impacts events have the capacity to create.

Protecting and promoting a high-quality environment, particularly in a country such as Ireland, is especially important since Ireland's tourism and events industry is dependent on its environmental resource base. In fact, it is this resource base that is used in promotional materials to attract tourists and event attendees to Ireland. For example, Fáilte Ireland (2016) remarked that Ireland is renowned for its 'clean green unspoilt image and scenery'. However, experience of event growth has demonstrated both the visual and physical effects of event activities to the environmental resource base in which events take place and, ultimately, depend (Gursoy and Kendall, 2006; Collins et al., 2009; Case, 2013; Maguire, 2020). Maguire (2020) discussed the severe pressures events place on the environment through requiring great amounts of resources as a result of human activity and demand and noted that such demand can inevitably cause modifications to the physical environment of host destinations. Jones (2018) reported that not planning for the implications caused to the environment as a result of events can cause long-term extensive damage and degradation and have as such become a significant cause for concern. In particular, areas of air, transport, waste, water, food and energy can significantly impact the use of resources, cause pollution, lead to land degradation, impair ecosystems and contribute to carbon emissions, which in turn affect the sustainability, longevity and quality of events moving forward (Collins and Cooper, 2016; Maguire and Hanrahan, 2016; Jones, 2018; Maguire, 2020). The importance of planning to offset carbon emissions, reduce pollution and sustainably manage resources is reflected in the way they are integrated in the

National Planning Frameworks, which have been developed in an effort to shape the future growth and development of destinations. However, recent reports from the EPA (2020) noted that the quality of the environment is 'not what it should be' and outlined that the outlook is not optimistic unless policy efforts are ramped up and integrated into international and national frameworks. Thus, the need to prioritise environmental impacts within planning practices for events is essential to preserving the key characteristics of the natural environment. A table of environmental impacts derived from international literature has been put forward (Table 3.1) to illustrate the potential environmental benefits and issues of events.

Table 3.1   Categorising environmental impacts

Positive environmental impacts	Negative environmental impacts	
Awareness of environmental issues	Landscape degradation and damage	Waste water generation
Long-term conservation of areas	Ecological/biodiversity damage	Mismanagement of sewage treatments
Preserving the environmental resource base quality	Traffic and transport impact	Mismanagement of catering and food facilities
Protection of biodiversity	Overcrowding	Mismanagement of sanitary facilities
Encouraging carbon offsetting	Energy consumption	
Encouraging resource efficiency/conservation	Water consumption	Pollution of ecosystems
Encouraging environmental monitoring/clean up	Climate change	Abandoned tents at campsites
	Generation of carbon emissions	Air, light and noise pollution
	Litter and waste generation	
	Drinking water often used in excess	
	Water quality often not maintained	

Source: Adapted and modified from Jeong and Faulkner (1996); Fredline et al. (2005); Collins et al. (2009); Raj and Musgrave (2009); Shanka and Alamiyo (2012); UNEP (2012); Case (2013); Jones (2014); Maguire and Hanrahan (2016); Maguire (2020).

Water and energy conservation at events is an area in need of attention as water can be consumed excessively at events. Yet, Maguire (2020) noted that it is an incremental provision at events for reasons of personal hygiene, sanitation and food preparation and is also a pre-requisite for event managers to provide drinking water stations for event attendees under national law (Jones, 2014). Therefore, the conservation of water together with the quality of water and treatment of wastewater should be a priority at events for reasons of public safety and environmental sustainability (EPA, 2012; Jones, 2014). Similarly, energy consumption from electricity and heating demands often required to roll out events can generate increased carbon emissions (Saayman and Saayman, 2012) and create a negative carbon effect on populations (Ceron and Dubois, 2003; Jones, 2014). This has been noted to contribute to the increasingly concerning issue of climate change (Mair, 2011), which is now the defining challenge of this century and is seen as an inhibitor that will slow or halt growth. Energy is fundamentally required for many event operations including but not limited to the operation of accommodation facilities, cooking requirements, stage operations, transport and travelling and operating entertainment devices (David, 2009a; Maguire and Hanrahan, 2017) but it has been reported that performance on climate change and carbon offsetting is very poor (EPA, 2020). Therefore, proactive efforts should be made to mitigate against carbon emissions from event activities and adapt to changing climate conditions. In fact, the EPA (2020) outlined the need to establish national environmental policy positions and to ensure the full implementation of current environmental policies already in place together with working to establish a greater link between the environment and health.

As a response to the Paris Agreement on climate change at the end of 2015, which was negotiated and agreed by 196 countries, an agreed international political consensus for global climate action was established (EC, 2017). Following this, a comprehensive report was conceived by the United Kingdom Festival Industry Group (2016) on the environmental impacts of events. This produced a dataset to reduce environmental event impacts associated with energy and climate change. Through climate action policies and national mitigation plans, events industries could commit to climate change mitigation by adopting standards for meaningful action on climate change and could effectively transition to low-carbon, climate-resilient, environmentally sustainable economies.

The mismanagement of resources at events has been reported to contribute to the ever concerning issue of pollution (UNEP, 2012). Likewise, issues of waste generation at events have been suggested to cause damage to the geological environment with unremoved rubbish from leftover food at catering and food services, depleting natural resources and contributing to air, water and soil pollution (Van der Wagen and White, 2010; Maguire and Hanrahan, 2016). These issues have become a primary environmental concern that warrants a sustainable approach to planning for events as they not only create visual impacts but also physical impacts, which can be both detrimental and irreversible (David, 2009b). In fact, air pollution is noted as the single largest environmental health risk in Europe and with events contributing significantly to air pollution this cannot be ignored.

Furthermore, overcrowding and congestion at events, while a health and safety issue (Goldblatt, 2010), poses an environmental threat to natural landscapes (UNCCD, 2014). Calls have been made to stop further deterioration of the natural environment that has been created by severe pressure due to human activities, to accelerate action to decarbonise and green the economy and to start to restore habitats and water bodies lost over time. This needs to be a key consideration of sustainable planning for event management (Kersulić et al., 2020). Similarly, transport affects the environment and has been acknowledged as the largest carbon contributor for events (Davenport and Switalski, 2006). The National Planning Framework for Ireland (2018) sets out to manage this issue by proposing that no non-zero-emission vehicles will be sold in Ireland after 2030. Therefore, considering the environment is one of the most basic resources for tourism and a core element of tourism products (Wall and Mathieson, 2006), a balanced approach to planning by policy makers is needed (Mowforth and Munt, 2016). Accordingly, the issue of abandoned tents at events has contributed to a waste generation problem (Maguire and Hanrahan, 2016). Hence, solutions are required to maximise the recycling of waste and to minimise landfill. This has become a critical objective for event managers and policy makers in recent years.

Given that the event sector is deeply rooted in the natural and built environment (OECD, 2004), it is important to maintain this image. An informed and consistent sustainable approach to planning for event management must therefore be implemented to secure the future long-term environmental sustainability of the events industry. Managing authorities everywhere have a responsibility to ensure events are conducted in a way that causes minimal harm to the environment (Case, 2013); they have the power to ensure environmental event impacts are planned and managed within a sustainability framework (Sharpley and Stone, 2011).

Although the tourism and events industries worldwide have been left devastated by the Covid-19 pandemic which has created a very difficult economic environment, the UNEP (2020) acknowledged that this period offered an opportunity to regenerate and rejuvenate the environmental resource base with fewer demands and human impacts being placed on resources. They also noted how this situation may build environmental and cultural awareness and respect and encourage responsible travel and behaviour. UNWTO (2020) noted that it represents an opportunity to accelerate sustainable consumption and production patterns and build back better tourism. However, to do this a fundamental focus must be placed on monitoring and evaluating environmental impacts (Maguire and McLoughlin, 2019; Maguire, 2020). In many developed destinations, for instance, managing authorities require event planners and organisers to submit environmental monitoring programme drafts before, during and after proposed events – in this way environmental impacts are measured and assessed at each stage of the event. Such evaluations can be used to ensure continuous improvement at events and enhance the reputation of events, thereby improving destination competitiveness (Maguire, 2019). If destinations wish to sustain growth and ensure their future economic output, then we need to monitor and measure environmental performance and sustainability efforts going forward and work towards ensuring that events minimise impacts to the environmental resource base. Through a sustainable approach to planning for event management as presented by Maguire (2020), policy makers could plan for and manage the process of planning for event management in a way that minimises negative impacts associated with events while maximising positive outcomes. Supporting monitoring mechanisms that would regularly capture such contributions and the value of ecosystem services through tourism at destination level would enable the tourism sector to capitalise on its conservation efforts according to UNWTO (2020). Furthermore, if destinations are to manage future growth in a planned, productive and sustainable way and ensure long-term economic, environmental and social sustainability, then they are going to have to address a number of issues in relation to environmental event sustainability, as addressing all environmental issues must be at the heart of a responsible recovery of the tourism sector. In fact, the resilience of tourism will depend on the sector's ability to balance the needs of people, planet and prosperity (UNWTO, 2020), thus, a comprehensive evaluation, monitoring and management system is essential to ensuring environmental event sustainability moving forward.

Environmental monitoring

The need to plan for and maintain a high-quality environment is crucial to progress towards a sustainable event industry (Case, 2013). Due to the adverse impacts of events on the environment, Case (2013) suggested there should be more of a focus on environmental assessment and monitoring processes. This has become an essential response to facilitating and regulating the protection and maintenance of the environmental resource base upon which events depend. In some developing destinations, managing authorities require event organisers to carry out an environmental monitoring programme before, during and after proposed events. The use of indicators as an environmental management tool can assist planners and organisers in facilitating an evidence-based approach to planning for events. There is a range of planning and management solutions and methods to the problems and issues associated with environmental consequences. These regulatory instruments include an EIA and SEA, which can be used to achieve desired levels of environmental protection and sustainability for event management around the globe. The consideration of these tools in the process of planning for event management can reduce or eliminate harmful environmental consequences. In fact, environmental assessments and monitoring systems are increasingly becoming an important part of the planning process of event management according to Maguire and McLoughlin (2019).

EIAs have been described as among the foremost tools available to national decision makers in their efforts to prevent environmental deterioration (Sniffen, 1995) and thus have become a crucial factor in determining the level of environmental risk associated with events (Raj and Musgrave, 2009). However, it has been noted that an EIA should be conducted before, during and after an event (Ferdinand and Kitchin, 2016) to clearly illustrate the transitional damage throughout the event. This can effectively demonstrate the damage and environmental degradation caused as a result of hosting an event and can improve the level of environmental protection with a view to enabling greater sustainability efforts in the events industry.

The SEA is similar to the EIA in that they share the same objectives and relate to each other within the same policy and planning process (Lee and Walsh, 1992). Additionally, both approaches are based on the principle where a preventative approach is utilised to facilitate environmental protection (Partidario, 2003; González et al., 2011). The SEA has become a legal requirement of member states in the European Union under the SEA Directive (2001/42EC) as set out by the European Commission in 2001 (EC, 2015). The legislation requires that all plans and programmes prepared by national, regional and local government authorities, which are likely to have a significant impact on the environment are subject to SEA procedures (DHPLG, 2015; NPF, 2018). As such, both approaches can be adopted and utilised as a tool for environmental protection in the process of planning for event management. Given that the primary objective of the SEA is to provide a high level of protection for the environment by contributing to the integration of environmental considerations into the preparation of specified plans and programmes (EC, 2005; Partidario, 2007), policy makers could develop a sustainable approach to planning for events through the development of event policies and plans.

DIT ACHIEV model

The DIT ACHIEV model – a tool for sustainable event management – has been suggested as a beneficial way to promote sustainability in event management practices (see Figure 3.1). Initially designed to develop indicators to mitigate against the negative impacts of tourism and guide a destination towards true sustainability, in later years it has been proposed to aid the sustainable management of events (Griffin, 2009). This model is therefore a significant development to the events management industry in Ireland as it has been designed specifically for an Irish setting.

The DIT-ACHIEV model is shaped into six specific fields of interest – administration, community, heritage, infrastructure, enterprise and visitor (Griffin, 2009) – designed to capture the pressures on the sustainability of an area. A seventh field, 'economic', was developed initially but was subsequently omitted due to questions in relation to its robustness as an indicator of a special event, which may be limited. Miller et al. (2012) suggested that perhaps it should have been included to fully serve as a management tool to identify key sustainability issues and to address those using indicators to gauge positive and negative changes over time. As such, it may be necessary to expand on the fields of interest to address broader event management sustainability issues to make indicators more explicit.

Despite being over a decade old, it is important to mention that the DIT-ACHIEV model has never been piloted or implemented in an event context. In order for it to make a valuable contribution towards implementing sustainable practices in event management, it needs to be tested. Furthermore, this model faces a challenge in relation to who, on a practical level is responsible for implementing it. Griffin (2009) noted that to progress sustainability in an event management context needs 'champions' who are willing to adopt the model and test its applicability both spatially and temporally. Miller et al. (2012) acknowledged that there might need to be a group or a touchstone serving as a response to give external advice and to provide guidance and expertise. This is further evidenced by the important role that local authorities in Ireland play, as they may be in an ideal position to implement this model given the regulatory role they hold towards events (see Maguire, 2020).

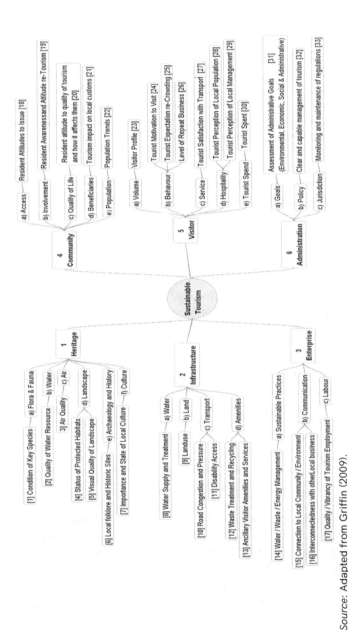

Source: Adapted from Griffin (2009).

Figure 3.1   The DIT ACHIEV model of sustainable event management

Sustainable indicator systems

The use of indicators for monitoring progress towards sustainability has been advocated and discussed by tourism researchers and policy makers over many years (UNWTO, 2004; Miller and Twining-Ward, 2005; Choi and Sirakaya, 2006; Griffin, 2009; Mowforth and Munt, 2009; EC, 2013b). Their use as essential instruments for policy development, regulation, enforcement and management procedures for destinations has been promoted since the 1990s (UNWTO, 1996). As a result, they have become the main recognised evaluation tool used to support sustainable tourism policy implementation (Choi and Sirakaya, 2006). Thus, having established that events are an important sector of Irish tourism, it is important to encourage and promote their development in a sustainable manner to ensure the long-term success of the industry.

The UNWTO identified indicators as: 'A set of measures to provide the necessary information to better understand the links between the impact of tourism on the cultural and natural setting in which this takes place and on which it is strongly dependent' (UNWTO, 1996: 12). As such, indicators are seen as catalysts to support sustainable planning processes (Mascarenhas et al., 2011). They can effectively quantify, measure, monitor, assess and communicate information efficiently and transparently, reducing the chances of making the wrong decisions (Maguire and McLoughlin, 2019). If used appropriately, they can enable stakeholders to benchmark their progress and performance in the future. GSTC (2013) and ETIS (EC, 2013a) have been reviewed for the purpose of this research as viable solutions to encourage greater levels of evidence-based planning for the environmental impacts of events.

Global sustainable tourism criteria for destinations

The GSTC-D is a global initiative aimed at managing and promoting sustainable tourism efforts worldwide. It was originally conceived as the beginning of a process to make sustainability the standard practice for all forms of tourism (GSTC, 2013). The criteria contained within the GSTC-D were mapped upon the 12 aims of sustainable tourism, which formed the starting point in selecting the GSTC criteria (UNEP and UNWTO, 2005). As such, one of its key objectives is to facilitate the adoption of universal principles, which strives to regulate tourism activities towards a more sustainable level. Therefore, it can play an incremental role in aiding the sustainable planning and management of tourism events. Born under the umbrella of the UNWTO, its mission is to:

'promote the widespread adoption of global sustainable tourism standards, ensuring that tourism and its activities contribute to conservation and poverty alleviation' (GSTC-D, 2015: 1). To achieve this goal, two sets of criteria were developed, one intended for hotels and operators (GSTC-HTO) and the other designed for destinations (GSTC-D). Developed in 2008, the criteria were updated in 2015 and have become a worldwide standard for tourism sustainability, available for adoption by governments, policy makers and destination planners. In particular, the GSTC-D is a specifically valuable development for initiating sustainability at destination level. These are defined in Table 3.2.

Table 3.2   The global sustainable tourism criteria for destinations

Demonstrate sustainable destination management	
A1. Sustainable development strategy A2. Destination management organisation A3. Monitoring A4. Tourism seasonality management A5. Climate change adaptation A6. Inventory of tourism assets and attractions A7. Planning regulations	A8. Access for all A9. Property acquisitions A10. Visitor satisfaction A11. Sustainability standards A12. Safety and security A13. Crisis and emergency management A14. Promotion
Maximise economic benefits to host community and minimise negative impacts	
B1. Economic monitoring B2. Local career opportunities B3. Public participation B4. Local community opinion B5. Local access	B6. Tourism awareness and education B7. Preventing exploitation B8. Supporting local entrepreneurs and fair trade B9. Support for community
Maximise benefits to communities, visitors and culture; minimise negative impacts	
C1. Attraction protection C2. Visitor management C3. Visitor behaviour	C4. Cultural heritage protection C5. Site interpretation C6. Intellectual property
Maximise benefits to the environment and minimise negative impacts	
D1. Environmental risks D2. Protection of sensitive environment D3. Water quality D4. Wildlife protection D5. Greenhouse gas emissions D6. Energy conservation; water management	D7. Water security D8. Water quality D9. Wastewater D10. Solid waste reduction D11. Light and noise pollution D12. Low-impact transportation

Source: Adapted from GSTC (2016).

The criteria are essentially the minimum requirement that any tourism-related business or organisation should aspire to reach in order to become economically, *environmentally*, socially and culturally sustainable. An advantage of this system is that it was developed with extensive public consultation, which has subsequently influenced the foundation of many national programmes and global policies establishing sustainable development in tourism. As a result, the criteria now serve as a framework for policy making, regulation, education and awareness intended for application by governments at all levels. Therefore, the contribution these criteria can make to the event industry cannot be underestimated and may be able to influence the process of sustainable planning for event management.

European Tourism Indicator System

Tourism has become an incremental asset of European Union economies and societies, supporting economic growth and activity to ensure the long-term competitiveness of the industry (UNCTAD, 2013) and thereby enhancing the quality of life of European Union residents. The European Commission has therefore committed itself to promoting the sustainable development of tourism in Europe. This has been prioritised through the introduction of a number of policy tools and legislative documents to facilitate sustainable planning and management practices by national and local governments. ETIS is the European Commission's most recent development, designed specifically for destinations to monitor performance and help destinations to develop and carry out their plans for greater sustainability with long-term vision (EC, 2016). It acts to enhance sustainable performance at destination level through the promotion of economic prosperity, social equality and environmental protection (Table 3.3).

An advantage of the ETIS is that it was developed as a result of lessons learned in the past from previous indicator systems and reflected upon some tools including the 12 aims of sustainable tourism and the GSTC. Thus, it has been acknowledged as a robust and effective management tool that provides data to help maximise sustainability at destination level (Maguire and McLoughlin, 2019). Having been officially launched in 2013 upon conducting a feasibility study with more than 100 European destinations, the feedback this tool has enabled since then has led to the development of a more updated and refined version of the ETIS (EC, 2016). The indicators from this tool may be beneficial guiding principles for measuring and monitoring event sustainability, enabling stakeholders to benchmark their progress and performance to make better and more informed management decisions to influence effective and comprehensive policies and plans (EC, 2013b). Therefore, the usefulness of this tool is that it can be expanded or contrasted to meet the needs of the destination, the interests of local stakeholders and to address specific sustainability issues that destinations face. Having recognised the ETIS as a useful tool for policy and decision makers at the local level; the application of this tool may prove invaluable for organisations seeking to monitor sustainable planning for events throughout Europe. By adopting and implementing such indicators, governments and policy makers can establish an evidence-based approach to event management planning whereby they can collect data and monitor and control event issues and impacts.

Table 3.3   European Tourism Indicator System

Destination management	
A.1. Sustainable tourism public policy	A.2. Customer satisfaction
Economic value	
B.1. Tourism flow (volume and value) at destination B.2. Quantity and quality if employment	B.3. Tourism enterprise(s) performance B.4. Tourism supply chain
Social and cultural impact	
C.1. Community/social impact C.2. Health and safety C.3. Gender equality	C.4. Inclusion/accessibility C.5. Protecting and enhancing cultural heritage, local identity and assets
Environmental impact	
D.1. Reducing transport impact D.2. Climate change D.3.Solid waste management	D.4. Sewage treatment D.5. Waste management D.6. Energy usage D.7. Landscape and biodiversity protection

Source: Adapted from EC (2016).

Going forward in environmental event impacts research

This chapter and the environmental sustainability issues and monitoring tools presented above have laid the foundation for future research in the domain of environmental event sustainability. A starting point for advancing this research would be to determine the applicability and effectiveness of the various tools in monitoring environmental sustainability performance. Going forward, it would be beneficial for researchers to identify and recognise the value of such holistic and comprehensive tools in transitioning the industry towards more sustainable thresholds and to therefore pilot such tools on real-world events in order to examine their suitability and feasibility. Maguire (2020) noted that any evaluation tools must be tested on real-world events and noted that only through testing its efficacy in applied contexts can the adoption of such tools be reinforced.

By testing the efficacy of such tools, future researchers could determine how comprehensive and consistent the tools are in facilitating greater levels of sustainability in the process of planning for environmental sustainability and assessing its value to the events industry. With the growing popularity of the events industry worldwide, the need to collect data, develop data sets, benchmark success and facilitate an evidence-informed approach to planning for environmental event sustainability would be beneficial to securing the future long-term competitiveness of the industry. Such data may also make way for valuable future longitudinal research on the topic. A longitudinal study could give a clear indication of any changes in the level of environmental event sustainability over time through the tools outlined above and would enable policy makers and event management organisations to track changes over time.

Without such an approach being adopted and utilised to better manage the environmental impacts associated with events, it would be difficult to establish any changes in respect of destinations transitioning towards environmental sustainability. Therefore, to embrace greater levels of sustainability in planning for event management in destinations moving forward, it would be useful to practitioners and researchers alike to undertake research in various destinations to determine the need for environmental event sustainability and to take action through the use of various tools and approaches as outlined in this chapter. This could provide more insights into environmental event sustainability and thereby broaden our comprehension and knowledge in different settings. Research in other destinations would help to identify alternative sustainable approaches to planning for events and enable comparisons to be made and best practice to be shared in the future.

Conclusion

This chapter has identified a fundamental need to place a priority on safeguarding the environmental resource base from event activities. Without an efficient and effective approach to environmental event sustainability, there is the potential for event industries to move beyond an acceptable level of environmental sustainability. As such, the need to plan to ensure that events take place within acceptable limits to the environmental resource base upon which events depend and in a way that caters for the increasingly growing and rapidly changing environment in which events now operate is essential. Without an acceptable level of environmental sustainability and valiant efforts being made towards planning for environmental sustainability at events, event activities will continue to create additional damage to the environment and also to society (Maguire, 2020). If destinations are to continue to be a competitive sector of tourism industries worldwide, policy makers must therefore act to safeguard the long-term environmental sustainability of event tourism products moving forward.

As much of the literature overlooks best practice approaches in achieving environmental event sustainability, this chapter attempts to draw attention to some approaches that have been developed to address sustainability issues and improve sustainability performance. Several tools have been suggested that can be adopted and utilised to facilitate a much needed evidence-informed approach to planning for event management moving forward. However, the need to test the efficacy of such tools in the context of event management planning in practice is essential. Therefore, the research recognises that calls need to be made to test such tools in studies of real-world events. The contribution of this research is to lead the way for practitioners and theorists to engage with discourse in relation to the implementation and transition towards environmental sustainability at events and to encourage the dissemination of best practice and lessons learned in environmental monitoring and management at events through various environmental sustainability tools and approaches. Moving forward, this may encourage destinations to effectively safeguard the environment from the impacts created by events and secure the future long-term competitiveness of the industry while garnering increased stakeholder support and taking away the tendency of destinations to view environmental issues as 'red tape bureaucracy' that merely tick regulatory boxes.

Without effective environmental sustainability efforts, it is difficult to comprehend how destinations can manage future growth in a planned, productive and sustainable way and ensure long-term economic, environmental and social sustainability moving forward. Therefore, if destinations, policy makers and event organisations wish to sustain the growth of the event sector and secure its future long-term sustainability, they need to work towards adopting and utilising a sustainable approach to planning for event management. Such an approach, if integrated as part of destination event licensing and regulatory processes, may facilitate improvements in relation to the current state of environmental sustainability for events. This may help to strengthen more sustainable planning for event management in future and provide a foundation with which to lay greater levels of environmental sustainability for event management moving forward.

References

Case, R. (2013), *Events and the Environment*. Routledge, London.

Ceron, J.P. and Dubois, G. (2003), Tourism and Climate Change: A Double Sense – the Case of France. Proceedings of the First International Conference on Tourism and Climate Change, Djerba, Tunisia. QTO, Madrid.

Choi, H. and Sirakaya, E. (2006), Sustainability Indicators for Managing Community Tourism. *Journal of Tourism Management*, 27(6), 1274–1289.

Collins, A. and Cooper, C. (2016), Measuring and Managing the Environmental Impacts of Festivals: The Contribution of the Ecological Footprint. *Journal of Sustainable Tourism*, 25(1), 1–15.

Collins, A., Jones, C. and Munday, M. (2009), Assessing the Environmental Impacts of Mega Sporting Events: Two Options? *Tourism Management*, 30, 828–837.

Davenport, J. and Switalski, T.A. (2006), Environmental Impacts of Transport Related to Tourism and Leisure Activities, in Davenport, J. and Davenport, J.L. (eds), *The Ecology of Transportation: Managing Mobility for the Environment*. Springer: London.

David, L. (2009a), Events and Tourism: An Environmental Approach and Impact Assessment. *Journal of Tourism, Challenges and Trends*, 2(2), 66–75.

David, L. (2009b), Environmental Impacts of Events, in Raj, R. and Musgrave, J. (eds), *Event Management and Sustainability*, CABI, Egham, 66–75.

Department of Housing Planning and Local Government (DHPLG) (2015), EIA and SEA, accessed 6 January at www.housing.gov.ie/planning/environmentalassessment/environmental-impact-assessment-eia/environmental-assessment

Dredge, D. and Whitford, M. (2011), Event Tourism Governance and the Public Sphere. *Journal of Sustainable Tourism*, 19(4–5), 479–499.

Environmental Protection Agency (EPA) (2012), SEA Effectiveness Review in Ireland: Action Plan 2012–2016, accessed 17 November 2020 at www.agriculture.gov.ie/media/migration/ruralenvironment/environment/seainformation/SeaActionPlan20122016.pdf

Environmental Protection Agency (EPA) (2020), Irelands Environment: An Integrated Assessment, accessed 3 January 2021 at www.epa.ie/media/EPA-Ireland%27s-Environment-2020-Summary.pdf

European Commission (EC) (2005), The SEA Manual: A Source Book on Strategic Environmental Assessment of Transport Infrastructure Plans and Programmes, accessed 7 January 2020 at http://ec.europa.eu/environment/archives/eia/sea-studies-and reports/pdf/beacon_manuel_en.pdf

European Commission (EC) (2013a), Enhancing the Competitiveness of Tourism in the EU, accessed 28 October 2020 at www.hotrec.eu/Documents/Document/20131009100029-Tourism_best_practices_-_full_report.pdf

European Commission (EC) (2013b), European Tourism Indicator System for Sustainable Destination Management, accessed 12 July 2019 at https://ec.europa.eu/growth/sectors/tourism/offer/sustainable/indicators_en

European Commission (EC) (2015), The SEA Directive (Directive 2001/42/EC), accessed 7 July 2020 at https://ec.europa.eu/environment/eia/sea-legalcontext.htm

European Commission (EC) (2016), European Tourism Indicator System for Sustainable Destination Management, accessed 20 December 2020 at http://ec.europa.eu/growth/sectors/tourism/offer/sustainable/indicators_en

European Commission (EC) (2017), Sustainable Tourism: Agenda for a Sustainable and Competitive European Tourism, accessed 4 February 2021 at http://eur-lex.europa.eu/legalcontent/EN/TXT/?uri=legissum:l10132

Fáilte Ireland (2016), Minister Ring Announces Funding of over €1m for Major Festivals and Events, accessed 4 March 2020 at www.failteireland.ie/Footer/MediaCentre/Minister-Ring-announces-funding-of-over-%E2%82%AC1m-for-ma.aspx

Ferdinand, N. and Kitchin, P. (2016), Events Management: An International Approach. Sage, London.

Fredline, L., Raybould, M., Jago, L. and Deery, M. (2005), Triple Bottom Line Event Evaluation: A Proposed Framework for Holistic Event Evaluation, accessed 8 September 2020 at www.researchgate.net/profile/Mike-Raybould/publication/40403798_Triple_Bottom_Line_Event_Evaluation_a_Proposed_Framework_for_Holisitic_Event_Evaluation/links/564bc8c408aeab8ed5e78a95/Triple-Bottom-Line-Event-Evaluation-a-Proposed-Framework-for-Holisitic-Event-Evaluation.pdf

Fredline, L., Jago, L. and Deery, M. (2013), The Social Impacts of Sports Events, in Fyall, A. and Garrod, B. (eds), Contemporary Cases in Sport Tourism. Goodfellow, Canada, 109–134.

Getz, D. and Page, S.J. (2016), Event Studies: Theory, Research and Policy for Planned Events. Routledge, London.

Global Sustainable Tourism Council (GSTC) (2013), Global Sustainable Tourism Criteria for Destinations, accessed 23 September 2020 at www.gstcouncil.org/gstc-criteria/gstc-destination-criteria/

Global Sustainable Tourism Council (GSTC) (2016), Certification and Accreditation, accessed 3 December 2020 at www.gstcouncil.org/for-destinations/

Global Sustainable Tourism Criteria for Destinations (GSTC-D) (2015), Overview of the Global Sustainable Tourism Criteria, accessed 7 November 2020 at www.gstcouncil.org/en/participate-in-gstc/gstc-member-application.html

Goldblatt, J. (2010), Special Events: A New Generation and the Next Frontier. Hoboken, NJ, John Wiley and Sons.

González, A., Gilmore, A., Foley, R., Sweeney, J. and Fry, J. (2011), Applying Geographic Information Systems to Support Strategic Environmental Assessment: Opportunities and Limitations in the Context of Irish Land-Use Plans. Environmental Impact Assessment Review, 31(3), 368–381.

Griffin, K. (2009), The DIT-ACHIEV Model: A Tool for Sustainable Event Management, in Raj, R. and Musgrave, J. (eds), Sustainability and Events, CABI, Oxford.

Gursoy, D. and Kendall, K.W. (2006), Hosting Mega Events: Modelling Locals Support. Annals of Tourism Research, 33(3), 603–628.

Jeong, G. and Faulkner, B. (1996), Resident Perceptions of Mega Event Impacts: The Taejon International Exposition Case. Festival Management and Event Tourism, 4, 2–11.

Jones, M. (2014), *Sustainable Event Management: A Practical Guide*. Routledge, London.

Jones, M. (2018), *Sustainable Event Management: A Practical Guide*. Earthscan, London.

Kersulić, A., Perić, M. and Wise, N. (2020), Assessing and Considering the Wider Impacts of Sport-Tourism Events: A Research Agenda Review of Sustainability and Strategic Planning Elements. *Sustainability*, 12(11), 4473.

Lee, N. and Walsh, F. (1992), Strategic Environmental Assessment: An Overview. *Project Appraisal*, 7, 126–136.

Liu, D. and Wilson, R. (2014), The Negative Impacts of Hosting Mega Sporting Events and Intention to Travel: A Test of the Crowding Out Effects Using the London 2012 Games as an Example. *International Journal of Sports Marketing and Sponsorship*, 15(3), 12–26.

Maguire K. (2019), Examining the Power Role of Local Authorities in Planning for Socio-economic Event Impacts. *Local Economy*, 34, 657–679.

Maguire, K. (2020), An Examination of the Level of Local Authority Sustainable Planning for Event Management: A Case Study of Ireland. *Journal of Sustainable Tourism*, 1–25.

Maguire K. and Hanrahan J. (2016), Local Authority Planning Provision for Event Management in Ireland: A Socio-Cultural Perspective, *Journal of Convention and Event Tourism*, 17, 129–158.

Maguire K. and Hanrahan J. (2017), Assessing the Economic Impact of Event Management in Ireland: A Local Authority Perspective. *Event Management*, 21, 333–346.

Maguire, K. and McLoughlin, E. (2019), An Evidence Informed Approach to Planning for Event Management in Ireland: An Examination of the European Tourism Indicator System. *Journal of Place Management and Development*, 13, 47–72.

Mair, J. (2011), Events and Climate Change: An Australian Perspective. *International Journal of Event and Festival Management*, 2(3), 245–253.

Mair, J. and Laing, J. (2013), Encouraging Pro-environmental Behaviour: The Role of Sustainability-Focused Events. *Journal of Sustainable Tourism*, 21(8), 1113–1128.

Mair, J. and Whitford, M. (2013), An Exploration of Event Research, Event Topics, Themes and Emerging Trends. *International Journal of Event and Festival Management*, 4(1), 6–30.

Mascarenhas, A., Coelho, P., Vaz, P., Dores, A. and Ramos, T.B. (2011), A Framework for Regional Sustainability Assessment: Developing Indicators for a Portuguese Region. *Sustainable Development*, 18(4), 211–219.

Miller, G. and Twinning-Ward, L. (2005), *Monitoring for a Sustainable Tourism Transition: The Challenges of Developing and Using Indicators*, CABI, Oxford.

Miller, G., Simpson, M. and Twinning-Ward, L. (2012), Study on the Feasibility of a European Tourism Indicator System for Sustainable Management at Destination Level, accessed 15 July 2020 at https://op.europa.eu/en/publication-detail/-/publication/3dc84d8b-fd50-4c27-bffc-5f046f607123

Mowforth, M. and Munt, I. (2009), *Tourism and Sustainability: Development and New Tourism in the Third World*, 3rd edn. Routledge, London.

Mowforth, M. and Munt, I. (2016), *Tourism and Sustainability: Development and New Tourism in the Third World*. Routledge, London.

National Planning Framework (NPF) (2018), Project Ireland 2040: National Planning Framework, accessed 23 April 2020 at http://npf.ie/

Organisation for Economic Co-operation and Development (OECD) (2004), Local Development Benefits from Staging Global Events: Achieving the Local Development Legacy from 2012, accessed 5 June 2020 at www.oecd.org

Partidario, M.R. (2003), Strategic Environmental Assessment (SEA) Current Practices, Future Demands and Capacity-Building Needs, accessed 5 August 2020 at www.iaia .org/pdf/Training/EIA/SEA/SEAManual.pdf

Partidario M.R. (2007), Scales and Associated Data: What Is Enough for SEA Needs? *Environmental Impact Assessment Review*, 27, 460–478.

Raj, R. and Musgrave, J. (2009), Event Management and Sustainability, CABI, Oxford.

Saayman, M. and Saayman, A. (2012), Determinants of Spending: An Evaluation of Three Major Sporting Events. *International Journal of Travel Research*, 14(2), 124–138.

Shanka, T. and Alamiyo, G. (2012), *Motivations to Visit Events/Festivals: An Exploratory Investigation*. Curtin University, Perth.

Sharpley, R. and Stone, P.R. (2011), Socio-Cultural Impacts of Events: Meanings, Authorized Transgression, and Social Capital, in Page, S. and Connell, J. (eds), *The Routledge Handbook of Events*. Routledge, London, 347–360.

Sniffen, J. (1995), UNEP Impact Assessment Meetings, in Mowforth, M. and Munt, I. (eds), *Tourism and Sustainability: New Tourism in the Third World*. Routledge, London.

UK Festival Industry Group (Powerful Thinking) (2016), The Show Must Go On, accessed 2 April 2020 at www.powerful-thinking.org.uk/vision2025

UNEP and UNWTO (2005), Making Tourism More Sustainable: A Guide for Policy-Makers, accessed 30 May 2020 at www.e-unwto.org/doi/book/10.18111/ 9789284408214

United Nations Conference on Trade and Development (UNCTAD) (2013), World Investment Report 2013, accessed 16 September 2020 at https://unctad.org/system/ files/official-document/wir2013_en.pdf

United Nations Convention to Combat Diversification (UNCCD) (2014), Land Degradation Neutrality: Resilience at Local, National and Regional Levels, accessed 5 May 2020 at www.unccd.int/lists/SiteDocumentLibrary/Publications/Land_Degrad _Nautrality_E_Web.pdf

United Nations Environment Programme (UNEP) (2012), Sustainable United Nations: Sustainable Events Guide: Give Your Large Event a Small Footprint, accessed 2 May 2020 at: worldcongress2012.iclei.org/fileadmin/templates/WC2012/Documents/ presentations/B3 Sustainable_Events_Guide.pdf

United Nations Environment Programme (UNEP) (2020), Recommendations on Plastic Pollution and Covid-19, accessed 6 September 2020 at www.oneplanetnetwork.org/ sustainable-tourism/recommendations-plastic-pollution-and-covid-19

United Nations World Tourism Organisation (UNWTO) (1996), *What Tourism Managers Need to Know: A Practical Guide to the Development and Use of Indicators of Sustainable Tourism*. WTO, Madrid.

United Nations World Tourism Organisation (UNWTO) (2004), Indicators of Sustainable Development for Tourism Destinations: A Guidebook. UNWTO, Madrid.

United Nations World Tourism Organisation (UNWTO) (2020), One Planet Vision for a Responsible Recovery of the Tourism Sector, accessed 6 November 2020 at: www .oneplanetnetwork.org/sustainable-tourism/covid-19-responsible-recovery-tourism

Van der Wagen, L. and White, L. (2010), *Event Management: For Tourism, Culture, Business and Sporting Events*. Pearson, Melbourne.

Wall, G. and Mathieson, A. (2006), *Tourism-Change, Impacts and Opportunities.* Pearson/Prentice Hall, Harlow.

Whitford, M., Phi, G.T. and Dredge, D. (2014), Principles and Practice: Indicators for Measuring Event Governance Performance. *Event Management*, 18(3), 387–403.

Wood, E. (2005), Measuring the Economic and Social Impacts of Local Authority Events. *International Journal of Public Sector Management*, 18(1), 37–53.

4. Social impacts of events

Nicholas Wise, Susanne Gellweiler, and Enqing Tian

Introduction

Much research from the events literature has focused on the importance of using events to develop and/or regenerate spaces and places (Schneider and Jacobson, 2019; Smith, 2012; Wise and Harris, 2019), build new destination images or brands (Hahm et al., 2019; Wise et al., 2015), or expand corporate and business interests (Hall, 2006). Scholars extend these understandings by referring to tangible benefits and the impacts that events have on place economies, destination planning, and the subsequent growth of tourism (Lauermann, 2019; Maguire, 2019; Maharaj 2015; Perić, 2018; Schausteck de Almeida et al., 2015). While it is important to address the role that events have on new or redeveloped facilities and infrastructures, and thus expansions for, or new investments in, events, leisure, and tourism, Andrews and Leopold (2013) and Moufakkir and Pernecky (2015) argue that within these avenues of research it is important to consider social and cultural impacts and the reactions of those who are ultimately "impacted" by event planning, hosting, developments, and management decisions. Research that considers transitioning economic bases sees planners and policy-makers directing decisions based on how to maintain a competitive advantage. But, as this may lead back to policies and investments aimed at developing spaces, the underlying social impacts that have an intangible impact on a place are part of an inherent and essential focus of research today concerning the impact of events. Concerning events and social impacts, Cowan (2016) argues that planning needs to be enabling so that residents are not met with barriers that limit their involvement. Much research that concerns social impacts of events critically assesses understandings through resident and community perspectives (e.g. Deery et al. 2012; Jepson and Clarke, 2015).

Broadly considering, social event impacts involve considerations of how members of a community, visitors, and event attendees engage with spaces and places (Gaffney, 2014), how events result in increased civic pride (Broudehoux, 2017), or how local well-being is transformed to include rather than exclude people from participating (Coakley and Souza, 2013). For instance, Jermyn (2001) categorized social impacts of events in four ways: hard outcomes, personal impacts, collective/group impacts, and civic/community impacts. Small (2007) identified six social event impact categories: inconvenience, community identity and cohesion, personal frustration, entertainment and socialization opportunities, community growth and development, and behavioral consequences. Relevant to these directions, Mao and Huang (2016) address three social impacts that events create: shape a new city image, promote community pride enhancement, and contribute to social development. The point on social development can refer to the celebration of cultural heritage, celebrating shared pasts, and reconfirming individual, community, and national identity—each shared and constructed through event experiences. Richards et al. (2013) and Wise and Harris (2019) argue that paying closer attention to intangible impacts influences planners and policy-makers to rethink decisions and consider the impacts that events create more holistically. Exploring and discussing differing trends associated with social impacts better allows researchers to critically position their debates and work with stakeholders to inform social and cultural policy. For instance, Smith (2012) assesses social impacts and social regeneration. Regeneration, again, is important to consider as a planning and policy concept because, and depending on the direction and impact of change in a particular setting, new developments can have adverse effects on social structures and on who is able to participate (Reis et al., 2013). The impetus of social impacts is to address how opportunities are further developed, and from a societal standpoint, these opportunities and experiences are linked to how people will benefit from hosting and planning for events (Wise and Perić, 2017).

Richards and Palmer (2010) argue that places need to keep up and respond to the pace of change or risk stagnation and decline. Given the vast expansion of (all types of) events in the past decade, places and destinations compete not only to host events, but to develop a new range of opportunities and attractions to destinations more attractive to consumers. These developments tend to focus on tangible gains and economic incentives, while the intangible impacts (on local populations who experience change happening around them) are secondary (Scholtz and Slabbert 2016; Smith 2005; Wise et al., 2021a). This focus on competitiveness and expanding for the purpose of economic productivity that encourages mass consumption aligns with competitiveness theory and planning techniques since the 1980s (Krugman, 1994). This influenced planning decisions through the 1990s which saw places transform unused or underused spaces, investing in event venues to bring economic activity back to places to add (economic) value to spaces and make places for consumption. Critical geographers and social theorists debated these capitalistic planning agendas (Harvey, 2012; Lefebvre, 1991), and many scholars looking at event spaces highlight the impact for local economies (Kim and Dombrosky, 2016), often forgoing who was being impacted by new developments—relating to Wise and Whittam's (2015) point about who regeneration is for.

With a focus on local and social impacts, scholars argue that competitiveness and contemporary planning agendas need to focus on creating additional value (Aquilino et al., 2019; Fytopoulou et al., 2021; Mendola and Volo, 2017; Wise et al., 2021b). Kubickova et al. (2017, 121) argue that social impacts pose a challenge because resident insight "might not inspire confidence in the impact that is directly attributable to tourism" or events to support economic growth. According to Wise et al. (2021b, 2431), "this position speaks back to performance-oriented research rationales solely concerned with tangible outcomes and economic deliverables". Crouch (2011) adds to this point that measuring and managing social impacts can pose a challenge for planners and policy-makers who seek to practically define approaches, and researchers who evaluate and critique approaches and outcomes. The next three sections of this chapter consider how social impacts of events are explored, measured, and managed going forward. The concluding section of the chapter puts emphasis on the need to consider well-being, quality of life, and social sustainability.

Exploring social impacts of events

According to Fredline et al. (2003, 26), "social impacts are defined as any impacts that potentially have an impact on quality of life for local residents. Thus, economic outcomes of events (such as employment opportunities) and environmental effects (such as litter) are included because perceptions of such impacts are likely to contribute to residents' overall reactions to an event." But a critical point that is not foreseen here, and alluded to above, is the need to consider issues of inclusion and exclusion (see Clark and Wise, 2018; Wise and Harris, 2017). Musgrave and Raj (2009) highlighted a number of positive and negative social event impacts. The positives include induced development and consumption (resulting in increased expenditures), promotional benefits that are long term, civic pride, community development, and new/increased employment opportunities. Negative impacts that result can include infrastructures not being maximized for future use, normal businesses being interrupted, resident exodus, lifestyle disruption, media reports not being supportive, community antagonism, security risks and issues, and unequal wealth distribution (Musgrave and Raj, 2009; Maguire, 2020).

Referring again to Lefebvre (1991) and Harvey (2012), who argue that the transformation of everyday spaces is appropriated by capital, they challenge us to continually question justice, access, and who has the right to consume. Their writing on the production of spaces, based on stipulations of control and power relations in unequal living/social environments, is widely accepted, and these issues are important for events researchers to address. Given current development and regeneration strategies touting "creative" efforts, the focus on consumption can sometimes distract from access (Cowan, 2016; Darcy, 2012). Thus, such top-down transformative measures which aim to "enhance" or "reproduce" a place image, add brand value, and/or generate new economic activity do not always consider how event planning and developments disrupt community foundations and social well-being (Murdoch, 2005). Inclusion and access in newly transformed urban spaces require the means to consume, and relate to Richards and Palmer's (2010) argument of meeting demands or risking stagnation. To Wise and Clark (2018), the processes of making and unmaking undermine different interest groups. There is also the dilemma of "creativity", which Richards (2020) highlights as a design principle for reproducing spaces and making places. But Wise and Clark (2018) challenge the term "creative" as merely a notion to brand places, and argue that it does not imply beneficial outcomes for all.

Putting emphasis on the role of the local community, and its contribution to events, it is important that communities leverage social outcomes (Đurkin and Wise, 2018) if social impacts are to be disseminated to the general public (see Misener and Mason, 2006). While some places rely on community initiatives, there is a need for decision-makers to step in and focus on promoting inclusive social policies to enable people to get/feel involved and participate. For example, a widely adapted focus on social capital has been an important conceptual focus and relates to Putnam's (2000) work that has greatly influenced sociological and political science research. Building on social capital, bonding capital has challenged events and community researchers to understand ties that help situate a greater sense of belonging, or sense of community (Aquilino et al., 2021; Wise, 2015). Much research has gained insight on how tourism has impacted a place from the standpoint of vested tourism stakeholders (e.g. Pulido-Fernández and Rodríguez-Díaz, 2016), but such insight is important to gain from the perspective of local residents as places invest heavily in changes (Fytopoulou et al., 2021; Wise et al., 2021b).

To outline issues concerning events and social impacts, from a policy stand-point governments and public-sector organizations need to further measure social impacts and social conditions because often what is proposed cannot always be met (Maharaj, 2017; Stell, 2014). Moreover, policy initiatives could do more at the local authority level to place efforts on improving local well-being (Clark et al., 2016; Hanrahan and Maguire, 2016), but just because something is proposed or intended does not mean that it is inclusive (Cowan, 2016; Rojek, 2013). Positive socio-cultural impacts are based on education, local experiences, improvements to residential facilities, maintaining cultural traditions and local artefacts, and increased civic pride is also a topical point of consideration (Smith, 2012; Spirou, 2011), but this can also include people's sense of being and their experiences and emotions towards an event (Gellweiler et al., 2019). For example, concerning tourism and social impacts, but likewise relevant to event planners and developers, the 1980 UNWTO Manila Declaration put emphasis on the need to consider social impacts. Given the growth and direction of tourism at the time, this focus on social impacts was to ensure just and socially sustainable futures in industries driven by financial bottom lines and maximizing economic impact. Events and tourism researchers as a response continue to address the declaration and the need to emphasize social legacy, or "softer" impacts in event studies (Getz and Page, 2016; Shipway and Fyall, 2012; Wise and Harris, 2019). Moreover, as Wise (2016, 32) argues: "numerous negative impacts on people and communities relate to the commodification of culture, violations of human rights, increased social problems, social demonstrations, loss of traditional industries, alterations in traditional codes (e.g. practices, values, religion) and community fragmentation". Lawless (2010) argues that social benefits and legacies are lost in the process as cities develop to host events, since funds are easily redistributed, or when hidden costs emerge.

Social impacts and social change are about altering people's outlooks and attitudes of their place (Deery et al. 2012). Moreover, designing studies where researchers seek to better understand how communities seek innovative ways to enhance social interactions can better allow researchers to work with and for a community through action research opposed to providing overviews of what might be needed to encourage change (see, for example, Conner, 2017; Wise, 2017). Thwaites et al. (2013) add that individual, social, and community capital provide researchers with different considerations and viewpoints as to how events impact people in local settings. By exploring social capital, researchers can understand the formation of networks, norms, and trusts in a local community and how and where collaboration helps enable people to set and meet shared objectives (Zhou and Kaplanidou, 2018). This is necessary because as places transform and develop to host future events and build attractions to add tourism and leisure opportunities, new developments will bring long-term impacts that can unite or divide people. Thus, stakeholder relations between public policy-makers, planners/developers, and the communities directly impacted challenge us to explore various and different visions of how events will impact on the people who reside in a place. Spirou (2011) critically sums up this point by arguing how some view investments in events and tourism as investments in someone else's interests—and do not always or necessarily favor what local residents need.

Measuring, analyzing, and managing social impacts of events

The purpose of measuring and analyzing the extent of social impacts following an event is to better understand if social transformation is achievable, and what future possibilities could lend to solutions that are favorable for populations affected by recent developments and hosting (Hall and Wise, 2019). Those most impacted and their concerns are not always publicized because their concerns can sit in the shadow of a new stadium or tribute spectacle highlights are what become synonymous with events and places. While event businesses and corporate investors involved with events gain exposure and get credit, there is also the need to address new enterprise or entrepreneurial activity among locals, as new businesses emerge from hosting events that have impacts locally and support communities (Jæger, 2020).

Yürük et al. (2017, 368) highlight that events "contribute to a sense of community, community pride, and spirit within host destinations, thus improving the quality of life of residents". Brolich et al. (2021) and Uysal et al. (2016) position the importance of well-being and quality of life. Directions from tourism, relevant to directions for events, suggest the need to address mediators between the impact of tourism, comparing impacts across different types of community residents, and investigating insights during different times and levels of development over time (Uysal et al., 2016). These points of focus can also direct researchers to consider anxieties and the level of stress that events put on local residents as well (Mooney et al., 2015). Quality of life and social behaviors direct researchers to well-being and impacts on people's mental health. According to Hansen et al. (2015, 1), being involved in meetings, training, or contributing to organizing events is "positively associated with each of the health parameters: good self-perceived health, good life-satisfaction, good self-esteem, and low anxiety and depression symptoms". A number of these directions are also explored in a recent edited collection by Jepson and Walters (2021). Here, equity and accessibility are at the forefront of critical considerations in event studies and event management research (Van Niekerk, 2017). Considerations for enhancing local quality of life is seen through job creation, improved and increased access to health facilities and care, new activities and entertainment options, upgraded park and recreation spaces, and new safety measures. Safety and crime incidents are complex, and the impacts locally can be felt by individuals through theft or alcohol/drug-related offences to wider issues including scams, violence, or wider threats linked to terrorist activity. These issues put pressures on local communities which can greatly disrupt everyday living environments.

Social impacts can result in a range of causal forces or stressors (Getz 2013). These include how expenditures and investments are directed (as people often ask: could money be spent on something else?) and how host–guest relations can result in problems or issues related to inclusion and exclusion. Furthermore, they encompass understanding the extent to which a community is involved, where event developments and activities are taking place and the role of the media in creating impressions of people and places. Events impact a range of different stakeholders, and when exploring social impacts it is particularly important to focus on resident perceptions (e.g. Fredline and Faulkner, 2000; Fytopoulou et al., 2021 ; Gursoy et al., 2017; Jordan et al., 2019; Li et al., 2018; Ma and Rotherham, 2016; Perić, 2018; van der Steen and Richards, 2019; Wise et al., 2021a). Here, scholars have used social exchange theory as a conceptual lens to explore local and resident perceptions to determine risks or costs (negative value) and benefits or rewards (positive value) (see Li et al., 2015; van der Steen and Richards, 2019). Social representations theory, is used as another approach to describe how values and attitudes are shared within a community based on past experiences or prior knowledge of something to understand perspectives when a bid is won or an event is hosted (Li et al., 2015). Relating back to social exchange theory, if residents form positive attitudes then they are more likely to engage in supportive behaviors.

Scholars argue that social impact research in events should take a longitudinal approach, i.e. to look at how events have impacted on communities and society over extended periods of time (see Gaffney, 2010; Wise et al., 2015). Various methodologies have been used in studies referenced through this chapter, but a key consideration when assessing social impacts is using subjective rather than objective measures because it can be difficult to develop objective social impact assessments given the scale of event, as they vary greatly and in impact from local community events like farmers' markets to global mega-sporting events. Several impact assessment tools or strategies have been considered to map and analyze different stakeholder concerns, but a key focus of social impact studies is community consultation to help inform planning decisions going forward (Allen et al., 2010), because the community can intervene by questioning/protesting decisions or voting out policy-makers when they run for re-election. A collaborative approach, according to Gursoy and Kendall (2006, 605), "encourages engagement, joint decision-making and [recognizes] collective responsibility to resolve conflicts or to advance vision". Most importantly, involving the community in decision-making allows them to recognize and realize impacts (Ntloko and Swart, 2008). This also points scholars to issues surrounding inclusion (involvement) and exclusion (isolation), which challenge authors to consider social justice, equity, and capital, which can impact on local well-being, participatory citizenship, and overall support. Here, Smith (2012) refers to degrees of citizen power (community control, where power is delegated, and partnerships), tokenism (placation, consultation, and extent of information), and non-participation (which can result in manipulation). The theoretical considerations discussed in this section relate to extrinsic and intrinsic ways of understanding social impacts (see Getz et al., 2019). Impact studies have been traditionally based on extrinsic models of community impact taking a macro-perspective where reactions and perspectives view the community as a single entity; whereas intrinsic models seek to explore and explain why support varies within a community.

Going forward in social impacts of events

Event organizations and developers focus on the promotion and branding of events and associated developments (Cudny, 2020). However, as framed and argued throughout this chapter, at all stages of an event lifecycle, researchers need to not only evaluate organizational impacts, but also the effect on people locally (across the socio-economic spectrum) because the scale of event impacts can often be concentrated, whereby some are included, whilst others are excluded. Scholars from various disciplines have long sought to understand notions of inclusion and exclusion concerning social impacts. As Van Der Merwe (2007) argues, tangible developments typically outweigh intangible impacts on communities. This is because corporate interests revolve around attracting investment and investors, which can result in community displacement, which results in local resistance (see Duignan et al., 2019). The development of an area for events often results in gentrification, which sees people who can no longer afford to reside in an area forced to move (Watt, 2013). Another critical perspective is offered by Maharaj (2017) concerning the creation of commercial restriction zones that resulted in displaced livelihoods among people engaged in fishing in Durban, South Africa. This crowding out is a form of economic displacement that has social consequences. While displacement often is viewed as forced, in some cases people will temporarily leave an area to avoid overcrowding (see Mules and Dwyer, 2005). Building on critical questions proposed above, to understand social impacts and who development is for, we also need to evaluate how local communities are actually impacted and by what standards researchers can measure these impacts (Wise, 2019). Despite proliferate events research, answering these questions from a social impact standpoint remains a challenge. This section refers to directions addressed by Chalip (2006, 2014), Deery et al. (2012), Getz (2013), Smith (2012), and Wise (2019) to help conceptualize social conditions to consider when evaluating event impacts.

Scholars point to the importance of enterprise opportunities because they provide training and skills acquisition that build human capital (Deery et al., 2012; Rojek, 2013; Wise and Harris, 2017) as well as confidence (Scott, 2020), which are economically and socially sustainable long term. These can also contribute to a greater local sense of community, placemaking and overall well-being through social interaction (Zhao and Wise, 2019). As such, increased employability and entrepreneurial activity can increase quality of life, especially in transitioning areas where residents have lived through event-oriented developments (Christie and Gibb, 2015; Wise, 2016; Wood, 2005). It is difficult to generalize research focusing on social and intangible impacts, and as discussed earlier on measuring impacts, bottom-up approaches and working closely with community stakeholders through inductive fieldwork is necessary if new (case-specific) knowledge is to emerge. For instance, Chalip's (2006, 2014) focus on social leveraging evidences the need to consider social outcomes based on social concerns. This is because of the liminality of events and how social impacts refer to social relations and social value. However, Chalip (2006) and Getz (2013) argue that various social elements (outcomes, concerns, relations, or associated value) are often inadequately measured. The concern here is that desired outcomes are merely proposed ideas (such as in a bid document), and thus frameworks to assess social impacts at different stages of an event lifecycle can lose focus—and if they lose focus they become overshadowed by economic impacts and demands for tangible evidence (Smith, 2012).

These issues point to the need to consider social conditions (Aquilino et al., 2019; Wise, 2019; Wise and Perić, 2017), as outlined in Table 4.1. Individual and social capital indicators are valuable to this discussion to reinforce the need to focus on how event-led developments altered the physical make-up of a community, thus considering how social benefits and sustained legacies can be achieved (see Agha et al., 2012; Chalip, 2014). Such "softer" impacts/ benefits can bring renewed attitudes and behaviors, based on how people feel involved, enthusiastic, or willing to participate (Camacho et al., 2019; Chalip and Fairley, 2019; Chien et al., 2012; Doumi et al., 2020; van der Steen and Richards, 2019). A common point from the articles referenced in the previous sentence is the need for clear and coherent policies and parallel relationships across stakeholders that are transparent. But as Smith (2012) and Perić et al. (2016) warn, managing how event impacts are leveraged remains a persistent challenge.

According to Wise (2019), identifying social conditions is a chance to provide a guiding framework for exploring, evaluating, and assessing social impacts in communities. Working directly with communities allows researchers to immerse themselves, which is a step towards more participatory approaches to research (Kindon, 2010; Ulian and Barbosa da Silva, 2020). Table 4.1 details 17 social conditions, organized around four guiding questions. While these questions are proposed and build on conceptual understandings from the literature, recent work has evaluated conditions proposed from Wise (2019) (see Aquilino et al., 2019; Wise et al., 2021b). The noted studies both took a quantitative measurement approach. So there is a need to explore and amend these conditions in different cases and through field-based research that respond to themes that emerge through work with and for communities, to offer new critical directions.

The first question is concerned with how local community stakeholders understand policies and what they feel they will gain (or not gain) from an event (Todd et al., 2016). This challenges researchers to gain a comprehensive understanding of policies and local relationships, including what support is available. Understanding this is necessary before moving on to the conditions associated with the second question on the need to explore experiences and involvement. Question 3 and associated social conditions move on to opportunities and insights on place and community. It is also important to understand if and how social policies are resulting in new involvement and opportunities for people in an events destination (see Gaffney, 2016). Local satisfaction and pride in place can be determined if we understand how people feel included or excluded, and this is where people will be critical of the impacts of new development. Moreover, and from community psychology and sociological standpoints, satisfaction and sense of community refer to membership, influence, shared emotional connections, and involvement (see McMillan and Chavis, 1986). The final question noted in Table 4.1 looks to the future, by exploring legacies, and whether future benefits are clear and socially sustainable. Grix

(2017) speaks directly to issues associated with legacy initiatives, highlighting again the difficulty to measure legacies, because they are also (often merely) proposed. Preuss (2007) argues, reinforced by Agha et al. (2012), that if events legacies are to be achieved, local stakeholders must be aware, informed, and involved. This guiding framework presents an attempt to explore the impacts of community change through social conditions that impact a range of local and community stakeholders when exploring social event impacts (Edwards, 2015).

Table 4.1   An overview of social conditions in social impact research

Question	Social conditions	What to observe and action
What does the community know about social impact plans and policies?	1. Clear policies on social benefits 2. Mutual understanding and tolerance among stakeholders 3. Local population is involved 4. Local population supports event initiatives	Identify key stakeholders Explore the extent of local knowledge and awareness Look into enthusiasm and participation
How do we go about measuring experiences and involvement of local community stakeholders?	5. Benefits from new infrastructures/venues 6. Mentorship/educational programs 7. Ability to start a local enterprise (to supply or support events) 8. Volunteer opportunities	Who is involved What programs exist Experience co-creation
What are the wider social opportunities?	9. Plans to minimize inclusion and exclusion 10. New opportunities (for youth, students, elderly, disabled, underprivileged, or underserved) 11. Place satisfaction (i.e. civic pride) 12. Increased sense of community and local identity	Community areas Social spaces How do people feel Reactions and behaviors
How do we work towards ensuring sustainable futures?	13. Co-management of venues/facilities 14. Access and ability to use venues/facilities 15. Legacy training initiatives 16. Participation incentives 17. Legacy agendas and benefits are clear	Who influences legacy Address power relations that exist and are limiting involvement Work with the community to determine solutions

Source: These 17 social conditions are adapted from and build on the 14 social conditions proposed by Wise (2019).

A review recently published by Mair et al. (2021) categorizes a range of social impacts relevant to mega-events. The authors explore the literature and identify eight key impact categories organized around two key themes: Theme 1 focusing on direct impact on residents (1. volunteering, education, and skills; 2. social cohesion, civic pride, and social capital; 3. inclusion and diversity; 4. sports participation, infrastructure, and health) and Theme 2 focusing on impacts on destination ecosystems (5. business and government networks; 6. destination branding; 7. disaster preparedness; 8. accessibility and accessible tourism) (Mair et al., 2021). For scholars studying the social impacts of events (at any scale), the social conditions discussed in this section provide some direction to critical questions, and the impact categories outlined and organized by Mair et al. (2021) will help guide researchers to explore critical and topical areas pertinent to contemporary research areas concerning event impacts. A consideration and focus on participation and active involvement, especially, is observed as an important area to consider going forward in social impact research (see, for example, Annear et al., 2019; Hansen et al., 2015; Reis et al., 2013; Ulian and Costa, 2015; Wise et al., 2021a, 2021b).

Conclusion

There are some considerable overlaps with Chapter 2 on economic impacts and Chapter 3 on environmental impacts with social impacts. Concerning socio-economic impacts, events can create jobs, but it is important to understand if these are temporary or will expand after an event. A successful event can see a new tourism economy emerge as a result of positive publicity, or how a destination showcases tourism opportunities and/or attractions. Socio-environmental impacts are also important to consider: these can include excessive noise, litter accumulation, and traffic congestion. These are not only unsightly, but can cause disruption and inconvenience to local residents, and the long-term consequences to the underlying environment can see people not engage with natural spaces as much and it takes away from a socially sustainable future (Wise, 2020; Ziakas, 2019). To Wallstam et al. (2020), exploring social impacts can allow researchers to work with stakeholders to inform effective policies that promote stakeholder involvement and give voice to local residents.

It is important to also consider social impacts of events in relation to competitiveness. Mendola and Volo (2017), who evaluated the assessment of destination competitiveness research, note that considerations of social prosperity and social development are acknowledged but underexplored. The authors further note that "the actual inclusion of well-being measurements is far from being achievable at this stage, yet that might be of high interest to many destinations" (Mendola and Volo, 2017, 551). Domínguez Vila et al. (2015) did attempt to address social impacts and accessibility, but looked at the perspective and impact of planning for consumption purposes opposed to local benefits. Given that there is much concern for evaluating economic performance indicators in events impact and competitiveness research, Aquilino et al. (2019) sought to explore a gap by developing a determinant dimension that assessed local social conditions and well-being. Such insight is important to consider locally because exploring impacts on residents directly can ultimately influence the success or failure of an event, and subsequently future tourism and leisure opportunities (Nadalipour et al., 2019).

There are a number of challenges when it comes to social impact assessments, and these include adequacy of indicators and theories of change, how unanticipated change is measured, how to know if enough valuable data has been collected, the reliability of self-reported data, financial proxies, and the ability to truly generalize findings given that the scale of events greatly varies. Richards and Marques (2016) highlight that considerations of impacts need to be continuous, promote stakeholder collaboration, and focus on the long term as opposed to the short term, stating that "monitoring and evaluation tend to concentrate on the short-term impacts produced by the event year itself, rather than the whole process from bid to legacy". This is a key consideration when exploring and evaluating social impacts, especially because demands and outcomes can change through an event lifecycle so continuous monitoring is needed to unremittingly and holistically understand how people and local communities are impacted by events. However, an important takeaway is that there is not a one-size-fits-all approach to measuring and that managing the social impacts of events will greatly vary because events differ based on scale, on local sites and situations, and on communities and cases which means that each event, case, and scenario needs to consider the needs and wants of the stakeholders.

References

Agha, N., Fairley, S., and Gibson, H. (2012), Considering legacy as a multi-dimensional construct: The legacy of the Olympic Games, *Sport Management Review* 15(1), 125–139.

Allen, J., O'Toole, W., Harris, R., and McDonnell, I. (2010), *Festival and Special Event Management*, Wiley, Oxford.

Andrews, H. and Leopold, T. (2013), *Events and the Social Sciences*, Routledge, London.

Annear, M.J., Shimizu, Y., and Kidokoro, T. (2019), Sports mega-event legacies and adult physical activity: A systematic literature review and research agenda, *European Journal of Sport Science* 19(5), 671–685.

Aquilino, L., Armenski, T., and Wise, N. (2019), Assessing the competitiveness of Matera and the Basilicata region (Italy) ahead of the 2019 European Capital of Culture, *Tourism and Hospitality Research* 19(4), 503–517.

Aquilino, L., Harris, J., and Wise, N. (2021), A sense of rurality: Events, placemaking and community participation in a small Welsh town, *Journal of Rural Studies* 83, 138–145.

Brolich, E., Perić, M., and Wise, N. (2021), Advice for Advent in Zagreb organizers: Insight into well-being and quality of life in Zagreb, in Jepson, A. and Walters, T. (eds), *Events and Wellbeing*, Routledge, London.

Broudehoux, A.-M. (2017), *Mega-Events and Urban Image Construction: Beijing and Rio de Janeiro*, Routledge, London.

Camacho, D.P., Alonso Dos Santos, M., and Duclos Bastias, D. (2019), The relationship between factors that contribute to support and future intentions in relation to a major sporting event, *Academia Revista Latinoamericana de Administración* 32(4), 442–454.

Chalip, L. (2006), Towards social leverage of sport events, *Journal of Sport and Tourism* 11(2), 109–127.

Chalip, L. (2014), From legacy to leverage, in Grix, J. (ed.), *Leveraging Legacies from Sports Mega-Events*, Palgrave Macmillan, London, 2–12.

Chalip, L. and Fairley, S. (2019), Thinking strategically about sport events, *Journal of Sport and Tourism* 23(4), 155–158.

Chien, P.M., Ritchie, B.W., Shipway, R., and Henderson, H. (2012), I am having a dilemma: Factors affecting resident support of event development in the community, *Journal of Travel Research* 51(4), 451–463.

Christie, L. and Gibb, K. (2015), A collaborative approach to event-led regeneration: The governance of legacy from the 2014 Commonwealth Games, *Local Economy* 30(8), 871–887.

Clark, J. and Wise, N. (2018), *Urban Renewal, Community and Participation: Theory, Policy and Practice*, Springer, Berlin.

Clark, J., Kearns, A., and Cleland, C. (2016), Spatial scale, time and process in mega-events: The complexity of host community perspectives on neighbourhood change, *Cities* 53, 87–97.

Coakley, J. and Souza, D.L. (2013), Sport mega-events: Can legacies and development be equitable and sustainable?, *Motriz Revista de Educação Física* 19, 580–589.

Conner, N. (2017), Sports and the social integration of migrants: Gaelic football, rugby football, and association football in South Dublin, in Koch, N. (ed.), *Critical Geographies of Sport*, Routledge, London, 190–206.

Cowan, A. (2016), *A Nice Place to Visit: Tourism and Urban Revitalization in the Postwar Rustbelt*, Temple University Press, Philadelphia, PA.

Crouch, G.I. (2011), Destination competitiveness: An analysis of determinant attributes, *Journal of Travel Research* 50, 27–45.

Cudny, W. (ed.) (2020), *Urban Events, Place Branding and Promotion*, Routledge, London.

Darcy, S. (2012), Disability, access, and inclusion in the event industry: A call for inclusive event research, *Event Management* 16(4), 259–265.

Deery, M., Jago, L., and Fredline, L. (2012), Rethinking social impacts of tourism research: A new research agenda, *Tourism Management* 33, 64–73.

Domínguez Vila, T., Darcy, S., and González, E.A. (2015), Competing for the disability tourism market: A comparative exploration of the factors of accessible tourism competitiveness in Spain and Australia, *Tourism Management* 47, 261–272.

Doumi, M., Kyriakaki, A., and Stavrinoudis, T. (2020), Small-scale cultural tourism events: Residents' perceptions on their quality and impacts, *Tourism Analysis* 25(2/3), 283–293.

Duignan, M.B., Pappalepore, I., and Everett, S. (2019), The "summer of discontent": Exclusion and communal resistance at the London 2012 Olympics, *Tourism Management* 70, 355–367.

Đurkin, J. and Wise, N. (2018), Managing community stakeholders in rural areas: Assessing the organisation of local sports events in Gorski kotar, Croatia, in Clarke, A. and Jepson, A. (eds), *Power, Construction and Meaning in Festivals and Events*, Routledge, London, 185–200.

Edwards, M.B. (2015), The role of sport in community capacity building: An examination of sport for development research and practice, *Sport Management Review* 18(1), 6–19.

Fredline, E. and Faulkner, B. (2000), Host communities reactions: A cluster analysis, *Annals of Tourism Research* 27(3), 763–784.

Fredline, L., Jago, L., and Deery, M. (2003), The development of a generic scale to measure social impacts of events, *Event Management* 8, 23–37.

Fytopoulou, E., Tampakis, S., Galatsidas, S., Karasmanaki, E., and Tsantopoulos, G. (2021), The role of events in local development: An analysis of residents' perspectives and visitor satisfaction, *Journal of Rural Studies* 82, 54–63.

Gaffney, C. (2010), Mega-events and socio-spatial dynamics in Rio de Janeiro, 1919–2016, *Journal of Latin American Geography* 9(1), 7–29.

Gaffney, C. (2014), A World Cup for whom? The impact of the 2014 World Cup on Brazilian football stadiums and cultures, in Fontes, P. and Holanda, B.B. (eds), *The Country of Football: Politics, Popular Culture, and the Beautiful Game in Brazil*, Oxford University Press, Oxford, 187–206.

Gaffney, C. (2016), The urban impacts of the 2014 World Cup in Brazil, in Gruneau, R. and Horne, J. (eds), *Mega-Events and Globalization: Capital and Spectacle in a Changing World Order*, Routledge, London, 167–185.

Gellweiler, S., Fletcher, T., and Wise, N. (2019), Exploring experiences and emotions sport event volunteers associate with "role exit", *International Review for the Sociology of Sport*, 54(4), 495–511.

Getz, D. (2013), *Event Tourism*, Cognizant, Putnam Valley, NY.

Getz, D. and Page, S.J. (2016), Progress and prospects for event tourism research, *Tourism Management* 52, 593–631.

Getz, D., Andersson, T.D., Armbrecht, J., and Lundberg, E. (2019), The value of festivals, in J. Mair (ed.), *The Routledge Handbook of Festivals*, Routledge, London, 22–30.

Grix, J. (2017), *Leveraging Mega-Event Legacies*, Routledge, London.

Gursoy, D. and Kendall, K.W. (2006), Hosting mega events: Modelling locals' support, *Annals of Tourism Research* 33(3), 603–623.

Gursoy, D., Yolal, M., Ribeiro, M.A., and Netto, A.P. (2017), Impact of trust on local residents' mega-event perceptions and their support, *Journal of Travel Research* 56(3), 393–406.

Hahm, J., Tasci, A.D.A., and Breiter Terry, D. (2019), The Olympic Games' impact on South Korea's image, *Journal of Destination Marketing and Management* 14, 100373.

Hall, C.M. (2006), Urban entrepreneurship, corporate interests and sports mega-events: The thin policies of competitiveness within the hard outcomes of neoliberalism, *The Sociological Review* 54(2), 59–70.

Hall, G. and Wise, N. (2019), Introduction: Sport and social transformation in Brazil, *Bulletin of Latin American Research* 38(3), 265–266.

Hanrahan, J. and Maguire, K. (2016), Local authority planning provision for event management in Ireland: A socio-cultural perspective, *Journal of Convention and Event Tourism*, 17(2), 129–158.

Hansen, E., Sund, E., Knudtsen, M.S., Krokstad, S., and Holmen, T.L. (2015), Cultural activity participation and associations with self-perceived health, life-satisfaction and mental health: The Young HUNT Study, Norway, *BMC Public Health*, 15, 544.

Harvey, D. (2012), *Rebel Cities: From the Right to the City to the Urban Revolution*, Verso, London.

Jæger, K. (2020), Event start-ups as catalysts for place, sport and tourism development: Moment scapes and geographical considerations, *Sport in Society* 23(1), 40–55.

Jepson, A.S. and Clarke, A. (eds) (2015), *Exploring Community Festivals and Events*, Routledge, London.

Jepson, A.S. and Walters, T. (eds) (2021), *Events and Well-Being*, Routledge, London.

Jermyn, H. (2001), *The Arts and Social Exclusion*, Arts Council of England, London.

Jordan, T., Gibson, F., Stinnett, B., and Howard, D. (2019), Stakeholder engagement in event planning: A case study of one rural community's process, *Event Management* 23(1), 61–74.

Kim, S. and Dombrosky, J. (2016), Economic impact of small scale event to the local economy: Case of Canfield Fair, *Journal of Tourism Insights* 7(1), 1–10.

Kindon, S. (2010), Participatory action research, in Hay, I. (ed.), *Qualitative Research Methods in Human Geography*, Oxford University Press, Oxford, 259–277.

Krugman, P. (1994), Competitiveness: A dangerous obsession, *Foreign Affairs* 73(2), 28–44.

Kubickova, M., Croes, R., and Rivera M. (2017), Human agency shaping tourism competitiveness and quality of life in developing economies, *Tourism Management Perspectives* 22, 120–131.

Lauermann, J. (2019), The urban politics of mega-events, grand promises meet local resistance, *Environment and Society* 10(1), 48–62.

Lawless, P. (2010), Urban regeneration: Is there a future?, *People, Place and Policy Online* 4, 24–28.

Lefebvre, H. (1991), *The Production of Space*, Blackwell, Oxford.

Li, H., Schein, D.D., Ravi, S. P., Song, W., and Gu, Y. (2018), Factors influencing residents' perceptions, attitudes and behavioral intention toward festivals and special events: A pre-event perspective, *Journal of Business Economics and Management* 19(2), 288–306.

Li, X., Hsu, C.H.C., and Lawton, L.J. (2015), Understanding residents' perception changes toward a mega-event through a dual-theory lens, *Journal of Travel Research* 54(3), 396–410.

Ma, S.C. and Rotherham, I.D. (2016), Residents' changed perceptions of sport event impacts: The case of the 2012 Tour de Taiwan, *Leisure Studies* 35(5), 616–637.

Maguire, K. (2019), Examining the power role of local authorities in planning for socio-economic event impacts, *Local Economy* 34(7), 657–679.

Maguire, K. (2020), An examination of the level of local authority sustainable planning for event management: A case study of Ireland, *Journal of Sustainable Tourism*, https://doi.org/10.1080/09669582.2020.1828431

Maharaj, B. (2015), The turn of the south? Social and economic impacts of mega-events in India, Brazil and South Africa, *Local Economy* 30(8), 983–999.

Maharaj, B. (2017), Contesting displacement and the struggle for survival: The case of subsistence fisher folk in Durban, South Africa, *Local Economy* 32(7), 744–762.

Mair, J., Chien, P.M., Kelly, S.J., and Derrington, S. (2021), Social impacts of mega-events: A systematic narrative review and research agenda, *Journal of Sustainable Tourism*, https://doi.org/10.1080/09669582.2020.1870989

Mao, L.L. and Huang, H. (2016), Social impact of Formula One Chinese Grand Prix: A comparison of local residents' perceptions based on the intrinsic dimension, *Sport Management Review* 19(3), 306–318.

McMillan, D. and Chavis, D. (1986), Sense of community: A definition and theory, *Journal of Community Psychology* 14(1), 6–23.

Mendola, D. and Volo, S. (2017), Building composite indicators in tourism studies: Measurements and applications in tourism destination competitiveness, *Tourism Management* 59, 541–553.

Misener, L. and Mason, D. (2006), Creating community networks: Can sporting events offer meaningful sources of social capital?, *Managing Leisure* 11(1), 39–56.

Mooney, G., McCall, V., and Paton, K. (2015), Exploring the use of large sporting events in the post-crash, post-welfare city: A "legacy" of increasing insecurity?, *Local Economy* 30(8), 910–924.

Moufakkir, O. and Pernecky, T. (eds) (2015), *Ideological, Social and Cultural Aspects of Events*, CABI, Wallingford.

Mules, T. and Dwyer, L. (2005), Public sector support for sport tourism events: The role of cost-benefit analysis, *Sport in Society* 8(2), 338–355.

Murdoch, S. (2005), Community development and urban regeneration, *Community Development Journal* 40(4), 439–446.

Musgrave, J. and Raj, R. (2009), Introduction to a conceptual framework for sustainable events, in Raj, R. and Musgrave, J. (eds), *Event Management and Sustainability*, CABI, Cambridge, MA, 1–12.

Nadalipour, Z., Imani Khoshkhoo, M.H., and Eftekhari, A.R. (2019), An integrated model of destination sustainable competitiveness, *Competitiveness Review* 29(4), 314–335.

Ntloko, N.J. and Swart, K. (2008), Sport tourism event impacts on the host community: A case study of Red Bull Big Wave Africa, *South African Journal for Research in Sport, Physical Education and Recreation* 30(2), 79–93.

Perić, M. (2018), Estimating the perceived socio-economic impacts of hosting large-scale sport tourism events, *Social Sciences* 7(10), 176.

Perić, M., Đurkin, J., and Wise, N. (2016), Leveraging small-scale sport events: Challenges of organising, delivering and managing sustainable outcomes in rural communities: The case of Gorski kotar, Croatia, *Sustainability* 8, 1337.

Preuss, H. (2007), *The Impact and Evaluation of Major Sporting Events*, Routledge, London.

Pulido-Fernández, J.I. and Rodríguez-Díaz, B. (2016), Reinterpreting the World Economic Forum's global tourism competitiveness index, *Tourism Management Perspectives* 20, 131–140.

Putnam, R. (2000), *Bowling Along: The Collapse and Revival of American Community*, Simon and Schuster, New York.

Reis, A.C., Sousa-Mast, F.R., and Vieira, M.C. (2013), Public policies and sports in marginalised communities: The case of Cidade de Deus, Rio de Janeiro, Brazil, *World Leisure Journal* 55(3), 229–251.

Richards, G. (2020), Designing creative places: The role of creative tourism, *Annals of Tourism Research* 85, 102922.

Richards, G. and Marques, L. (2016), Bidding for success? Impacts of the European Capital of Culture bid, *Scandinavian Journal of Hospitality and Tourism* 16(2), 180–195.

Richards, G. and Palmer, R. (2010), *Eventful Cities: Cultural Management and Urban Revitalisation*, Butterworth-Heinemann, Oxford.

Richards, G., de Brito, M., and Wilks, L. (2013), *Exploring the Social Impacts of Events*, Routledge, London.

Rojek, C. (2013), *Event Power: How Global Events Manage and Manipulate*, SAGE, London.

Schausteck de Almeida, B., Bolsmann, C., Júnior, W.M., and de Souza, J. (2015), Rationales, rhetoric and realities: FIFA's World Cup in South Africa 2010 and Brazil 2014, *International Review for the Sociology of Sport* 50(3), 265–282.

Schneider, W. and Jacobson, K. (2019), *Transforming Cities: Paradigms and Potentials of Urban Development within the "European Capital of Culture"*, Olms Verlag, Hildesheim.

Scholtz, M. and Slabbert, E. (2016), The relevance of the tangible and intangible social impacts of tourism on selected South African communities, *Journal of Tourism and Cultural Change* 14(2), 107–128.

Scott, D.S. (2020), The confidence delusion: A sociological exploration of participants' confidence in sport-for-development, *International Review for the Sociology of Sport* 55(4), 383–398.

Shipway, R. and Fyall, A. (2012), *International Sports Events: Impacts, Experiences and Identities*, Routledge, London.

Small, K. (2007), Social dimensions of community festivals: An application of factor analysis in the development of the social impact perception (sip) scale, *Event Management* 11(1), 45–55.

Smith, A. (2005), Conceptualizing image change: The reimagining of Barcelona, *Tourism Geographies* 7, 398–423.

Smith, A. (2012), *Events and Urban Regeneration: The Strategic Use of Events to Revitalise Cities*, Routledge, London.

Spirou, C. (2011), *Urban Tourism and Urban Change: Cities in a Global Economy*, Routledge, London.

Stell, M. (2014), Candidate cities, citizens and the Commonwealth Games: The limits of aspiration, in Dun, S., Spracklen, K., and Wise, N. (eds), *Game Changer: The Transformative Potential of Sport*, ID Press, Oxford, 127–142.

Thwaites, K., Mathers, A., and Simkins, I. (2013), *Socially Restorative Urbanism*, Routledge, London.

Todd, L., Leask, A., and Ensor, J. (2016), Understanding primary stakeholders' multiple roles in hallmark event tourism management, *Tourism Management* 59, 494–509.

Ulian F. and Barbosa da Silva, R. (2020), Using mobile methods to analyze physical activity in the district of Itaquera, São Paulo, Brazil, *Sport in Society* 23(1), 24–39.

Ulian, F. and Costa, A.M.M. (2015), The legacy of the FIFA World Cup 2014: Urban mobility in five Brazilian cities, *Revista InSIET* 2(2), 23–37.

Uysal, M., Sirgy, M.J., Woo, E., and Kim, H. (2016), Quality of life (QOL) and well-being research in tourism, *Tourism Management* 53, 244–261.

Van Der Merwe, J. (2007), Political analysis of South Africa's hosting of the rugby and cricket World Cups: Lessons for the 2010 football World Cup and beyond?, *Politikon* 34(1), 67–81.

van der Steen, T. and Richards, G. (2019), Factors affecting resident support for a hallmark cultural event: The 2018 European Capital of Culture in Valletta, Malta, *Journal of Policy Research in Tourism, Leisure and Events*, https://doi.org/10.1080/19407963.2019.1696352

Van Niekerk, M. (2017), Contemporary issues in events, festivals and destination management, *International Journal of Contemporary Hospitality Management* 29(3), 842–847.

Wallstam, M., Ioannides, D., and Pettersson, R. (2020), Evaluating the social impacts of events: In search of unified indicators for effective policymaking, *Journal of Policy Research in Tourism, Leisure and Events* 12(2), 122–141.

Watt, P. (2013), "It's not for us": Regeneration, the 2012 Olympics and the gentrification of East London, *City* 17(1), 99–118.

Wise, N. (2015), Placing sense of community, *Journal of Community Psychology* 43(7), 920–929.

Wise, N. (2016), Outlining triple bottom line contexts in urban tourism regeneration, *Cities* 53, 30–34.

Wise, N. (2017), In the shadow of mega-events: The value of ethnography in sports geography, in Koch, N. (ed.), *Critical Geographies of Sport*, Routledge, London, 220–234.

Wise, N. (2019), Towards a more enabling representation: Framing an emergent conceptual approach to measure social conditions following mega-event transformation in Manaus, Brazil, *Bulletin of Latin American Research* 38(3), 300–316.

Wise, N. (2020), Eventful futures and triple bottom line impacts: BRICS, image regeneration and competitiveness, *Journal of Place Management and Development* 13(1), 89–100.

Wise, N. and Clark, J. (eds) (2018), *Urban Transformations: Geographies of Renewal and Creative Change*, Routledge, London.

Wise, N. and Harris, J. (eds) (2017), *Sport, Events, Tourism and Regeneration*, Routledge, London.

Wise, N. and Harris, J. (eds) (2019), *Events, Places and Societies*, Routledge, London.

Wise, N. and Perić, M. (2017), Sports tourism, regeneration and social impacts: New opportunities and directions for research, the case of Medulin, Croatia, in Bellini, A. and Pasquinelli, C. (eds), *Tourism in the City: Towards an Integrative Agenda on Urban Tourism*, Springer, Berlin, 311–320.

Wise, N. and Whittam, G. (2015), Editorial: Regeneration, enterprise, sport and tourism, *Local Economy* 30(8), 867–870.

Wise, N., Đurkin Badurina, J., and Perić, M. (2021a), Assessing residents' perceptions of urban placemaking prior to hosting a major cultural event, *International Journal of Event and Festival Management* 12(1), 51–69.

Wise, N., Đurkin Badurina, J., and Perić, M. (2021b), Pre-event competitiveness: Exploring residents' perceptions of place management and local impacts, *International Journal of Contemporary Hospitality Management* 33(7).

Wise, N., Flinn, J., and Mulec, I. (2015), The Exit Festival: Contesting political pasts, impacts on youth culture and regenerating the image of Serbia and Novi Sad, in

Moufakkir, O. and Pernecky, T. (eds), *Ideological, Social and Cultural Aspects of Events*, CABI, Wallingford, 60–73.

Wood, E.H. (2005), Measuring the economic and social impacts of local authority events, *International Journal of Public Sector Management* 18(1), 37–53.

Yürük, P., Akyol, A., and Şimşek, G.G. (2017), Analyzing the effects of social impacts of events on satisfaction and loyalty, *Tourism Management* 60, 367–378.

Zhao, Y. and Wise, N. (2019), Evaluating the intersection between "green events" and sense of community at Liverpool's Lark Lane Farmers Market, *Journal of Community Psychology* 47(5), 1118–1130.

Zhou, R. and Kaplanidou, K. (2018), Building social capital from sport event participation: An exploration of the social impacts of participatory sport events on the community, *Sport Management Review* 21(5), 491–503.

Ziakas, V. (2019), Issues, patterns and strategies in the development of event portfolios: Configuring models, design and policy, *Journal of Policy Research in Tourism, Leisure and Events* 11(9), 121–158.

PART II

Research themes and case examples

5. Convention events

Jeeyeon Jeannie Hahm

Conventions, the convention industry, and convention centers

A convention is defined by the Events Industry Council (EIC) as a "gathering of delegates, representatives, and members of a membership or industry organization convened for a common purpose. Common features include educational sessions, committee meetings, social functions, and meetings to conduct the governance business of the organization. Conventions are typically recurring events with specific, established timing" (EIC, 2020). It is also known as a congress or conference. While the term convention is typically used in the United States, the term congress is generally used in Europe. Compared to congresses or conventions, conferences are usually shorter in duration with specific objectives, and are mostly on a smaller scale (EIC, 2020). Some conventions include an exhibition component. These events are also known as trade shows or trade fairs. The characteristics of these events are that businesses (exhibitors) display products, services, or promotional materials to attendees visiting their exhibits on the show floor. The primary focus is on business-to-business relationships (EIC, 2020). If the consumer/buyer/attendee is the general public, these events are referred to as consumer shows, public shows, or gate shows—the primary focus is on business-to-consumer relationships. Altogether, the industry typically refers to these events as business events or MICE (meeting, incentive, conference/congress, and exhibition) events.

Conventions are a key source of income for associations. Attendees pay registration fees, sponsors support the event while benefiting from their exposure to attendees, and exhibitors pay for the opportunity to showcase their products and services to a well-targeted group of attendees. Exhibitors spend a lot of money to participate at a convention but it is at a lower cost compared to making sales trips to meet potential buyers individually (Fenich, 2019). The amount of business that is generated by conventions is substantiated. The enormous impact of convention or business events has been well documented in industry reports and in academic research (e.g., Dwyer et al., 2000a, 2000b; Jones and Li, 2015). There are millions of people around the world that travel to attend conventions. These activities provide social, cultural, and economic benefits to host destinations (Dwyer et al., 2000a). Of the positive impacts, the economic benefits of conventions are substantial. It is well known that business travelers tend to spend more at a destination than the average leisure traveler (Davidson and Cope, 2003). Conventions create a strong multiplier effect on the economy that reaches beyond lodging, restaurants, attractions, retail, and transportation (Kim and Chon, 2009). According to a study commissioned by the EIC in 2018 and conducted by Oxford Economics, business events generated a total of $2.5 trillion in global business sales in 2017 (see again, EIC, 2020). The industry supported 26 million global jobs and $1.5 trillion of gross domestic product. The massive economic impact of the business events sector is demonstrated by the fact that it generated more direct output than other major global industries, such as consumer electronics, computers, and office equipment.

The convention industry has seen dramatic growth over the past several decades (Spiller, 2002) while experiencing some variation along the way due to external factors such as the economy, globalization, cost of travel, oil prices, and terrorism (Cetron and DeMicco, 2004). In recognition of the massive economic impact of conventions, destinations have been investing in convention infrastructure development since the 1960s. The building boom occurred during the 1980s and 1990s (Cetron and DeMicco, 2004), with acceleration in the 1990s continuing into the year 2000 (Rogers, 2008). The September 11 terrorist attacks exacerbated the already declining growth in 2001 (Cetron and DeMicco, 2004). The industry bounced back from 2004 to 2007 with moderate to dramatic growth in planner budgets, overall attendance, attendee spending, number of meetings, and length of meetings. Then, the recession in the United States at the end of 2007 to 2009 negatively hit the industry again (MPI, 2010). The major blow that no one could have predicted happened in 2020 with the COVID-19 pandemic. This was worse than any other time in history because the entire world came to a standstill. The economic loss for convention centers, other venues, and many businesses that rely on conventions has been in the billions. As of early 2021, the industry is slowly getting back by implementing safety protocols, limiting in-person attendance, and hosting hybrid or virtual events. The volatile global environment continues to create challenges for convention organizers to continue with their events and attract attendees.

The venues where many conventions, congresses, or conferences are held, convention centers, are economic drivers of the local community. Cities have been spending millions of dollars to build convention centers and further expand them to increase their hosting capacities. Along with convention center development, infrastructure surrounding the facility is expanded including hotels, restaurants, transportation, and roads. It is estimated that between 2002 and 2011, cities in the United States invested $13 billion in convention center construction, expansion, and remodeling (Sanders, 2014). In addition, meeting space at convention centers has expanded from 36.4 million square feet in 1989 to 70.5 million square feet in 2011 (Sanders, 2014). In more recent years, major convention destinations have been devoting millions of dollars on upgrading and modernizing their facilities. Convention centers are traditionally known to be massive blocky warehouse-like structures with lots of space to handle large events rather than attractive architectural beauties. However, a transformation in convention center design has been happening in recent years with consideration of the attendees and meeting planners. City governments have been hiring architects to design a stunning exterior incorporating more glass than blocked walls. When the Orange County Convention Center (OCCC) located in Orlando, Florida almost doubled its total size by adding another building to it several years ago, in addition to the glass-walled pre-function areas, the architect created grand arched entries while making them efficient and elegant exposed structures. This has given the building its distinctive and welcoming look that is well known today (Walter P. Moore, 2020). Miami hired top architects to redesign the exterior of its convention center. The façade has more than 500 oversize fins of aluminum and glass to resemble an ocean wave (Peterson, 2019).

The interior design philosophy of convention centers has been improving by incorporating design elements that provide "warmth" and an inviting feel compared to the "cold" look and feel of its utilitarian spaces. Meeting planners are asking for more hotel-quality interiors with flexibility of space. Convention centers have been adding accent artwork (e.g., sculptures, paintings), modern light fixtures, comfortable furniture, and geometric-designed carpets. There is an increase in integrating local flavor into the designs. In terms of space and show floor design, centers are focusing on different configurations and different uses of space that can enhance engagement while staying relevant and entertaining (Fenich, 2019). Some new features seen in recent years include hubs (or pop-up meeting rooms), education centers, interactive spaces, and tech centers (Fenich, 2019). As such, the needs and wants of meeting planners and attendees have been challenging convention centers to reimagine their designs and space usage.

A substantial part of the remodeling and upgrades for convention centers has been related to sustainability and technology. About a decade ago, the concept of green meetings started to gain attention. The EIC created the APEX/ASTM Environmentally Sustainable Meeting Standards in 2013 that meeting venues can follow to demonstrate and validate their sustainability commitments (EIC, 2020). Some of the criteria include: maintaining energy-efficient practices throughout the building, performing energy audits, using LED technology and generating renewable energy on-site; taking steps to ensure high air quality, from incentivizing attendees and workers to reduce their carbon footprint through alternative transportation options; and measuring waste and recycling, regularly setting aggressive targets for waste diversion, providing a composting program, and eliminating single-use plastics (Alderton, 2019). Additionally, convention centers are adding solar panels on rooftops, rooftop gardens with honeybees, indoor vertical hydroponic gardens, and food donation programs. Many convention centers share the responsibility to reduce their environmental impact, recognizing the number of events and the volume of people they host and the enormous amount of economic activity they generate. Sustainability for convention centers has become an expectation and norm among event organizers, meeting planners, and attendees. In the United States, convention centers have been investing in earning Leadership in Energy and Environmental Design (LEED) certification, a globally recognized green building rating system. The David L. Lawrence Convention Center located in Pittsburgh, Pennsylvania was the first convention center in the United States to achieve LEED Gold certification in 2003 when it opened. At the time, it was recognized as the largest green building in the world (Exhibit City News, 2017). Currently, the center holds a LEED Platinum building status along with the Oregon Convention Center, which are the only convention centers to have earned the highest designation in the United States.

Technology has become an imperative concern in recent years and more so when the world had to promptly adapt to virtual and hybrid meetings during the pandemic. Convention centers have been working diligently to upgrade existing or add new technology in response to planners' needs and wants. Common upgrades that centers have been working on are adding more bandwidth and improving Wi-Fi and cellphone reception. Some advanced features that are being considered include high-tech audiovisual equipment in meeting spaces, 4K LED screens, smart building systems, meeting room key cards, digital signage, 3D printers, virtual reality experiences (including virtual site tours), cyber security tools, and convertible seating arrangements (e.g., the Swiss Tech Convention Center) (Social Tables, n.d.). When it comes to technology, functionality is the most important aspect. Technology availability and functionality can make or break an event, which affects future business. There is no benefit to having impressive high-tech gear if it does not function seamlessly. Technology needs to function well while increasing productivity, efficiency, and engagement.

Orange County Convention Center

The OCCC is located in Orlando, Florida, just 15 minutes from Orlando International Airport. The multi-award-winning convention center is currently the second largest convention facility in North America showcasing two beautiful buildings. The West Concourse features over 1 million square feet of exhibition space, 49 meeting rooms, 141 breakout rooms, a ballroom, a multi-purpose room, a theater, a lecture hall, boardrooms, a business center, a full-service restaurant, and four food courts. A 1,500 foot Oversight Pedestrian Bridge with moving sidewalks connects the West to the North/South Concourse. The North/South Concourse showcases unique architecture and tropical ambiance designed for flexibility and functionality. This concourse features less than a million square feet of exhibition space, general assembly areas, 25 meeting rooms, 94 breakout rooms, two full-service restaurants, four food courts, and two business centers (OCCC, 2020b). There are 116,000 hotel rooms in the surrounding area with 5,000 directly connected to the center by pedestrian bridges. On average, the OCCC hosts nearly 200 events annually. These events include 115 conventions and trade shows that attract more than 1.5 million attendees, providing approximately $3 billion in economic impact to the Central Florida region each year (OCCC, 2020a).

The mission of the center is economic development. The International Association of Amusement Parks and Attractions' (IAAPA) annual convention generates one of the highest economic impacts to Central Florida. The association has met at the convention center for the past 15 years, except for three times, and is on the books until 2030. The show attracts about 40,000 attendees from over 100 countries. Basically, an amusement park is built on the show floor with rides, rope courses, large inflatables, video games, and bowling, to name a few (Winston, 2020). It is not just the size and capability to host a large show but it is the relationships the center builds with their clients that bring them back year after year.

During the fiscal year 2019–2020, before the COVID-19 pandemic, the OCCC had success with an estimated 667,000 attendees across 79 events, generating an economic impact of $1.49 billion estimated. Since March 2020, 78 conventions were canceled with an estimated economic impact of $2.1

billion, as of January 2021 (OCCC, 2021b). The center managed to reschedule 103 events for the 2021 fiscal year, as of February 2021, with 25 to 40 more gatherings expected (Northstar Meetings Group, 2021). The center hosted its first in-person trade show "Together Again Expo" in July 2020 with more than 1,400 people in attendance. It was the first show held at the center since March 2020. From March to December 2020, the center welcomed more than 50 events under modified operations. In the fall of 2020, the IAAPA, National Business Aviation Association, and American Dental Association's annual meetings were back at the center (Winston, 2020). In December 2020, the center hosted three major conventions – the American Kennel Club National Championship presented by Royal Canin (est. 6,000 people with an economic impact of $15.4 million), Olympia Fitness and Performance Weekend (economic impact of $7.7 million), and the Central Florida International Auto Show (est. 13,000 people) (OCCC, 2021a). These large-scale conventions have been held safely without incident (Northstar Meetings Group, 2021).

When the outbreak of COVID-19 started, many convention centers stepped up to help. Facilities were converted into makeshift medical facilities, testing sites, and PPE storage and distribution sites. The OCCC was not an exception with its community impact. The center offered its large parking lot as a coronavirus testing site. With the availability of vaccinations in December 2020, it has transformed into a large-scale vaccination site. At the same time, testing is still going on in one area in a remote parking garage and will continue (Doyle, 2021).

The OCCC is leading the industry as a model for safely hosting live events. In response to the COVID-19 pandemic, safety has been the primary focus for the center. Some precautions that were taken include more hand sanitizer stations, staggered attendance suggestions, specific entries and exits, wider aisles with directional signage, floor stickers, temperature checks, and enhanced cleaning. The OCCC was one of the first convention centers in the United States to become GBAC Star certified, a third-party validation of rigorous sanitation protocols, in coronavirus cleaning and prevention (OCCC, 2020a; Winston, 2020). This is an effort that venues are taking to bring back live events safely. The center released a Recovery and Resiliency Plan in June 2020 that outlines new safety protocols for meeting rooms, food and beverage service, audiovisual equipment, and so on (Northstar Meetings Group, 2021). The center has been collaborating with area hospitals, Orlando Health, for several offerings such as medically certified communication materials, 24/7 medical concierge, customized medical plan guidance, planner access to a medical expert, access to PPE for attendees, and medical advisory services to an event's host hotels and transportation vendors (Winston, 2020).

Another area of concentration is related to innovative and sophisticated technology. The center launched the OCCC Executive Studio, which is a new state-of-the-art digital broadcast center for hybrid conventions and trade shows. An event of any size can access the digital equipment to produce interactive hybrid events that will offer amazing audiovisual experiences (Wilson, 2020). The studio also features a stage and classroom-style seating that allows the crowd to be physically distanced (Northstar Meetings Group, 2021). The OCCC turned out to be a major success story during the pandemic by being one of the only convention centers that has hosted large-scale events safely (Ferrante, 2021). The center continues to evolve with its innovations in the convention industry. While many of the enhancements laid out for the five-year renovation plan have been completed (e.g., technology, digital signage, and meeting spaces), the $605 million expansion of the convention center has been postponed until transient tax revenues in the county are recovered (Winston, 2020).

Research directions

Academic research in the field of conventions or MICE has evolved over the years. Since Weber and Chon's (2002) *Convention tourism: International research and industry perspectives*, several books have been published on the subject (e.g., Davidson and Cope, 2003; Davidson and Rogers, 2006; Davidson et al., 2009; Mair, 2013). Academic articles have reviewed MICE research conducted over the years (e.g., Getz and Page, 2016; Lee and Back, 2005; Lee and Lee, 2014; Mair, 2012; Weber and Ladkin, 2004; Yoo and Weber, 2005). Existing research on MICE can be organized into six broad categories: (1) economic impact of conventions (e.g., Dwyer et al., 2000b; Jones and Li, 2015; Malek and Kim, 2016); (2) convention site/destination selection of planners/ organizers (e.g., Chen, 2006; Clark and McCleary, 1995; Crouch and Louviere, 2004; DiPietro et al., 2008; Elston and Draper, 2012; Fawzy and Samra, 2008); (3) meeting participation decision-making process of attendees (e.g., Jago and Deery, 2005; Lee and Back, 2007; Mair and Thompson, 2009; Oppermann and Chon, 1997; Yoo and Chon, 2008); (4) attendee satisfaction and loyalty (e.g., Hahm et al., 2016; Jung and Tanford, 2017; Severt et al., 2007); (5) destination marketing organization's marketing and operation strategy (e.g., Abbey and Link, 1994; Park and Kim, 2017); and (6) conference and meeting technology (e.g., Cantallops and Salvi, 2014), which is a relatively new topic of interest.

Studies of economic impact of conventions and exhibitions started in the early 1990s. This line of research continued into the mid-2000s to recent years. Researchers have expressed the difficulty in consistently measuring the economic impacts of MICE activity for a destination. The economic benefits of hosting a convention are not captured by the convention center. The activities associated with the convention are mostly leaked into the local community as attendees and visitors stay and spend at places other than the convention center (Jones and Li, 2015). It has been found that international convention attendees spend more than leisure tourists and often bring others (i.e., family or friends), mixing business and pleasure (Dwyer, 2002). More recent studies on the subject of economic impact have broadened its focus on knowledge diffusion, networking, collaboration, innovation, and educational outcomes (Foley et al., 2013). Research should continue with a broader approach to the discussion of economic impacts by spotlighting business event legacies and their impact on the destination.

A popular area of research in the field of conventions is related to convention site or destination selection. This line of research focuses on the perspectives of meeting planners or convention organizers. There are many characteristics that planners need to consider when choosing the convention site, both venue and destination. These factors include quality, accessibility, availability, size, cost, value, safety and security, reputation/image, additional attractions, and so on. More recently, uniqueness, technology, sustainability, and safety have emerged as critical concerns. The investigations conducted in these studies have led to identifying the most important and least important criteria for planners. Since the COVID-19 pandemic, safety and security related to health and medical concerns have been the most important factors. Ultimately, researchers have acknowledged that planners should use different criteria in the selection of a site, which should be based on the type of event and the objective of the event.

Another stream of research concentrates on the perspectives of the attendees. These studies have examined the behavior of attendees by identifying motivators (and/or inhibitors) to attend a convention, observing the decision-making process to attend, or investigating satisfaction and loyalty. A major success factor for conventions is attendance. However, attendees have a variety of conventions, conferences, meetings, and tradeshows that they can choose to attend, making it challenging for organizers. Attendees tend to hold multiple memberships and their needs and wants have been changing with increased experience. The decision to attend a convention is complex, similar to selecting a destination for leisure. Therefore, it is critical to understand attendees' personal needs and wants (e.g., networking, education, professional enhancement), financial factors, inhibiting factors, perceptions of the organizer, event, and destination for a successful event. These factors have been found to influence satisfaction. Moreover, researchers have identified a strong relationship between satisfaction and loyalty. More recently, there has been an effort to adopt psychological constructs to provide deeper insights to attendee behavior (e.g., sense of community) (Hahm et al., 2016).

There has been a major advancement in MICE research over the past two decades. It is anticipated that academic research in this area will continue to progress further. There are journals being developed and special issues being published in the area of events. Event researchers need to be innovative in their research endeavors by conducting interdisciplinary research and incorporating theories to provide a stronger foundation to explaining the phenomenon. The MICE industry was forced to rethink conventions due to the pandemic. It is anticipated that research centered on the impact of the pandemic will increase. Moreover, future research will continue to concentrate on less explored but popular topics such as technology, risk or crisis management, social and environmental impacts, aging, and climate change effects. In terms of methodology, researchers should consider different research designs, such as qualitative research, mixed methods, or experimental designs.

References

Abbey, J. and Link, C. (1994), The convention and meetings sector: Its operation and research needs, in Brent Ritchie, J.R. and Goeldner, C.R. (eds), *Travel, tourism and hospitality research: A handbook for managers and researchers* (2nd edn), John Wiley, New York.

Alderton, M. (2019), 5 environmentally friendly convention centers for hosting green meetings, assessed 23 March 2021 at www.northstarmeetingsgroup.com/Planning-Tips-and-Trends/Site-Selection/Green-Sustainable-Convention-Centers

Cantallops, A. and Salvi, F. (2014), New consumer behavior: A review of research on eWOM and hotels, *International Journal of Hospitality Management* 36, 41–51.

Cetron, M. and DeMicco, F. (2004), Trends for meetings and expositions industry, *FIU Hospitality Review* 22(1), 47–68.

Chen, C. (2006), Applying the analytical hierarchy process (AHP) approach to convention site selection, *Journal of Travel Research* 45(2), 167–174.

Clark, J. and McCleary, K. (1995), Influencing associations' site-selection process, *Cornell Hotel and Restaurant Administration Quarterly* 36(2), 61–68.

Crouch, G. and Louviere, J. (2004), The determinants of convention site selection: A logistic choice model from experimental data, *Journal of Travel Research* 43(2), 118–130.

Davidson, R. and Cope, B. (2003), *Business travel: Conferences, incentive travel, exhibitions, corporate hospitality and corporate travel*, Prentice Hall, Upper Saddle River, NJ.

Davidson, R. and Rogers, T. (2006), *Marketing destinations and venues for conferences, conventions and business events*, Butterworth-Heinemann, Oxford.

Davidson, R., Holloway, C., and Humphreys, C. (2009), *The business of tourism*, Prentice Hall, Upper Saddle River, NJ.

DiPietro, R., Breiter, D., Rompf, P., and Godlewska, M. (2008), An exploratory study of differences among meeting and exhibition planners in their destination selection criteria, *Journal of Convention and Event Tourism* 9(4), 258–276.

Doyle, A. (2021), Convention centers pivot to offer a shot of hope, assessed 24 January 2021 at www.tradeshowexecutive.com/convention-centers-pivot-to-offer-a-shot-of-hope/

Dwyer, L. (2002), Economic contribution of convention tourism: Conceptual and empirical issues, in Weber, K. and Chon, K.S. (eds), *Convention tourism: International research and industry perspectives* (pp. 21–36), CABI, Boston, MA.

Dwyer, L., Mellor, R., Mistilis, N., and Mules, T. (2000a), A framework for assessing tangible and intangible impacts of events and conventions, *Event Management* 6(3), 175–189.

Dwyer, L., Mellor, R., Mistilis, N., and Mules, T. (2000b), Forecasting the economic impacts of events and conventions, *Event Management* 6(3), 191–204.

Elston, K. and Draper, J. (2012), A review of meeting planner site selection criteria research, *Journal of Convention and Event Tourism* 13(3), 203–220.

Events Industry Council (EIC) (2020), 2018 global economic significance of business events, assessed 24 January 2021 at https://insights.eventscouncil.org/Full-Article/2018-global-economic-significance-of-business-events

Exhibit City News (2017), Pittsburgh's David L. Lawrence Convention Center gains LEED Platinum re-certification, assessed 24 January 2021 at https://exhibitcitynews.com/pittsburghs-david-l-lawrence-convention-center-gains-leed-platinum-recertification/

Fawzy, A. and Samra, Y.A. (2008), A conceptual model for understanding associations' site selection process: An organizational buyer behavior perspective, *Journal of Convention and Event Tourism* 9(2), 119–136.

Fenich, G. (2019), *Meetings, expositions, events, and conventions: An introduction to the industry*, Pearson, New York.

Ferrante, F. (2021), U.S. trade shows: Orlando, Dallas, Atlanta lead the way, assessed 21 March 2021 at www.tradeshowexecutive.com/u-s-trade-shows-orlando-dallas-atlanta-lead-the-way/

Foley, C., Schlenker, K., Edwards, D., and Lewis-Smith, L. (2013), Determining business event legacies beyond the tourism spend: An Australian case study approach, *Event Management* 17(3), 311–322.

Getz, D. and Page, S.J. (2016), Progress and prospects for event tourism research, *Tourism Management* 52, 593–631.

Hahm, J., Breiter, D., Severt, K., Wang, Y., and Fjelstul, J. (2016), The relationship between sense of community and satisfaction on future intentions to attend an association's annual meeting, *Tourism Management* 52, 151–160.

Jago, L. and Deery, M. (2005), Relationships and factors influencing convention decision-making, *Journal of Convention and Event Tourism* 7(1), 23–41.

Jones, C. and Li, S. (2015), The economic importance of meetings and conferences: A satellite account approach, *Annals of Tourism Research* 52, 117–133.

Jung, S. and Tanford, S. (2017), What contributes to convention attendee satisfaction and loyalty? A meta-analysis, *Journal of Convention and Event Tourism* 18(2), 118–134.

Kim, S.S. and Chon, K. (2009), An economic impact analysis of the Korean exhibition industry, *International Journal of Tourism Research* 11(3), 311–318.

Lee, M.J. and Back, K. (2005), A review of convention and meeting management research, *Journal of Convention and Event Tourism* 7(2), 1–19.

Lee, M.J. and Back, K. (2007), Association members' meeting participation behaviors: Development of Meeting Participation Model, *Journal of Travel and Tourism Marketing* 22(2), 15–33.

Lee, M.J. and Lee, S. (2014), Subject areas and future research agendas in exhibition research: Visitors' and organizers' perspectives, *Event Management* 18(3), 377–386.

Mair, J. (2012), A review of business events literature, *Event Management* 16(2), 133–141.

Mair, J. (2013), *Conferences and conventions: A research perspective*, Routledge, Abingdon.

Mair, J. and Thompson, K. (2009), The UK association conference attendance decision-making process, *Tourism Management* 30(3), 400–409.

Malek, K. and Kim, J. (2016), Convention attendance and gaming volume in South Korean casinos, *International Journal of Event and Festival Management* 7(1), 66–80.

Meeting Professionals International (MPI) (2010), *FutureWatch 2010: A comparative outlook on the global business of meetings*, Meeting Professional International.

Northstar Meetings Group (2021), What's open in Orlando right now, assessed 20 February 2021 at www.northstarmeetingsgroup.com/orlando-what-is-open

Oppermann, M. and Chon, K. (1997), Convention participation decision-making process, *Annals of Tourism Research* 24(1), 178–191.

Orange County Convention Center (OCCC) (2020a), About the Orange County Convention Center, assessed 24 January 2021 at www.occc.net/About-Us

Orange County Convention Center (OCCC) (2020b), Fact sheet, assessed 24 January 2021 at https://view.publitas.com/orange-county-convention-center/fact-sheet-service-partners/page/1

Orange County Convention Center (OCCC) (2021a), Orange County Convention Center continues to generate economic impact and support community amid global pandemic, assessed 24 January 2021 at www.occc.net/About-Us-Media-Relations-Press-Releases/ArticleID/296/OCCC-Economic-Impact

Orange County Convention Center (OCCC) (2021b), Orange County Convention Center event updates, assessed 24 January 2021 at www.occc.net/Updates

Park, H. and Kim, D. (2017), In pursuit of an environmentally friendly convention industry: A sustainability framework and guidelines for a green convention, *International Journal of Contemporary Hospitality Management* 29(3), 1028–1051.

Peterson, B. (2019), Convention centers across major U.S. cities expand and renovate, assessed 24 January 2021 at www.northstarmeetingsgroup.com/Planning-Tips-and-Trends/Site-Selection/new-expanded-Convention-Centers-United-States

Rogers, T. (2008), *Conferences and conventions: A global industry* (2nd edn), Butterworth-Heinemann, Oxford.

Sanders, H. (2014), *Convention center follies: Politics, power, and public investments in American cities*, University of Pennsylvania Press, Philadelphia, PA.

Severt, D., Wang, Y., Chen, P., and Breiter, D. (2007), Examining the motivation, perceived performance, and behavioral intentions of convention attendees: Evidence from a regional conference, *Tourism Management* 28(2), 399–408.

Social Tables (n.d.), 15 technology upgrades your convention center needs now, assessed 23 March 2021 at www.socialtables.com/blog/event-technology/convention-center-upgrade/

Spiller, J. (2002), History of convention tourism, in Weber, K. and Chon, K. (eds), *Convention tourism: International research and industry perspectives* (pp. 3–19), Haworth, New York.

Walter P. Moore (2020), Orange County Convention Center phase V expansion, assessed 24 January 2021 at www.walterpmoore.com/projects/orange-county-convention-center-phase-v-expansion

Weber, K. and Chon, K. (2002), *Convention tourism: International research and industry perspectives*, Haworth, New York.

Weber, K. and Ladkin, A. (2004), Trends affecting the convention industry in the 21st century, *Journal of Convention and Event Tourism* 6(4), 47–63.

Wilson, H.K. (2020), On the road to recovery: OCCC, DLCC and MCCNO, assessed 24 January 2021 at https://exhibitcitynews.com/on-the-road-to-recovery-occc-dlcc-mccno/

Winston, S. (2020), Greater Orlando gets back to business, assessed 24 January 2021 at www.smartmeetings.com/destination_article/greater-orlando-business?fbclid=IwAR3J2S5YXQN0w6SoBFZUfNEi3BRdrVqt-HtXfYfIysvyYBzoa-YTFyf-UNM

Yoo, J.E. and Chon, K.S. (2008), Factors affecting convention participation decision-making: Developing a measurement scale, *Journal of Travel Research* 47(1), 113–122.

Yoo, J.E. and Weber, K. (2005), Progress in convention tourism research, *Journal of Hospitality and Tourism Research* 29(2), 194–222.

6. Sports tourism and event impacts

Marko Perić, Jelena Đurkin Badurina, and Nicholas Wise

Sports tourism

Sports tourism is a niche form of tourism that is gaining popularity and thus expanding opportunities around the world (Parker, 2019). In fact, sports tourism is considered the fastest growing sector of the travel industry according to the United Nations World Tourism Organization. There are three 'types' of sports tourists: participatory, event-based, and celebratory (Parker, 2019). Thus, sports tourism ranges from general recreational activities (with some or no competition) to high-profile competitions. Tourists also travel around their respective countries and internationally to follow their sporting teams or attend mega-events. Celebratory forms of sports tourism include visits to museums, places, or areas where the focus is on remembrance. Each of these perspectives to sports tourism can create a range of event impacts for both participants and the host community.

From an academic standpoint, sports tourism is defined by Weed and Bull (2009) as the overlap and interactions between people, places, and activities, and these can be active (i.e. when people directly compete in sport or recreation) and passive (i.e. when people spectate), building on the above-noted points. It is noted that sports tourism activity is common in the summer. But some destinations are looking to create sports tourism opportunities in winter months and also hold training camps and special events in the winter time as a way of using this industry to overcome seasonality (in destinations like Croatia). Recent studies focusing on Croatia have looked at the role of events as a chance to extend the impact of tourism and create new sporting activities in a destination (see Đurkin and Wise, 2018; Đurkin Badurina et al., 2020; Perić and Wise, 2015; Wise and Perić, 2017; Wise et al., 2017; Wise et al., 2019).

Over the past few decades studies on sports tourism have greatly expanded (Weed, 2009), but more consideration of the directions and range of impacts that sports tourism generates is needed when we consider events (see Kersulić et al., 2020).

While much work considers success and economic impact considerations (e.g. Kaplanidou et al., 2013), there are a number of critical challenges of sports tourism that are addressed in the literature that relate to event impacts. For instance, sports tourism activities can be invasive of space, and cause disruptions locally as well as overcrowding and excess noise (see Higham, 1999). Host–guest interactions can be both positive and negative depending on the circumstances, with some of the concern here relevant to issues addressed in the previous sentence. The economic potential is usually high and social impacts include a renewed or enhanced pride in place and new entertainment or leisure opportunities locally (Ohmann et al., 2006). There are also concerns that lead to negative impacts and these include long lines that result in waiting (which can put a strain on locals), price gouging, high amounts of trash left behind, and destruction of property. In addition to the noted economic and social impacts, there can be adverse environmental impacts. Addressed by Grofelnik et al. (2020), environmental impacts of sports tourism are increasingly visible from the extended transportation of participants and attendees, thus generating significant carbon dioxide emissions.

Risnjak Trail running events in Gorski kotar

Croatia is a tourism-dependent country with an 11 billion euro tourism revenue, which comprises about 20 percent of the country's gross domestic product (Croatian Bureau of Statistics, 2020). Croatia is a country that sees its tourism industry suffer from seasonality (with some of the highest rates of tourism seasonality in the Mediterranean region). In seeking ways to overcome this economic burden and sustain tourism during times of the year when the industry goes almost dormant, there is a national initiative to develop year-round tourism across the whole country, including continental regions of the country that are still less tourism developed (Wise et al., 2019). However, while seeking to expand the economic potential of tourism in Croatia year-round, there are strong desires to preserve the natural environment. This is key to the identity of the country and crucial to Croatia's destination branding, as the country seeks to initiate and design new tourism products in less-developed continental (inland) destinations (Perić et al., 2017).

One of these less-developed tourism areas in Croatia is the mountainous region of Gorski kotar, which has ideal landscapes and is full of event and recreational potential throughout the year (Institute for Tourism, 2019; Wise et al., 2019). Numerous local sports facilities are scattered among towns and municipalities in Gorski kotar, but these are mostly oriented to satisfying local recreational needs, especially in terms of winter sports such as skating, sledding, Nordic walking, and biathlon. Apart from that, there are some football pitches and several school sports halls that are not designed for professional sport nor for big events (Wise et al., 2019). The local focus arguably limits the wider economic impact potential for this remote region, and sports tourism-oriented events are seen as a way of capturing attention to promote the region. For instance, trail running, mountain biking, trekking, sport fishing, skiing/sledding, and cross-country skiing are the most popular outdoor sports tourism activities in the region and have much potential given the natural settings and resources. In total, there are around 40 different sports activities registered in Gorski kotar, of which three quarters are manifested in an organised manner as sporting events (Perić et al., 2016b). Approximately 80–90 different sports events (mostly one-day events) are organised each year in Gorski kotar, gathering around 11,000 competitors (active sports tourists) and 9,000 spectators (passive sports tourists).

Aligned with conceptual insight from Weed and Bull (2009) and Pine and Gilmore (1998), classifications of activities in Gorski kotar belong to 'event sports tourism' and 'sports participation tourism' which encompass the entertainment and escapist realms of experience (see Perić et al., 2016b). Most activities and events take place during the summer while approximately one third are in the winter or are year round. The provision of events is usually by local sports associations and clubs, but joint organisation by public and private sectors is common too. The private sector (which is profit-oriented) organises several events, and these have been quite successful. Regardless of the provider, participation fees need to be paid for most of the events. In return, participants receive race packs and gifts and are offered food and beverage services that are prepared and consumed in collaboration with local caterers. Due to low attendance (on average around 100–130 competitors and the same number of spectators per event), limited media attention (primarily through social networks and local radio) and reluctance of major sponsors to be involved, all the events are small-scale. Thus, sports tourism in Gorski kotar represents an intriguing topic for further examination, and more research is needed to consider the range of event impacts, as this chapter will outline by focusing on the Risnjak Trail, a well-established international trail running event in Gorski kotar with significant local impacts.

The one-day Risnjak Trail event in the Risnjak National Park is organised by a private firm (Ad Natura Sport) and a sports club (Ad Natura) from Rijeka in cooperation with regional and local tourism boards, local authorities, and a public institution (Risnjak National Park). Held in a natural area since 2013, the event carrying capacity is limited to 500 participants and has become one of the most attended sporting events in Gorski kotar. The Risnjak Trail is part of the trail running series Kvarner Trails where multiple races are gathered under a regional trail running brand (see Figure 6.1).

Source: Photograph by Marko Perić.

Figure 6.1   Start and finish lines at the Risnjak Trail

To break down the event impacts, and to offer relevant directions to scholars, researchers, and smaller-scale sports tourism events, we outline results aligned with economic, environmental, and socio-cultural impacts. From a budgeting and economic impact standpoint, a challenge that event organisers face when planning for sports tourism events is setting fees and determining what is included. This can limit participation if participants and attendees are unclear about the benefits of getting involved in an event. The strategy of setting the appropriate fee is part of the overall intention of the managing director of the Risnjak Trail to position this event among the top trail races in Croatia and the race fee plays a significant role in those efforts (Perić and Slavić, 2019, 177). Such fees, when multiplied with the number of participants, generate significant revenue and extra money is earned by selling the footwear and clothing of a major sponsor.

In the first few years, collected revenue was hardly enough to cover the operating costs of the organisation, so Risnjak Trail relied on additional support from local authorities and private sponsorship. Since 2017, the event has recorded a profit, as the managing director interviewed (in February 2018) highlights: 'It was hard to break even at the beginning, but now the situation is better, the event is well recognised, we have regular attendees, we made our organisation more efficient and now the event is sustainable.'

This event generates positive impacts for the local community, too, as they are not overburdened by tourists as the event is one-day and attendees do not stay in the destination for a longer period. The average length of stay of trail runners seems to be shorter than other outdoor tourists (Perić et al., 2019) suggesting that participation in this event is the main motive to visit the destination. While most of the Risnjak Trail attendees were one-day visitors, the average length of stay varied between one and two days and the average daily expenditure was around 50–55 euro. Considering the fact that at least half of this amount relates to race fees, one can say that this is not a game of big numbers, but it still generates some benefits to local stakeholders and Gorski kotar collectively.

However, the managing director feels that the exchange of benefits between the event and the area is not reciprocal. The support the event receives from the local authorities and tourist boards is mainly declarative, while financial support is scarce. The managing director's initiatives to involve local stakeholders to provide additional entertainment programmes failed, and he is in charge of the whole event programme, as explained:

> The atmosphere is very important for our participants, it helps people relax and feel good at the event. It seems to me that I am left to myself. I invited local folklore society to present but it was unsuccessful. Sometimes, there is a stand with homemade agricultural products, but this stand is here for every weekend, so it is not event related. I have to organise the music and loudspeaker and to play the role of the event host on my own.

This rather reluctant response from the local community stakeholders in terms of supporting the event with local products, services, and/or an entertaining programme could be due to the general limitations and issues related to hosting sport events in rural communities, especially with lacking social and human capital, but also generally tight local budgets and financial limitations (Đurkin and Wise, 2018). Having in mind scarce public financial resources, local public-sector stakeholders might be more inclined to financially support sports events organised by local sports associations, rather than an event organised by a for-profit firm from outside of the community.

Besides acting as an economic resource, sport can be a communication and territorial marketing tool (Perrin-Malterre, 2018). As is the case with other outdoor sporting events, one of the key resources for the Risnjak Trail organisation is the natural setting. Risnjak Trail takes place within a protected mountainous area of the Risnjak National Park, which goes beyond a physical resource and represents a true attraction and a main motivation to participate. This is emphasised on the Kvarner Trails website homepage (of which Risnjak Trail is a part) where it is stated 'Join Us & Run Beautiful Kvarner Trails. Just Nature & Running' (Ad Natura Sport, 2020).

The managing director is well aware of this fact and that he has to establish procedures to protect the environment such as the use of provisional hiking trail markers, penalisation, and/or disqualification of participants who litter along the course (except at designated aid stations), post-race course inspection and the dismantling and transport of assembly facilities, etc. The total work devoted to environmental issues in the planning and implementation phase is significant, and pro-environmental behaviour of event attendees is additionally communicated in promotional materials and race rules and regulations. In such ways, environmental protection is considered an investment that results in many benefits for an organisation's business model (Coles et al., 2016; Perić et al., 2019). The ultimate result is that there is no major negative impact on the environment.

Many staff are involved in the implementation of event activities. There is the core team, which consists of 10 people, and around 50 volunteers, mostly from the nearby town of Rijeka. However, even in the core team responsible for event planning and realisation only one team member (i.e. the managing director) is employed while others volunteer, in most cases from year to year. Other volunteers are deployed along the course and aid stations. The process of volunteer selection is planned; those registered for volunteering are interviewed about their motivation, and for those who are hired, one-day training is provided. Volunteers have a complimentary lunch and refreshments and the possibility to acquire new skills; volunteering at events is always an opportunity to have fun and make acquaintances with other people and their cultures. The managing director of the Risnjak race highlighted pride as another aspect of being part of the organisation: first, there is a job to do: 'Fun comes later … and when everything went well, at the end of the day I think we can all be proud of ourselves.'

Outdoor activities attract people motivated by enjoying nature and searching for an escape from their daily routine to decrease stress levels and help maintain their health and weight as well as their overall wellbeing. In terms of other socio-cultural impacts that might be incurred by sports events, the prevailing impression is that Risnjak Trail, due to the limited engagement of the local community in organisation and implementation of the event, to some extent lacks social leveraging elements such as local capacity building and achieving a 'liminal' atmosphere for participants by providing a unique entertainment programme for the local community, visitors, and participants (Perić et al., 2016a).

Future directions

Sports tourism has the potential to create a range of economic, environmental, and socio-cultural event impacts, despite the scale and scope of the event. Depending on the case, the focus may evolve around links to natural settings, which in turn can limit economic impacts, but simultaneously strengthen socio-cultural impacts because people will not feel overburdened by hosting events in their communities (especially in rural locales). It is argued that most of the economic benefits are captured by private companies and the sports clubs that organise the event, but the public institution Risnjak National Park and other local accommodation providers record above-average consumption on the weekend of the event, too. Despite these business opportunities, it seems that other local stakeholders fail to recognise this event as a contributor to des- tination image and their businesses. Reasons why people may fail to recognise how this event can contribute to destination image and business success may lie in the relatively short duration of the event. This is because local stakehold- ers perceive that as the event is being organised and implemented by some- body from the 'outside', profit-oriented intentions take away from the local benefits. On the positive side, environmental and safety impacts are negligible because of precise environmental and security protection rules and measures. The main socio-cultural impacts are the benefits of volunteering as well as improved wellbeing of the attendees. However, the potential socio-cultural impacts for local stakeholders are not developed to their full extent, due to the low level of involvement of local community public and private stakeholders in the event planning and implementation.

During the last few years (apart from 2020 due to Covid-19), Risnjak Trail has reached its planned attendance and a further increase in the size of the event might harm the environment. Therefore, to become more recognisable and competitive and achieve additional positive impacts without increasing the number of participants event organisers should:

- try to expand the partner network by involving other stakeholders interested in providing additional event services like entertainment for attendees, event merchandise, or accommodation;
- establish and cherish long-term relationships with existing as well as new volunteers;
- cherish long-term relationships with existing attendees and try to attract new ones with additional marketing efforts – one idea could be to make participation on the Risnjak Trail (by being one of the limited number of participants) a matter of a prestige for trail runners;
- encourage attendees to come with family and friends, therefore encouraging spending in the region; and
- design this event to stay environmentally friendly, that is, to reinforce the pro-environmental behaviour of attendees and respect and protect nature.

A synergy between public and private parties is needed to complement the story that lies behind this event. Therefore, public stakeholders should ensure dissemination of event information and help with the implementation of environmental protection and security measures. Also, considering the example of Risnjak Trail, the local/regional authorities should:

- encourage local stakeholders to join and enrich this event by providing additional content (fair merchandise, entertainment for families and children, etc.);
- renovate existing and develop new sports infrastructure; and
- in partnership with key local stakeholders, encourage initiation of new events and outdoor sports activities that are promising for Gorski kotar and accessible to the entire population, especially for youngsters, such as mountain biking, hiking, sport fishing, sledding, etc.

A one-size-fits-all solution does not exist and event organisers and other public and private partners should use these recommendations as a guide in designing their management and marketing strategies and business models. Referring to Perrin-Malterre (2018) and Perić and Slavić (2019), Risnjak Trail has a relatively small and incremental effect over one weekend of the year, but improvement and replication of this business model to a number of other events through the year would give an impetus to the distinctiveness and competitiveness of Gorski kotar as tourist destination. This would surely be beneficial in case of external factors such as the Covid-19 pandemic in

2020–2021 that can totally paralyse tourism activities and negatively affect all local stakeholders.

Academic contributions to future event organisation and implementation should be oriented on the analysis of best practice cases and studying methods for the achievement of a positive economic and social impact of small-scale outdoor sports events organised in less-developed rural regions such as Gorski kotar.

References

Ad Natura Sport (2020), Risnjak Trail, assessed 26 May 2020 at http://en.kvarnertrails .com/general-info1.html

Coles, T., Warren, N., Borden, D.S., and Dinan, C. (2016), Business models among SMTEs: Identifying attitudes to environmental costs and their implications for sustainable tourism, *Journal of Sustainable Tourism* 25(4), 471–488.

Croatian Bureau of Statistics (2020), Tourist arrivals and nights in 2019, first release, number: 4.3.2, assessed 22 May 2020 at https://mint.gov.hr/UserDocsImages//AAA _2020_ABC/c_dokumenti//200228_DZS_turizam2019.pdf

Đurkin, J. and Wise, N. (2018), Managing community stakeholders in rural areas: Assessing the organisation of local sports events in Gorski kotar, Croatia, in Clarke, A. and Jepson, A. (eds), *Power, Construction and Meaning in Festivals and Events*, Routledge, London, 185–200.

Đurkin Badurina, J., Perić, M., and Vitezić, V. (2020), Potential for the regeneration of rural areas through local involvement in the organisation of sport events, *Managing Sport and Leisure*, doi: 10.1080/23750472.2020.1829990

Grofelnik, H., Perić, M., and Wise, N. (2020), Applying carbon footprint method possibilities to the sustainable development of sports tourism, *WIT Transactions on Ecology and the Environment*, 248, 153–163.

Higham, J. (1999), Commentary: Sport as an avenue of tourism development: An analysis of the positive and negative impacts of sport tourism, *Current Issues in Tourism*, 2(1), 82–90.

Institute for Tourism (2019), *Master plan turističkog razvoja Gorskog kotara [Master Plan of Tourist Development of Gorski Kotar]*, Horwath HTL, Zagreb.

Kaplanidou, K., Kerwin, S., and Karadakis, K. (2013), Understanding sport event success: Exploring perceptions of sport event consumers and event providers. *Journal of Sport and Tourism* 18(3), 137–159.

Kersulić, A., Perić, M., and Wise, N. (2020), Assessing and considering the wider impacts of sport-tourism events: A research agenda review of sustainability and strategic planning elements, *Sustainability*, 12(11), 4473.

Ohmann, S., Jones, I., and Wilkes, K. (2006), The perceived social impacts of the 2006 Football World Cup on Munich residents, *Journal of Sport and Tourism* 11(2), 129–152.

Parker, R. (2019), The remarkable growth of sport tourism, *Human Kinetics*, accessed 26 January 2021 at https://humankinetics.me/2019/04/04/the-remarkable-growth-of -sport-tourism/

Perić, M. and Slavić, N. (2019), Event sport tourism business models: The case of trail running, *Sport, Business and Management: An International Journal* 9(2), 164–184.

Perić, M. and Wise, N. (2015), Understanding the delivery of experience: Conceptualising business models and sports tourism: Assessing two case studies in Istria, Croatia, *Local Economy* 30(8), 1000–1016.

Perić, M., Đurkin J., and Wise N. (2016a), Leveraging small-scale sport events: Challenges of organising, delivering and managing sustainable outcomes in rural communities: The case of Gorski kotar, Croatia, *Sustainability* 8(12), 1–17.

Perić, M., Škorić, S., and Jurčević, V. (2016b), Sport tourism supply in Gorski kotar (Croatia): Analysis and possible recommendations for providers, *Acta Turistica* 28(1), 49–71.

Perić, M., Čuić Tanković, A., and Đurkin, J. (2017), Role of brand personality traits in creating an umbrella brand for small-scale sports events: Case of Gorski kotar, Croatia, *Društvena istraživanja: časopis za opća društvena pitanja* 26(4), 561–581.

Perić, M., Vitezić, V., and Đurkin Badurina, J. (2019), Business models for active outdoor sport event tourism experiences, *Tourism Management Perspectives* 32, 100561.

Perrin-Malterre, C. (2018), Tourism diversification process around trail running in the Pays of Allevard (Isère), *Journal of Sport and Tourism* 22(1), 67–82.

Pine, B.J. and Gilmore, J.H. (1998), Welcome to the experience economy, *Harvard Business Review* 76(4) (July–August), 97–105.

Weed, M. (2009), Progress in sports tourism research? A meta-review and exploration of futures, *Tourism Management* 30(5), 616–628.

Weed, M. and Bull, C. (2009), *Sport Tourism: Participants, Policy and Providers*, 2nd edn, Elsevier Butterworth Heinemann, Oxford.

Wise, N. and Perić, M. (2017), Sports tourism, regeneration and social impacts: New opportunities and directions for research, the case of Medulin, Croatia, in *Tourism in the City: Towards and Integrative Agenda on Urban Tourism*, edited by N. Bellini and C. Pasquinelli (pp. 311–320), Springer Vieweg, Berlin.

Wise, N., Perić, M., and Armenski, T. (2017), The role of sports tourism and events to regenerate and sustain off-season tourism in Istria, Croatia: Addressing perspectives from industry managers and planners, in *Sport, Events, Tourism and Regeneration*, edited by N. Wise and J. Harris (pp. 179–192), Routledge, London.

Wise, N., Perić, M., and Đurkin, J. (2019), Benchmarking service delivery for sports tourism and events: Lessons for Gorski Kotar, Croatia from Pokljuka, Slovenia, *European Journal of Tourism Research* 22, 107–128.

7. Religious events and commercialization

Flávia Ulian and Angela Fileno da Silva

Cultural and religious events

The Constitution of the Federal Republic of Brazil, promulgated in 1988, defines Brazilian cultural heritage in its 216th article as consisting: "of the assets of a tangible and intangible nature, which bear reference to the identity, action and memory of the various groups that form the Brazilian society" (Brasil, 2020, 114). In 2000, a decree promulgated by the National Institute of Historic and Artistic Heritage (in Portuguese: Instituto do Patrimônio Histórico e Artístico Nacional, IPHAN) – an institution of the Brazilian federal government responsible for the preservation, conservation and safeguarding of the country's assets of a tangible and intangible nature – instituted the registry of the intangible heritage. This resulted in the creation of the Intangible Heritage National Program (in Portuguese: Programa Nacional de Patrimônio Imaterial, PNPI), enabling the identification, safeguarding and promotion of the assets of intangible nature that form the Brazilian cultural heritage (Brasil, 2000).

In 2016 came the regulation of the PNPI, following the conceptualization of the 2003 Convention for the Safeguarding of the Intangible Cultural Heritage/ United Nations Educational, Scientific and Cultural Organisation. In this sense, IPHAN considers being part of the intangible heritage as:

> the uses, representations, expressions, knowledge, and techniques … that the communities, groups and in some cases, individuals may recognise as integral part of their cultural heritage. This intangible cultural heritage, that is passed on through generations, is constantly recreated by the communities and groups according to their surroundings, their interaction with nature and its history, instilling in them a sense of identity and continuity and contributing thus to promote the respect for cultural diversity and human creativity. (IPHAN, 2016)

IPHAN designated a festival dedicated to Senhor Bom Jesus do Bonfim in 2013. This festival, held in Salvador, the capital city of Bahia, in the Book of Celebrations Register, "where rituals and festivals that have registered the collective experience of work, religiosity, entertainment and other social life practices are inscribed" (Brasil, 2000).

The Festa do Bonfim is considered the largest and most popular religious expression in Bahia. The one held in January 2021 marked 276 uninterrupted years of celebration. According to Gonçalves (2019), it recognizes the existence of intangible heritage, since the Constitution of the Federal Republic of Brazil expanded the view on culture, diversity and ethnicity, contributing to the promotion of intangible heritage and stimulating the preservation of the popular festival. The author points out: "the field of heritage involves many actors such as: the local populations and their associations, the government representatives, the commodification of ethnic cultures, the diffusion of events and actions through digital medias, international institutions, the mass media and the education (education system) and national culture" (Gonçalves, 2019, 202). Still, Gonçalves (2019) refers to the importance of not only maintaining the intangible heritage that festivals represent, but also the importance of recognizing African heritage. In this way, these events mark the ethnic Afro Brazilian component present in such commemorations.

Historically speaking, religious celebrations, civic festivals and sporting and cultural events have been taking place and creating a logistical structure to facilitate these practices, themselves becoming tourist attractions. Societies of different cultures recognize the need to perform creative communal activities, and given these are cultural practices that have long existed, adding a touristic element can commercialize an event. With cultural meanings practiced publicly, celebrations and collective rituals that contribute to the identity reinforcement of a particular group of people can get lost if it becomes over-commercialized (Quinn, 2009; Melo et al., 2015).

Heritage and cultural events exert an important role in the cultural, political and economic context of a country or region. Moreover, such events can promote a location (Marujo, 2014). According to Melo et al. (2015), there are undeniable positive impacts derived from cultural events – especially regarding the economic aspects and their benefits in the development of places (see also Wise and Harris, 2019). Therefore, scholars need to question to what extent residents are consulted about their interest in the celebration of the event. These impacts need to be balanced, especially when the events become tourist attractions and pass through a process of "touristification", which can result in the event losing its identity or some of its initially intended meaning.

Furthermore, there is a worry that this phenomenon is accompanied by a centralization and concentration of income, a so-called "merchandise festival", with low appropriation of profits by the poorest segments of the population (Serpa, 2007). This is also seen in local living environments like the favelas in Brazil, which are sometimes changed to attract tourists (Wise et al., 2019).

In Brazil, culture has been widely used to promote tourist destinations (OECD, 2009). The intangible cultural heritage represented by the Festa do Bonfim creates, in the city of Salvador, a local distinction in the face of globalization. Many studies dedicated to the understanding of event tourism emphasize the segment's capacity to attract people to the places in which they are held, working against seasonality, and causing positive economic impacts (Getz and Page, 2016). This economic emphasis, however, can obscure the environmental and sociocultural impacts that occur following these events. Thus, event tourism needs to be promoted in a socially and culturally sustainable manner, especially since "sustainability in tourism requires hosts to be positively disposed towards developments, so as to enhance the tourists' experience and contribute to the destination's attractiveness" (Quinn, 2009, 4). This matter becomes even more complex once we deal with the relationship between event tourism and cultural tourism. Due to the fragility of heritage assets, it is necessary to minimize the adverse impacts that arise from creative tourism activity (Richards, 2020).

Managing cultural heritage requires the application of specific knowledge for the transformation of cultural heritage assets into tourism resources (see Jimura, 2018; Wise and Jimura, 2020). This management, however, must above all preserve them and relate them to a broad social and economic context. There are serious threats to heritage when there is massification, lack of authenticity and the non-routing of the benefits that tourism may pass on to heritage (Gonzales, 2009). Serpa (2007, 109) is equally critical when heritage "becomes 'the scenery' for the festival", rendering itself something homogenic and "exhibitionist". Today, the celebrations dedicated to Senhor do Bonfim are part of a broad historical process. This chapter discusses how the festival was appropriated by the black population of Salvador during the nineteenth and twentieth centuries, given new meaning considering local contexts and is currently enjoyed by national and foreign tourists as an affirmation of ethnic identity. The idea is to understand how the Festa do Bonfim resisted the "commercialization of ethnic cultures" (Gonçalves, 2019).

The Lavagem do Bonfim

Founded by Portugal, Salvador was the capital of Brazil from 1549 to 1763. In 2020, according to estimates from the Brazilian Institute of Geography and Statistics (in Portuguese: Instituto Brasileiro de Geografia e Estatística, IBGE), the population of the city was 2,886,698. At the beginning of 2019, the projection of Salvador's tourist gross domestic product (GDP) was R$5.7 billion, 8.2 percent of the city's total GDP (PRODETUR – Salvador, 2020). According to data from the Observatório do Turismo da Bahia (2019–2020), the months of January and February receive the greatest numbers of national and international tourists in the municipality, because this is when the three major events held by the city occur: New Year celebrations, the Festa do Bonfim and Carnival. The washing of the stairs of the Bonfim Basilica is the stage of the festival that brings together the largest number of participants, integrating the calendar of events of tourist interest to the city of Salvador.

The cult of Senhor Bom Jesus do Bonfim has Portuguese origins. The devotion was brought to Brazil in 1745, by Theodózio Faria (Nunes Neto, 2019). The religious Bonfim Brotherhood is considered one of the longest and most complex in Salvador and in Brazil. Religious brotherhoods are lay devotions, belonging to the Catholic Church and linked to a saint. Until the end of the nineteenth century, most of these associations were organized according to ethnic-racial criteria. Some brotherhoods were exclusively for the white population, while others had their membership restricted to certain black ethnic groups, the so-called black men's brotherhoods.

The festival offered to the saint of devotion is a time when members of the brotherhoods come together. On this occasion faithful people and sympathizers participate in celebrations that combine profane and ecclesiastical activities. The Bonfim Brotherhood started in 1745, and in 1754 part of the works of the Basilica, on the Itapagipe Hill, were concluded (Groetelaars, 1983). This is a significant milestone for the devotion, as it marks the moment when the current Festa do Bonfim started to delineate itself from the point of view of its geographical location (Figure 7.1) and the set of rituals that comprise it.

Since the nineteenth century, the devotion festival has begun on the Saturday after Three Kings' Day. On this day there are nine prayer meetings. On the Thursday the Lavagem do Bonfim is celebrated, an occasion in which Catholic and Candomblé rituals cross each other forming a complex mosaic of meaning (Nunes Neto, 2019). This is a fundamental element for the understanding of

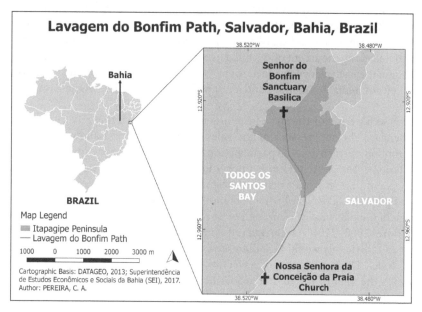

Figure 7.1   Map showing the location of the Lavagem do Bonfim path in
Salvador, Brazil

the black participation in the rituals. When the water carried by the *baianas* is poured into the nave of the Basilica, a gap is opened to the exercise of Candomblé. Amid a Catholic, Portuguese and white festival, an African rite is publicly and collectively performed to Oxalá (Ott, 1969). On the Sunday, a mass marks the end of the novena and the cycle of ecclesiastical celebrations, with fireworks traditionally marking the end of the commemorations. However, for many participants the festival has not then ended. Pilgrims remain in the square of the Basilica, where they spend Sunday night at food and game stalls and in guitar and samba circles (Guimarães, 1994).

In 1860, Prince Maximilian I of Habsburg (Habsburgo, 1982, 123) was in Salvador and attended the ceremonies inside the church. His report of the pilgrimage from Cidade Baixa to Itapagipe exposed the black participation at the stage of the greatest popular mobilization in the cycle of the Bonfim celebrations. During the route the "black crowd pressed together, laughing curiously and chattering" and, in improvised kitchens in the streets, black women sold food to the population. Goods were offered in baskets and in glass cases even inside the church, where "all sort of religious trinkets, amulets, candles and eatables" were sold. Subverting the silence that should be observed inside the church, these women announced their offerings and aroused the gluttony of the faithful (Habsburgo, 1982, 125, 129). Querino (1922, 119) highlights that the presence of "festival stalls" were "provided with toys of all kinds" and distributed along the ascent of the hill. Here we find the games as another component of the festival, which added to the "street organ players, ambulant vendors of refreshments, sweets etc." and amplified the profane share of the Lavagem.

Seen as a period of rupture of the order, the festival became a fixture on the calendar. The suppression of the rules during this period allowed the consumption of spirit and the participation of individuals already "exalted" in the interior of the church. Drunkenness during the festival was tolerated to such an extent that, in years when the treasurer of the devotion was more "pleasant and playful", "a barrel of wine and another of spirit, to stimulate the enthusiasm of the pilgrims" was ordered to be placed in the middle of the churchyard (Priore, 2000, 119). As Duvignaud adds (1983, 68), festivals were moments when individuals would face themselves with a "world without structure and no code". During the time of slavery, the Festa do Bonfim was an occasion in which the vigil of the master would become milder, and it was possible for slaves to get drunk, dance and devote themselves to orixás (Silva, 2014).

In 1860, as brooms scrubbed the Basilica floor, one of the profound moments of the suppression of rules took place. During the rite execution, the youth were allowed to "flirt" inside the temple, the women were allowed to exhibit "the naked bust and the beautiful shoulders" and the "old black man with a white head, slightly drunk" was allowed to enter the ceremony (Querino, 1922, 119). According to Spix (1938, 122), "the noise and the unrestrained joy" of the Lavagem do Bonfim were part of the commemoration in which "different human races in promiscuity" participated. By blurring the boundaries and bringing whites and blacks together, the festival was viewed negatively by some individuals. The scene of disorder generated protests among the religious and the Bahia elite, who opposed the combination that united the celebration of Bonfim to the African ritual associated with Oxalá and believed that the washing disrespected "the customs, morals and religion" (Habsburgo, 1982, 248).

In the nineteenth century, the cycle of celebrations around the Bonfim brought to light the participation of the black in the Bahian slave society. Affirming their existence, the black population took to the streets causing a stir with their drums. New networks of relationships and identity construction were established. Thus, thinking about the paths through which the celebration of Bonfim acquired African contours becomes useful when we reflect on the current meanings of this cycle of celebration and its appropriation by tourist activity.

Future directions

In 1889, the Lavagem do Bonfim was banned by the Archbishop of Bahia. The abolition of slavery in Brazil had occurred the year before and it was a time when the white population feared the backlash of the newly freed. It was deemed necessary to make the boundaries between whites and blacks more evident. For this reason, it was believed that the ritual of the Lavagem, which blurred ethnic boundaries and mixed individuals and religions, had to be purged.

Prevented from entering the church, the devotees began to wash in front of the Basilica. Soon, this space was forbidden to the participants who began to wash the steps of the temple. Although pursued and stigmatized, the black population was responsible for guaranteeing the maintenance of a ritual that has been transformed into the Ethnic Afro event that we see today, resisting its commodification in Bahia and elsewhere across Brazil.

At this point, considering Melo et al. (2015), there is a need to question how far the choices of this population were taken into consideration (and respected) in the process that transformed the traditional Lavagem do Bonfim into a tourist event. This question is also related to how the local community perceives itself as part of the tourist attraction. More recently the discussion has broadened to questions related to the "touristification" of territories, to the "spectaculariza-tion" of events (Serpa, 2007) and, within limits, to the "overtourism" bringing about "tourismphobia" (Dominguez, 2018). In general, researchers view with apprehension the growth of what they consider to be the most evident negative impacts of the spread of mass tourism.

At the Lavagem do Bonfim it is possible to notice the permanent tension between devotees, responsible for the symbolic content of the ritual, and the economic agents and the state, engaged in making profit from the event. Furthermore, the tension between the involved actors in these disputes reveals the economic and power asymmetries between the local population, the Bahia state policy-makers and the business community – all key tourism stakehold-ers. Articles in Portuguese highlight the positive economic impacts provided by the appropriation of traditional events by tourism, such as that of the

Tourism Office of Bahia State (in Portuguese: Secretaria de Turismo do Estado da Bahia) about ethnic-Afro tourism held in the state. Although the document argues that that segment is "an instrument of social reparation", with tourism being capable of benefiting the Afro descendant population, the document does not specify how its participation in the gains from this segment would come about (Bahia, 2009, 7).

In spite of the developmentalist foundations that relate the Lavagem do Bonfim to the economic gains determined throughout the productive chain of tourism, it is important to question how the poorest population – that, in Salvador, is also Afro descendant – can integrate the event beyond the street commerce of food, beverages and souvenirs, an activity known to be precarious and unprofitable. In 2021, with imposed limits due to the Covid-19 pandemic, the Festa do Bonfim underwent adaptations. The masses and novenas were held in person, even with a restricted number of the faithful and internet broadcasts. The main changes occurred on the day of the Cortejo and Lavagem do Bonfim, an occasion responsible for gathering the largest contingent of devotees and tourists.

On this day, the image of Senhor do Bonfim, placed on a Fire Department car, traveled the traditional procession route. Devotees greeted the procession from their windows, while some faithful dressed in white and using masks waited in the streets for the image to pass. At the end of the procession, the rector of the Basilica gave a blessing from the balcony of the church. The Lavagem was suspended as the rite made social distancing impossible. The adaptation of the Bonfim festival is an indication of the strength of the devotion. Even without tourists, the event took place. Its symbolic content has not been lost despite the appropriations made by tourism. Going forward, more work on the symbolic content of religious events and pilgrimages will help research on the social impacts of place and identity.

This chapter demonstrates how the black population of Salvador has resisted the ecclesiastical attempts to end the Lavagem during a religious event. The effort of the church was in vain, as the ritual that associates Senhor do Bonfim to Oxalá is still in practice today. We believe that this process has contributed to keeping the event going, having a positive impact for this intangible heritage to keep existing, although numerous social and cultural impacts have been seen as discussed in this chapter. In this sense, we highlight that future research requires an understanding of the Festa do Bonfim, given the relationship between tourism and the local population, as the history of the event can serve as a guide when determining perceptions about traditional events that have been given new meaning over time. An important understanding is how core foundations are preserved. We consider this to be an important direction when shaping public policies, which require commitment to ensure a balance in the relationship between the local community and the different sectors linked to tourism. We finish this chapter with a question for future studies focusing on religious and cultural events: How can stakeholders guarantee that a festival does not become "spectacularized" just to meet the demands of tourists?

References

Bahia (2009), Secretaria de Turismo, Superintendência de Serviços Turísticos – SUSET, *Turismo Étnico-Afro na Bahia*. Fundação Pedro Calmon, Salvador.

Brasil (2000), Decreto Nº 3.551, de 4 de agosto de 2000, Institui o registro de bens culturais de natureza imaterial que constituem o patrimônio cultural brasileiro, cria o Programa Nacional do Patrimônio Imaterial e dá outras providências. Presidência da República, Casa Civil, Subchefia para Assuntos Jurídicos, Brasília.

Brasil (2020), Constituição da República Federativa do Brasil: texto constitucional promulgado em 5 de outubro de 1988, compilado até a Emenda Constitucional no. 108/2020. Senado Federal, Coordenação de Edições Técnicas, Brasília.

Dominguez, A.Q. (2018), Turismofobia, ou o Turismo como fetiche, *Revista do Centro de Pesquisa e Formação*.

Duvignaud, J. (1983), *Festas e civilizações*. Edições U.F. do Ceará/Tempo Brasileiro, Fortaleza/Rio de Janeiro.

Getz, D. and Page, S.J. (2016), Progress and prospects for event tourism research, *Tourism Management*, 52, 593–631.

Gonçalves, M.A.R. (2019), A Feira das Iabás em Madureira/Rio de Janeiro: comida, música e cultura afro-brasileira, *Patrimônio e Memória*, 15(1), 200–219.

Gonzalez, Maria Velasco (2009), Gestión turística del patrimonio cultural: enfoques para um desarrollo sostenible del turismo cultural. *Cuadernos de turismo*, 23, 237–253.

Groetelaars, M. M. (1983) *Quem é o Senhor do Bonfim? O significado do Senhor do Bonfim na vida do povo da Bahia*. Vozes, Petrópolis.

Guimarães, E.A.M. (1994), *Religião popular, festa e sagrado. Catolicismo popular e afro-brasilidade na festa do Bonfim*. UFBA, dissertação de mestrado, Salvador.

Habsburgo, M. (1982), *Bahia 1860. Esboços de Viagem*. Tempo Brasileiro/Fundação Cultural do Estado da Bahia, Rio de Janeiro/Bahia.

IBGE (2020) *População estimada*: IBGE, Diretoria de Pesquisas, Coordenação de População e Indicadores Sociais, Estimativas da população residente com data de referência 1o de julho de 2020)

IPHAN (2016), Portaria Nº 200, de 18 de maio de 2016. Dispõe sobre a regulamentação do Programa Nacional do Patrimônio Imaterial – PNPI. Brasília. http://portal.iphan .gov.br/uploads/legislacao/portaria_n_200_de_15_de_maio_de_2016.pdf, assessed January 28, 2021.

Jimura, T. (2018), *World Heritage Sites: Tourism, Local Communities and Conservation Activities*. CABI, Boston, MA.

Marujo, N. (2014), Turismo e eventos especiais: a Festa da Flor na Ilha da Madeira, *Tourism and Management Studies*, 10(2), 26–31.

Melo, J.J.M., Araújo-Maciel, A.P. and Figueiredo, S.J.L. (2015), Eventos Culturais como estratégia de fomento do turismo: análise do Festival Folclórico de Parintins (AM), *Revista Brasileira de Ecoturismo*, 8(2), 251–272.

Nunes Neto, F.A. (2019), *A invenção de uma tradição*. UFBA, tese de doutorado, Salvador.

OECD (2009), *The Impact of Culture on Tourism*. OECD, Paris.

Ott, C. (1969), A transformação do culto da morte da Igreja do Bonfim em santuário de fertilidade. *Afro-Ásia*, 8–9, 35–39.

Priore, M.D. (2000), *Festas e utopias no Brasil colonial*. Brasiliense, São Paulo.

PRODETUR – Salvador (2020), *Plano Estratégico de Marketing Turístico de Salvador*. Prefeitura Municipal de Salvador/Horwath HTL, Salvador/Bahia.

Querino, M. (1922), *A Bahia de Outro'ora, vultos e factos populares*, 2nd edn. Livraria Econômica, Bahia.

Quinn, B. (2009), Festivals, events and tourism, in Jamal, T. and Robinson, M. (eds), *The SAGE Handbook of Tourism Studies*, Sage , New York, 483–503.

Richards, G. (2020), Designing creative places: The role of creative tourism, *Annals of Tourism Research*, 85, 102922.

Serpa, A. (2007), *O espaço público na cidade contemporânea*. Contexto, São Paulo.

Silva, A.F. da (2014), *Amanhã é dia santo: circularidades atlânticas e a comunidade brasileira na Costa da Mina*. Fapesp/Alameda, São Paulo.

Spix, J.B.V. (1938), *Através da Bahia, excerptos da obra Reise in Brasilien*, 3rd edn. Editora Nacional, São Paulo.

Wise, N. and Harris, J (eds) (2019), *Events, Places and Societies*. London. Routledge.

Wise, N. and Jimura, T. (eds) (2020), *Tourism, Cultural Heritage, and Urban Regeneration*. Springer, Berlin.

Wise, N., Polidoro, M., Hall, G. and Uvinha, R.R. (2019), User-generated insight of Rio's Rocinha favela tour: Authentic attraction or vulnerable living environment?, *Local Economy*, 34(7), 680–698.

8. Events and intangible cultural heritage

Takamitsu Jimura

Intangible cultural heritage

This chapter sheds light on intangible cultural heritage (hereafter ICH) and its relationships with events. As an area of study, ICH became noticeable in academia during the 1980s (Jimura, 2019). Since then, ICH has been examined in various but often interconnected subject fields, including heritage and cultural studies, history, anthropology, museology and semiotics, as well as in tourism and events studies. This implies that ICH is an interdisciplinary area of study and has been explored by many different approaches. In the real world, the United Nations Educational, Scientific and Cultural Organisation (hereafter UNESCO) has been playing a central role in the recognition and conservation of ICH around the world since the late 1980s. This has also been demonstrated by the Recommendation on the Safeguarding of Traditional Culture and Folklore (1989), the Director-General's initiative to create a new programme for the ICH (1992), and the Proclamation of Masterpieces of the Oral and Intangible Heritage of Humanity (2001) (Aikawa-Faure, 2020). Such a series of interrelated movements, especially the Proclamation, led to the adoption of the Convention for the Safeguarding of ICH (hereafter ICH Convention) in 2003 at the UNESCO General Conference (Jimura, 2019). Thus, it would not be a coincidence that ICH has been investigated more widely and intensely in academia since 2003 (Jimura, 2019). Of these studies, some focus on the ICH Convention (e.g. Kurin, 2004; Bortolotto, 2007), whilst others explore ICH more broadly (e.g. Lenzerini, 2011; Lixinski, 2013).

Regarding the content of the ICH Convention, Article 1 shows its purposes as follows:

a. to safeguard the intangible cultural heritage;

b.   to ensure respect for the intangible cultural heritage of the communities, groups and individuals concerned;
c.   to raise awareness at the local, national and international levels of the importance of the intangible cultural heritage, and of ensuring mutual appreciation thereof; and
d.   to provide for international cooperation and assistance (UNESCO, n.d.).

To achieve the purposes specified in Article 1, Article 2.1 defines what ICH is in the context of the ICH Convention as follows:

> the practices, representations, expressions, knowledge, skills – as well as the instruments, objects, artefacts and cultural spaces associated therewith – that communities, groups and, in some cases, individuals recognise as part of their cultural heritage. This ICH, transmitted from generation to generation, is constantly recreated by communities and groups in response to their environment, their interaction with nature and their history, and provides them with a sense of identity and continuity, thus promoting respect for cultural diversity and human creativity. For the purposes of this Convention, consideration will be given solely to such ICH as is compatible with existing international human rights instruments, as well as with the requirements of mutual respect among communities, groups and individuals, and of sustainable development. (UNESCO, n.d.)

In relation to Article 2.1, Article 2.2 demonstrates typical kinds of ICH protected through the ICH Convention as follows:

a.   oral traditions and expressions, including language as a vehicle of ICH;
b.   performing arts;
c.   social practices, rituals and festive events;
d.   knowledge and practices concerning nature and the universe; and
e.   traditional craftsmanship. (UNESCO, n.d.)

When considering ICH and events, as Article 2.2 of the ICH Convention indicates, 'events' is one of the representative examples of ICH. Wise and Jimura (2020) examine the interrelationships between tourism, cultural heritage and urban regeneration. In their book, the power of festivals and events is confirmed in terms of its impacts on tourism and urban regeneration (Jimura and Wise, 2020). Concerning the associations between ICH and events, a variety of ICH has been functioning as the main theme(s) of events throughout history. Such ICH includes religions, foods and drinks, arts, books (literature), dances/performing arts, films/television programmes and sports (Jimura, 2022). These sorts of ICH work as central themes of events and are often related with the lives and interests of people who are connected with certain ICH. This signifies that ICH and events featuring specific ICH would reflect the cultural backgrounds and characteristics of the places where the ICH roots and events are held at least to some extent.

Amongst the events featuring diverse ICH, those highlighting a religion are commonly found throughout the globe. Nevertheless, there are clear differences in the principles and practices of religious events depending on religion and regionality. To cite a case, each of the world's major religions, such as Christianity, Islam, Hinduism, Buddhism and Judaism, has its own religious events. A certain degree of commonalities or similarities in the purposes and implementations of religious events are confirmed beyond regionality, but there are also some divergences by country or region. For instance, how to celebrate Easter or Holy Week in Christianity is different – and depends on a country's cultural and historic background. Semana Santa is a Christian event that is held in Spain and other Christian (Catholic) countries with Spanish influences, but is not found in other Christian nations. On the other hand, Shintoism is a religion unique to Japan; therefore, Shinto events can be found only in Japan. For example, Aoi Matsuri is a Shinto event held in May annually in Kyoto. Although there are uncountable Shinto events all over Japan, each Shinto event reflects the individuality and regionality on its aims and practices. Most of these religious events initially developed as local events in which the main participants and audience were local residents. As time goes by, however, some religious events, including Aoi Matsuri, have become tourism resources, attracting visitors from outside local communities.

In addition to religions, sports, particularly traditional or national sports, are appreciated, utilised and conserved as ICH (Niu and Yu, 2008) and have also been acting as key themes of events all over the world. Probably the most famous and established sporting events are the Olympics and Paralympics. Jimura's (2020) study on Tokyo 2020 (which was rescheduled to 2021) reveals how this mega-sporting event has changed the cityscape of its hosting city and could work together with Japan's recent inbound tourism boom to revitalise Tokyo and Japan as a whole, especially their economy. As stated at the beginning, the main topic of this chapter is ICH and its connections with events. The following section focuses on fireworks as a typical example of Japan's traditional ICH and fireworks displays as major events featuring this ICH. The next section also discusses the impacts of fireworks displays on local communities and other stakeholder groups.

Fireworks (*hanabi*) and fireworks displays (*hanabi-taikai*) in Japan

Japan's fireworks are called *hanabi*, which literally means flowery fires. *Hanabi* have been entertaining Japanese people since the seventeenth century. Gunpowder is an essential element of *hanabi*. It is believed that gunpowder was imported to Japan together with Chinese-style guns and then with European-style guns by the middle of the sixteenth century. At that time, Japan was full of constant battles amongst many different domains. Due to this unstable social condition, there were a lot of demands for gunpowder, guns and their craftsmen. Considering all of these factors, it could be assumed that the know-how of *hanabi* making arrived in Japan when gunpowder and guns were introduced to Japan.

In the early seventeenth century, the whole of Japan was unified by Ieyasu Tokugawa and the Edo period (1603–1868) began. The Edo period is known as a very peaceful era without civil conflict or wars against foreign countries, and gun production was strictly cracked down by the Tokugawa Shogunate (Honda, 2008). Thus, it is considered that gunpowder craftsmen began to produce fireworks (*hanabi*) instead of gunpowder (Kamieshu, 2016). This triggered the birth of today's *hanabi* craftsmen (*hanabishi*), companies and stores. It is generally believed that the first Japanese person who experienced a firework was the aforementioned Ieyasu Tokugawa, who watched the firework brought to Japan by a foreign merchant in 1612 (Honda, 2008; Kamieshu, 2016). In 1659, Japan's oldest *hanabi* company and store, Kagiya, was established in Edo (today's Tokyo) (Honda, 2008). The *hanabi* Kagiya sold at that time were small fireworks such as Japanese sparklers (*senko-hanabi*) and pinwheels (*nezumi-hanabi*) that were enjoyed by families and with neighbours. It is generally agreed that Japan's oldest fireworks display (*hanabi-taikai*) is Sumidagawa Hanabi-taikai, whose history can be traced back to Ryogoku Kawabiraki in 1733 (Honda, 2008; Kamieshu, 2016). During the Edo period, the *hanabi* that bloomed in the night sky during *hanabi-taikai* were not colourful at all, but were just dark yellow because of a low ignition temperature (e.g. 1700 Celsius) and a limited variety of colour substances (Aogaki, 1987). *Hanabi* in *hanabi-taikai* began to be colourful during the Meiji period (1868–1912) and the Taisho period (1912–1926), thanks to the import of new and advanced chemicals from overseas (Aogaki, 1987).

The *hanabi* launched during *hanabi-taikai* are still being improved in many senses, in their colours and designs. Figure 8.1 shows colourful *hanabi* with a sophisticated design launched during Kumano Ohanabi-taikai held in Kumano City, Mie Prefecture. The knowledge and skills required for the production, launch and safety of *hanabi* used for *hanabi-taikai* have been conserved and advanced by each *hanabishi*, groups of *hanabishi* and *hanabi* companies, from generation to generation. Today, *hanabi* and *hanabi-taikai* are widely recognised by Japanese people as a seasonal tradition of Japan's summer as well as Japan's ICH. There are some possible reasons why summer is regarded as a season of *hanabi* and *hanabi-taikai* in Japan. One of the commonly accepted reasons is that *hanabi* was originally launched to console the souls of families' ancestors and people who had lost their lives. In Japanese Buddhism, *obon* is a traditional event held in July or August and aims to welcome the spirits of families' ancestors returning to their home during the *obon* period. Therefore, summer has been established as a peak *hanabi* season and currently numerous *hanabi-taikai* are organised in summer across Japan.

Source: Photograph by Hiromi Morita.

Figure 8.1   Hanabi at Kumano Ohanabi-taikai

Hanabi-taikai vary in terms of history, the number and variety of *hanabi* launched, the number and type of viewers and venues and their fee policy. Like religious events, initially the majority of *hanabi-taikai* emerged as community events whose main spectators were local residents, including families, children and youngsters. Some *hanabi-taikai* have developed into major regional or even national events, usually held in summer, that attract not only local residents but people from around Japan. Of such major *hanabi-taikai*, Omagari no Hanabi (Daisen City, Akita Prefecture), Tsuchiura Zenkoku Hanabi Kyogi-taikai (Tsuchiura City, Ibaraki Prefecture) and Nagaoka Ohanabi-taikai (Nagaoka City, Niigata Prefecture) are generally viewed as the top three *hanabi-taikai* events of Japan (Maruyama, 2016).

As discussed above, varied kinds of ICH can serve as key themes for events, and *hanabi* is one such ICH in Japan. In social sciences and the subject field of events studies, the impacts of events have been widely researched, and relevant to this chapter is recognising that economic and social impacts have been studied extensively (e.g. Dwyer et al., 2006; Deery and Jago, 2010; Wise and Harris, 2019) followed by environmental impacts (e.g. David, 2009; Maguire, 2020). As for the impacts of fireworks displays, their environmental impacts have been much more examined, especially in the study fields belonging to natural sciences, rather than considering how these events create economic and social impacts. Thus, there is a need to look at various impacts of fireworks displays, particularly their economic and social impacts. The following discussion will refer to the top three *hanabi-taikai* events of Japan.

First, the social impacts of events have been utilised as a key justification for holding events (Richards et al., 2013). These impacts can be understood as changes in people's way of life, or alterations in the quality of key stakeholders of events including local residents and visitors (Sharpley and Stone, 2012). In the case of *hanabi-taikai* in Japan, even the majority of today's main *hanabi-taikai* initially started as local events, often as religious ones. In fact, the root of Omagari was a socialising opportunity and pastime enjoyed amongst local peasants and landlords, and then developed into a fireworks oblation to Suwa Shrine in 1910 (Isurugi, 2012). The origin of Nagaoka is also a local religious festival that began in 1892 (Isurugi, 2012). Today, both Omagari and Nagaoka are organised annually in August and have been established as important summer traditions of these cities. In contrast, Tsuchiura started in 1925 as a local commemorative event and has been held in the autumn annually because it is also acknowledged as a significant harvest festival (Isurugi, 2012).

Over around a century, many *hanabi-taikai* originally began as local events and have developed into regional or national *hanabi-taikai* as represented by Omagari, Tsuchiura and Nagaoka. In this process, social meanings of these events have also altered. Currently, Omagari and Tsuchiura play a role as major national *hanabi* competitions where *hanabishi* from all over Japan compete by demonstrating their great skills and ideas through the displays of their cutting-edge *hanabi* productions. Given these two major *hanabi-taikai* and the fact that the majority of *hanabi-taikai* are held in the summer, it could be stated that the social impacts of *hanabi-taikai* include not only the conservation of Japan's seasonal, typically summer, traditions at local, regional and national levels but also the inheritance of knowledge and skills of *hanabishi* to Japan's future generations. On the other hand, Nagaoka is not organised as a *hanabi* competition. Instead, it has retained its commemorative character and has also involved praying for recovery from natural disasters (e.g. the 2011 Tohoku Earthquake and Tsunami) and pandemic diseases (e.g. COVID-19) in recent years. In this sense, the social impacts of *hanabi-taikai* like Nagaoka include raising people's awareness of various important issues for humankind and society as well as uniting people across Japan. Through the development of *hanabi-taikai* as popular tourism resources for a wider audience; hosting cities of famous *hanabi-taikai* can enhance their recognition amongst people in Japan. However, the ties between *hanabi-taikai* and local communities may have weakened and/or the uniqueness of each *hanabi-taikai* may have been lost through such a process. Changes in the quality of events often become clear in the commoditisation process such as evolving into tourism resources (Jimura, 2022). Such social impacts can also be understood as damaging the authenticity of traditional *hanabi-taikai*. Furthermore, many *hanabi-taikai* whose primary purpose is to work as tourism resources have begun recently (e.g. Yokohama Sparkling Twilight since 2012).

When local *hanabi-taikai* have turned into regional and national ones, they become more tourist-focused. As mentioned above, this can cause negative rather than positive social impacts on local communities. However, this commoditisation process can bring positive rather than negative economic impacts to local communities. The hosting cities of the top three *hanabi-taikai* are not large municipalities in terms of their populations (around 80,000 in Daisen City, around 140,000 in Tsuchiura City and around 280,000 in Nagaoka City), and do not have major visitor attractions except their *hanabi-taikai*. Moreover, none of them are situated close to Japan's metropolises. Nevertheless, a large number of spectators come to the hosting cities on the days of their *hanabi-taikai* (around 750,000 to Omagari (Daisen City), around 650,000 to Tsuchiura City and around 1 million to Nagaoka City) (Walker Plus, 2020). This implies that a vast amount of economic revenue can be brought to the hosting cities and prefectures. In fact, it is estimated that direct spending by the spectators of Omagari 2010 is around 5 billion Japanese Yen, which is over 48 million United States dollars (FIDEA, 2010). If such financial revenues surpass the operating costs of *hanabi-taikai*, they are evaluated as financially successful events. When *hanabi-taikai* were annual local events enjoyed only within local communities, their operating costs were not a major issue mainly due to their small size. Currently, however, the operating costs of *hanabi-taikai* are a vital issue for their organisers who are typically local governments and chambers of commerce. Traditionally, sponsorship from local enterprises or local branches of large companies, subsidies from local governments and donations from the general public, including local people, have been the main financial sources of the operating budgets of *hanabi-taikai*, especially the major ones. Lately, however, many local businesses and governments have reduced their financial support for *hanabi-taikai* due to a long-term recession. Consequently, many *hanabi-taikai* have been struggling with a smaller operating budget. To tackle this difficulty, many major *hanabi-taikai*, including the top three, started selling paid seats to spectators (typically 1,000–4,000 Japanese Yen, or 9–38 United States dollars per person) to enjoy *hanabi* comfortably. As the majority of spectators who purchase paid seats are non-local visitors, they can bring financial benefits from outside of the holding cities. The introduction of paid seats also meets the benefit principle and could ensure a certain level of fairness amongst all the spectators.

Lastly, the environmental impacts of *hanabi-taikai* are discussed in the context of events and tourism studies. The most common environmental impact would be a large amount of rubbish left by spectators during and after *hanabi-taikai*. It often costs the organisers a lot to clean up. Sometimes, moreover, the fragments of fireworks balls are not all collected after *hanabi-taikai* due to collection costs, and this could cause negative impacts on the natural environment, including riverbeds or coast soils and river or sea waters (Inaba, 2016).

Research directions

Considering the key points and discussions presented so far in this chapter, these final paragraphs suggest some ideas of future research on events and ICH. First, as there are a countless number of events featuring the same kind of ICH all over the world, it would be worth investigating how the purposes and practices of the events highlighting the same sort of ICH (e.g. fireworks displays) can differ by country (e.g. Japan and the United Kingdom). Such a comparative study would reveal the factors, particularly social and/or cultural, that can cause the differences in the purposes and practices of the ICT events amongst varied areas.

Each ICH has associations with certain individuals, communities and/or groups. In light of the ICH Convention adopted by UNESCO, however, each ICH should not only be respected by these key stakeholders who have direct links to the ICH, but be appreciated widely by people and organisations that do not have direct relations with the ICH. This signifies that the assistance required for the conservation of the ICH should be provided at local, national and international levels, and this can lead to proper conservation of the ICH for a prolonged period. This is a vital mission for all types of ICH across the world, and future studies on events and ICH should help relevant stakeholders to achieve this aim. To this end, it is crucial in future research to identify similarities and variations amongst stakeholders of certain ICH events in the levels of their interests in, understanding of and attachments to the ICH. These stakeholders comprise those who have direct associations with the ICH and/ or the ICH event (e.g. local governments, conservation bodies and local communities) and those who do not have such links (e.g. non-local visitors, media and researchers). The findings of this research would be helpful for the former, especially policy makers such as local governments, to develop or improve the conservation plans and management practices of the ICH and ICH event, and their awareness-raising activities targeting local people as well as tourists.

Regarding the impacts of events, traditionally their social and economic impacts rather than their environmental impacts have been the main study subjects in events and tourism studies. Concerning fireworks displays, however, their environmental impacts have been paid more attention to than their social or economic impacts, and these environmental impacts have been examined in natural sciences rather than social sciences. This phenomenon can still be confirmed even if the scope of studies is further narrowed down to the impacts of Japan's fireworks displays (*hanabi-taikai*). For this reason there is a need for events studies to examine the various impacts of fireworks displays, especially those focusing on their economic and social impacts. In reality, however, the economic, social and environmental impacts of events and others (e.g. political impacts) are often interrelated. For instance, the development of local *hanabi-taikai* into regional or even national *hanabi-taikai*, which are well known amongst Japanese people as key summer attractions, implies such interrelations amongst different kinds of event impacts. As a fireworks display becomes popular amongst outsiders such as tourists, it may begin to detract from its association with a certain locality/region and local communities (social impact). This may provoke an increase in the visitor numbers that can generate additional revenue for the hosting city of the fireworks display (economic impact), although it can also cause an increase in the amount of rubbish (environmental impact).

Given these possible ideas of future research on ICH and events in which key theme is a specific ICH, event organisers need to reconsider the meaning of the events in diverse contexts, particularly in the local context. Thus, a holistic approach that can explore not only the various impacts of an ICH event but also the interrelationships amongst these impacts should be adopted in future research. This attitude aims to achieve a comprehensive understanding of the impacts of an ICH event and to consider what needs to be maintained and what should be changed for the successful future of the ICH event. Such research is essential to conserve the ICH itself and to keep running the ICH event over a long period without losing the original meaning of both the ICH and the ICH event.

References

Aikawa-Faure, N. (2020) Article 31: Transitional Clause on the Relationship to the Proclamation of Masterpieces of the Oral and Intangible Heritage of Humanity. In: Blake, J and Lixinski, L. (eds), *The 2003 UNESCO Intangible Heritage Convention: A Commentary*. Oxford: Oxford University Press, pp. 408–431.

Aogaki, R. (1987) Color of Fire Works and Flame Reaktion [in Japanese]. *Kagaku to Kyoiku, 35*(5), 417–419.

Bortolotto, C. (2007) From Objects to Processes: UNESCO's 'Intangible Cultural Heritage'. *Journal of Museum Ethnography, 19,* 21–33.

David, L. (2009) Environmental Impacts of Events. In Raj, R. and Musgrave, J. (eds), *Event Management and Sustainability*. Wallingford: CABI, pp. 66–75.

Deery, M. and Jago, L. (2010) Social Impacts of Events and the Role of Anti-Social Behaviour. *International Journal of Event and Festival Management, 1*(1), 8–28.

Dwyer, L., Forsyth, P. and Spurr, R. (2006) Assessing the Economic Impacts of Events: A Computable General Equilibrium Approach. *Journal of Travel Research, 45*(1), 59–66.

FIDEA (2010) *Dai84kai zenkoku-hanabi-kyogi-taikai 'Omagari no Hanabi' kaisai ni tomonau keizai-hakyu-koka* (Economic Impacts of Omagari 2010) [in Japanese]. Available at: www.f-ric.co.jp/report/research/2010/1010.pdf (accessed 6 July 2020).

Honda, M. (2008) Small Talk on Fireworks in Japan [in Japanese]. *Journal of the Japanese Association for Petroleum Technology, 73*(4), 281–286.

Inaba, R. (2016) Environmentally-Friendly Fireworks [in Japanese]. *Japanese Journal of Occupational Medicine and Traumatology, 64,* 213–216.

Isurugi, S. (2012) Hanabi no machi Omagari (Omagari: A City of Fireworks) [in Japanese]. *Chiikikosogaku Kenkyukyoiku Hokoku, 2,* 29–39.

Jimura, T. (2019) *World Heritage Sites: Tourism, Local Communities, and Conservation Activities*. Wallingford: CABI.

Jimura, T. (2020) Changing Faces of Tokyo: Regeneration, Tourism and Tokyo 2020. In Wise, N. and Jimura, T. (eds), *Tourism, Cultural Heritage and Urban Regeneration: Changing Spaces in Historical Places*. Cham: Springer, pp. 141–155.

Jimura, T. (2022) *Cultural Heritage and Tourism in Japan*. London: Routledge.

Jimura, T. and Wise, N. (2020) Expanding Perspectives in Tourism, Cultural Heritage and Urban Regeneration. In Wise, N. and Jimura, T. (eds), *Tourism, Cultural Heritage and Urban Regeneration: Changing Spaces in Historical Places*. Cham: Springer, pp. 205–213.

Kamieshu, N. (2016) Manatsu no Fubutsushi – Hanabi (Seasonal Feature of Japan's Mid-summer – Fireworks) [in Japanese]. Available at: www.homes.co.jp/cont/press/reform/reform_00377/ (accessed 27 June 2020).

Kurin, R. (2004) Safeguarding Intangible Cultural Heritage in the 2003 UNESCO Convention: A Critical Appraisal. *Museum International, 56*(1–2), 66–77.

Lenzerini, F. (2011) Intangible Cultural Heritage: The Living Culture of Peoples. *European Journal of International Law, 22*(1), 101–120.

Lixinski, L. (2013) *Intangible Cultural Heritage in International Law*. Oxford: Oxford University Press.

Maguire, K. (2020) An Examination of the Level of Local Authority Sustainable Planning for Event Management: A Case Study of Ireland. *Journal of Sustainable Tourism*, 1–26.

Maruyama, Y. (2016) Chinkon no Hanabi no Minzokugaku (Folklore of Fireworks for the Dead Souls) [in Japanese]. *Nihongakuho, 35*, 25–45.

Niu, A.J. and Yu, D.H. (2008) Development of Traditional Sport on Perspective of Protection of Intangible Cultural Heritage. *Journal of Wuhan Institute of Physical Education, 42*(1), 90.

Richards, G., De Brito, M. and Wilks, L. (2013) *Exploring the Social Impacts of Events*. London: Routledge.

Sharpley, R. and Stone, P. (2012). Socio-Cultural Impacts of Events: Meanings, Authorized Transgression, and Social Capital. In Page, S. and Connell, J. (eds), *The Routledge Handbook of Events*. London: Routledge, pp. 347–361.

UNESCO (n.d.) Text of the Convention for the Safeguarding of the Intangible Cultural Heritage. Available at: https://ich.unesco.org/en/convention (accessed 23 June 2020).

Walker Plus (2020) Hanabi-taikai 2020 [in Japanese]. Available at: https://hanabi.walkerplus.com/ (accessed 6 July 2020).

Wise, N. and Harris, J. (eds) (2019) *Events, Places and Societies*. London: Routledge.

Wise, N. and Jimura, T. (eds) (2020) *Tourism, Cultural Heritage and Urban Regeneration: Changing Spaces in Historical Places*. Cham: Springer.

9. Transformational atmospheres of international sporting events

Jada Lindblom

Affective atmospheres

Influenced by cultural geography scholarship and a heightened interest in affect and emotion, tourism and events scholars have begun to pay greater attention to the concept of *atmospheres*. Inspired in part by the influential work of philosopher Gernot Böhme, Edensor (2012) describes atmospheres as a mental or emotive "tone" imbued within a particular environment, which, when powerful, may draw people in and be experienced personally through mood. Anderson (2009, 78) considers atmospheres as "collective affects," suggesting an atmosphere to be the "shared ground from which subjective states and their attendant feelings and emotions emerge." Reflecting a similar notion of collectivity and transferability, Stewart (2011, 452) envisions atmospheres as "intensities" that pool together, creating "not an inert context but a force field in which people find themselves," imbued with expressivity, potentiality, and a sense of composition for the present moment. Applying these ideas within tourism scholarship, Volgger and Pfister (2020, 2) suggest that this atmospherically attuned direction offers a "corrective re-turn to a more holistically conceived living space which is perceived with all senses and sits at the interface between matter and idea to rebalance idealistic and materialistic worldviews." Concurring with Sobecka (2018), Volgger and Pfister (2020, 2) suggest that the atmospheric turn in tourism scholarship may be valuable in assisting a "refocus on the ubiquitous but invisible substrate penetrating all things" – uncovering layers which may otherwise seem inaccessible. Furthermore, Volgger and Pfister (2020) note, attention to atmospheres may align with contemporary, commercial desires for tourism practices and experiences that are more sustainable and "locally embedded," reflecting the intertwining of socio-cultural and economic factors within the realm of tourism.

When considering the roles of atmospheres in tourism, leisure, and events, an atmosphere is a complex dimension to control, yet can play a critical role in visitor, attendee, or customer experience and satisfaction. In the context of restaurants, for instance, variables including lighting, décor, colors, cleanliness, odors, music, noise level, and temperature collectively contribute to the atmosphere, impacting customer satisfaction (Sulek and Hensley, 2004). Atmospheres are noted to be important factors for theme park experience design (Kao et al., 2008; McCarthy, 2019) and prominent in perceptions of tourism transportation options, such as airplanes (Lin, 2015). Examinations of atmospheres may help to describe a place or event's essence, depicting settings as "tranquil" or "relaxing" (as in San Martin and Del Bosque, 2008), or "vibrant," "memorable," and "social" (as in Stefansdottir, 2018). While visitors' affective conceptualizations of destinations have been recognized as highly influential to the development of place image, the affective, atmospheric dimensions of places have not always been consistently evaluated in place image research (Royo-Vela, 2009). However, recent tourism research has shown increasing attention to the implications of atmospheres, for instance how affective perceptions of atmospheric cues may influence word-of-mouth promotion (Loureiro et al., 2020).

Affective atmospheres arise as a particularly important concept for understanding both the expectations and the impacts associated with larger-scale events, such as international sporting events. With high levels of production, these events may be intentionally designed to create immersive environments in which attendees feel transported to a different version of the host city, or seemingly a different place entirely that only exists for the duration of the event. In studying a large-scale, international sporting event, McGillivray (2019) describes this phenomenon through the concept of the "Live City," in which affective atmospheres are intentionally created through the hosting of a large event, positioning the city as a setting of expansive consumptive potential. The affective atmospheres of events and tourism attractions may be designed and controlled by their managers to some extent, but they are also co-created by participants within the setting, who may have varying degrees of agency in determining the affective nature of the event (Edensor and Sumartojo, 2015). Similarly, Stefansdottir (2018) emphasizes that there is an ongoing process at work of affective co-creation between an environment and an inhabitant, as they leave impressions upon one another. These impressions do not only occur in the moment; events, in particular, may be preconceived by the attendee/participant to be affective in a certain way, as noted by Edensor

(2010). Repeat event attendees, especially, may anticipate a certain affective atmosphere when they return (Edensor, 2012).

Events are commonly associated with affective and emotional experiences of excitement, anticipation, and enjoyment, but locational and social contexts may create a more nuanced range of outcomes. Stadiums used for live sports events have been noted to elicit high levels of arousal and pleasure amongst attendees (Uhrich and Benkenstein, 2010). The celebratory atmospheres of large sporting events may positively contribute to residents' subjective well-being (Schlegel et al., 2017) or foster a general positive perception of the host city atmosphere, which may be linked with a sense of urban regeneration (Ohmann et al., 2006). Cities may specifically employ the development of sporting events and related facilities in hopes of such goals of urban image regeneration (Gratton, et al., 2005) and to bolster tourism appeal in transitional destinations (Wise and Harris, 2017). Smaller international sporting events have been noted for their potential to yield community benefits such as enhanced pride, unity, and a sense of euphoria, with possibly fewer negative community impacts (Taks et al., 2015). Social impacts of events are not limited to positive outcomes such as senses of celebration and unity: sporting events, in particular, are recognized for their ability to emphasize divisions between groups of people, such as teams or fan groups (Bertoli, 2017). Research pertaining to the Olympic Games finds that sentiments of nationalism may operate via affective atmospheres, propelled by a range of factors including event marketing narratives, music, and corporate sponsorships (Closs Stephens, 2016). The emotional and affective evocations of sporting events in turn present a wide range of economic and social implications (Uhrich and Koenigstorfer, 2009).

The Red Bull Cliff Diving World Series in Mostar, Bosnia and Herzegovina

Since 2015, the city of Mostar, Bosnia and Herzegovina has hosted a stop on the Red Bull Cliff Diving World Series tour. Mostar's natural beauty and historic setting provide a striking backdrop for the diving competition and related events. However, the city remains notorious for having experienced some of the worst physical damage and fatalities during the Bosnian War, from 1992 to 1995 (Bollens, 2007), which created long-term impacts upon the city's heritage sites and place image (Wise, 2020). Fought between the city's own religious-ethnic subpopulations (as well as outside forces), the war has had lasting social impacts in Mostar that are often exhibited through affective dimensions in the everyday lives of residents (Laketa, 2016). The city's subpopulations have remained largely divided, geographically and socially, although some signs of progress in reunification have become more apparent of late (Carabelli, 2018).

In recent years, the weekend-long Red Bull event has centered around *Stari Most* (the Old Bridge), a UNESCO World Heritage Site that was reconstructed in the early 2000s following its notable wartime destruction (see Figure 9.1). The bridge has been central to a local, centuries' old tradition of high diving. Mostar is one of only a few stops in the Red Bull series to have been included on the tour annually. The event attracts tourists as well as locals, who can enjoy the competitive events as well as side offerings such as a free street festival of regional musical performers. Research from another destination on the Red Bull Cliff Diving World Series tour has indicated a generally high level of satisfaction amongst residents pertaining to the event's economic contributions to the region, plus some recognition of positive impacts related to social and cultural development (Avelar et al., 2021). Mostar's war history and noted social divisions makes the city a particularly interesting context for studying the community impacts of an international sporting event that attracts local as well as foreign interest and attendance.

This research on the Red Bull event was conducted as part of a broader, multi-methods investigation of the community impacts of tourism in Mostar. This event-specific study focuses mainly on interview findings, which are supported by coinciding results from a quantitative component. Fourteen adult residents of Mostar (and nearby suburbs/villages) were recruited via snowball sampling methods to participate in multi-day research that included a three-part interview as well as a place-based, experiential component. This sample was delimited to younger adult residents (mean age 27; range 18–42), with a specific interest in learning about the experiences and perceptions of residents who grew up during and in the aftermath of the war. The semi-structured interviews included questions about the participants' lived experiences in the city as well as their opinions and perceptions about tourism, special events, and tourism sites in Mostar. The topic of the Red Bull event commonly emerged in the interviews unprompted before specific questions pertaining to the event were asked at the very end of the interview process.

A resident survey ($n = 408$) preceded the qualitative, interview-based component of this research. Several questions in the survey instrument specifically addressed the Red Bull Cliff Diving World Series event and its location, the Old Bridge. Four questions were adapted from the scale developed by Kim et al. (2015) addressing the social impacts of hosting events (in part adapted from

Source: Photograph by Jada Lindblom.

Figure 9.1   A competitor prepares to dive atop Mostar's Old Bridge

Crompton, 2004). Findings from the survey revealed very positive perceptions overall of the Red Bull event's social impacts, with all mean scores between 6 (strongly agree) and 7 (very strongly agree) on the seven-point Likert-type scale. These items included: "the event enhances community pride" ($M = 6.45$, $SD = 1.24$); "the event enhances the sense of being a part of a community" ($M = 6.37$, $SD = 1.25$); "the event provides the incentive for the preservation of local culture" ($M = 6.34$, $SD = 1.26$); and "the event reinforces community spirit" ($M = 6.33$, $SD = 1.34$). Additional survey questions revealed positive perceptions of tourism development in Mostar, generally speaking, and positive responses to the presence of tourists in the city. Respondents associated the presence of tourists at the Old Bridge site, specifically, with strong feelings of pride, happiness, and satisfaction, as well as a moderately high perceived sense of surprise (see Lindblom et al., 2020).

While the interview protocol was designed with the intention of learning about the affective and emotional impacts of tourism upon residents in Mostar, no questions directly addressed the concept of *atmosphere*. Inductively, this arose across the interviews as an important theme. Interview participants frequently noted how the Red Bull event altered the city's atmospheres in ways that seemed highly transformative. Perceptions of the event and its associated atmospheres were nearly all positive, reflecting themes of fun, excitement, liveliness, sociability, pride, and success. A few respondents noted negative perceptions, such as complaints about discomfort including crowding and the high summer temperatures at the outdoor venue, or that the event's high-adrenaline, action sports emphasis was not to their personal liking. However, the topic of crowding was commonly expressed in positive terms, too, in that it represented perceptions of popularity, urban vibrancy, and local economic benefit.

Many participants expressed that the appeal of the event resulted as a combination of contributing factors, most notably the excitement and entertainment value of the high-level competition and good feelings from seeing the city filled with people, both locals and tourists. The popularity of the event seemed to inspire a sense of hopefulness for the city – that Mostar could be known for something like beautiful scenery and fun gatherings, rather than war damage, fatalities, and social divisions. One participant who was a teen during the war reflected upon this dichotomy, expressing that the Red Bull competition was an excellent event for anyone to attend "if you like *life*." She elaborated:

> It's an incredible experience just from the fact that, okay, it's in our hometown, it's a lot of publicity for the city. But at the same time, what [the athletes] are doing up there is so incredible. Like you just *live* it. You look at them, the *energy*. The atmosphere is great.

Another participant expressed similar thoughts, again identifying the atmosphere of the event as its main point of appeal. He explained how its high-adrenaline sports focus was critical for creating a certain type of atmosphere:

> Everything is *pumped*, and then the music, and the announcements, and the preparation for the jumping; *they're going to jump from their hands!*, you know? The total silence and then when they go down, the crowd explodes at the same time, and if they do a good jump, a lot of comments.

One young male interviewee expressed that the appeal of the event was difficult to articulate, yet undeniably special: "It's just something you've got to go and see and feel … It's not something that you can describe with words."

For one young woman who had moved to Mostar after the war, the event was notable for how it represented a profound sensory shift in the city:

> It shows the best of Mostar. It's like you *hear* it, like it's *all people*, and *talking*, and *crowded*, and *happy* and, I don't know, everything is *full*. All these restaurants now are empty, but they are full at that time. So I think it's like Mostar is *a place to be* at that time of the year.

Many participants mentioned that the city felt like a different and improved place during the Red Bull weekend – more "exciting" and "cosmopolitan." Several of the participants expressed that the event provided an excellent example of the possibilities of tourism and special events in Mostar, in ways that could be fun for locals as well as visitors. While tourism, as an industry, has been a growing influence in Mostar over the past decade, the event weekend provided a taste of what the city could look and feel like if it were to become even more established as a popular destination.

The interview participants commonly noted how relevant it was that Mostar has its own tradition of high diving from the bridge. This point allowed residents to feel a deepened sense of connection and pride associated with the event; yet, many participants noted that Red Bull was able to turn the sport of high diving into something even more exciting and engaging for spectators than what the traditional diving offered:

> The Old Bridge is beautiful on its own. There are people diving from the Old Bridge [regularly] but they [the spectators] are not going to experience the atmosphere that the Red Bull Cliff Diving brings to Mostar. They're not going to experience, like, the air that you can cut with a knife. There is so much going on, wherever you turn. There is a concert here, there is a concert there, there's a street performance there … Wherever you go, there is always something that takes your mind away.

The reputation as well as the programming style of the event sponsor, Red Bull, were important factors in generating positive affective atmospheres. Participants often spoke of the event's easily detectable "good energy," air of excitement, and emphases on having fun and bringing people together. In a city known for lasting internal conflict and divisions amongst its population, participants reflected that having a well-known international organizing body (that attracts interest from athletes and fans from around the world) helps to create a more neutral and welcoming space in Mostar. This positioning allows the event to facilitate feelings of pride, happiness, and fulfillment across a broader range of residents. The international context of the event helped imbue positivity into an emotionally and culturally complex local site (the Old Bridge) that for many residents held difficult memories and associations.

Amongst the participants, there was a broad recognition that Bosnia and Herzegovina's international reputation still suffers due to the war history, and the positive energy of the event, as publicized internationally on television and online, helped to dismantle some of the country's persistent stigmas and preconceived notions left over from the war.

Research directions

The interviews with Mostar residents emphasized the reciprocal and co-produced nature of atmospheres. While the excitement of the high diving and international-level competition created an enjoyable and highly antic-ipated experience for attendees, the residents' further reflections about the event – viewing it as an indicator of post-war economic and social progress and a changing international reputation – in turn added to the general sense of positivity associated with the event. Widely, participants agreed that Red Bull brought something good to their city, and it was a source of pride to be included on the "elite," global tour. As a recurrent happening, residents showed a high level of familiarity with the event and expressed that they look forward to the city's fun, lively, and sociable atmosphere during the event period. Its festivities, from the competition itself to the associated music fes-tival and other side events, each alter the city's ambience and create affective atmospheres representing a powerful sense of transformation, capable of "taking [one's] mind away."

In this post-war city, which has experienced the lasting impacts of widespread violence and destruction, this sense of transformation occurs in different ways. In the moment, on a personal and experiential level, residents may feel as if they are transported to a completely different place when attending; they may feel their own moods shift dramatically. On a broader scale and scope, the event works to generate senses of hope and opportunity as residents are able to picture a different sort of future for the city, modelled through this particular event.

The case of Mostar and the Red Bull Cliff Diving World Series illustrates how the most seemingly general event goals, such as creating fun environments aimed at bringing people together, may become more tangibly meaningful and important in places where fun and togetherness have not always seemed so commonplace or likely. In understanding how an international event may be transformative to a host city, the concept of atmospheres becomes crucial. As some of the interview comments in this study expressed, the positive impacts of an event may not be easily assessed or articulated; they may be subjective, multi-sensory, and/or reflective of a long and complex personal history with a place. Attention to the atmospheres created by events helps to reveal their emotional, affective, and social impacts, allowing for metrics of success to more wholeheartedly address community-based issues and concerns in ways that attendee counts and economic figures alone cannot describe.

This research reiterates the importance of evaluating event impacts from social perspectives as well as economic metrics, reflecting findings from other research pertaining to event impacts in the transitional regions of former Yugoslavia (e.g., Đurkin Badurina et al., 2020; Wise and Perić, 2017). The case of Mostar emphasizes how local history and social context may deeply influence the ways in which an event may impact a host community. In choosing a host city, event organizers should consider the potential for an event to be inclusive of the entire local population and positively transformative upon the local community, and also consider how their own identity and affiliations may impact outcomes. Supplemental, complementary aspects of the event, such as street festivals that serve residents as well as visitors, may compound the potential positive impacts of an event. For events that will likely repeat annually in the same city, community research methods such as resident surveys, interviews, and focus groups may help organizers build upon perceived benefits while minimizing or mitigating negative impacts. Research specifically attuned to affective, atmospheric considerations may glean insights regarding the components that most notably impact the creation of positively perceived atmospheres.

In this research, the multi-sensory experience (namely sights and sounds) of the live event, the perceived high quality of event organization and production, and the accessibility of free-of-cost and inclusive side events seemed to contribute substantially to positive atmospheric perceptions. These perceptions were largely centered upon notions of excitement, fun, togetherness, local pride, urban renewal, and destination reimaging. By combining an international perspective with an orientation toward leisure enjoyment and sociality, the Red Bull event creates spaces of perceived neutrality and inclusivity in places known for representations of cultural affiliations and divisions. These spaces open opportunities for healing as well as imagining new social and economic possibilities.

This research suggests an encouraging outlook for other post-conflict cities that hope to benefit from special events toward goals of revitalizing their image and offerings. Importantly, the findings also serve as a reminder for researchers and planners of the importance of a place's own heritage, residents' own interest in the event, and the community's level of visitor readiness in providing a supportive hosting environment. In concordance with Chalip (2006), there is much evidence from Mostar that the positive, celebratory, and social environment created by sporting events may be leveraged, if carefully planned, to help address local issues and serve broader community development goals. Considering the perceived importance of atmospheres in residents' assessment of the quality, appeal, and impacts of an event, there is still much opportunity for future research to investigate the factors and preconditions of events that are most conducive to creating positive, transformative atmospheres in host communities. While it is tempting, and common, for event producers to try to manipulate and design certain types of atmospheres, interested researchers should not assume such fixity and predetermination, and instead keep in mind the organic, fluid, and co-produced nature of atmospheres. Since atmospheres are subjective, ever changing, and often nebulous, this is a line of inquiry well suited for creative and in-depth qualitative (or mixed-methods) research tuned to understanding the richness of personal experiences.

References

Anderson, B. (2009), Affective Atmospheres, *Emotion, Space and Society* 2(2), 77–81.

Avelar M., Sousa Á., and Menezes A. (2021), The Impacts of Sport Tourism Events: The Red Bull Cliff Diving World Series Case in the Azores Islands, in de Carvalho J.V., Rocha Á., Liberato, P., and Peña A. (eds), *ICOTTS 2020: Advances in Tourism, Technology and Systems*. Springer, Singapore.

Bertoli, A.D. (2017), Nationalism and Conflict: Lessons from International Sports, *International Studies Quarterly* 61(4), 835–849.

Bollens, S.A. (2007), *Cities, Nationalism and Democratization*. Routledge, New York.

Carabelli, G. (2018), *The Divided City and the Grassroots: The (Un)Making of Ethnic Divisions in Mostar*. Palgrave Macmillan, London.

Chalip, L. (2006), Towards Social Leverage of Sport Events. *Journal of Sport and Tourism* 11(2), 109–127.

Closs Stephens, A. (2016), The Affective Atmospheres of Nationalism, *Cultural Geographies* 23(2), 181–198.

Crompton, J. (2004), Beyond Economic Impact: An Alternative Rationale for the Public Subsidy of Major League Sports Facilities, *Journal of Sport Management* 18(1), 40–58.

Đurkin Badurina, J., Perić, M., and Vitezić, V. (2020), Potential for the Regeneration of Rural Areas through Local Involvement in the Organisation of Sport Events, *Managing Sport and Leisure*, 1–18.

Edensor, T. (2010), Aurora Landscapes: Affective Atmospheres of Light and Dark, in Benediktsson, K., and Lund, K.A. (eds), *Conversations with Landscape*. Routledge, London, 227–240.

Edensor, T. (2012), Illuminated Atmospheres: Anticipating and Reproducing the Flow of Affective Experience in Blackpool, *Environment and Planning D: Society and Space* 30(6), 1103–1122.

Edensor, T., and Sumartojo, S. (2015), Designing Atmospheres: Introduction to Special Issue, *Visual Communication* 14(3), 251–265.

Gratton, C., Shibli, S., and Coleman, R. (2005), Sport and Economic Regeneration in Cities, *Urban Studies* 42(5–6), 985–999.

Kao, Y.F., Huang, L.S., and Wu, C.H. (2008), Effects of Theatrical Elements on Experiential Quality and Loyalty Intentions for Theme Parks, *Asia Pacific Journal of Tourism Research* 13(2), 163–174.

Kim, W., Jun, H.M., Walker, M., and Drane, D. (2015), Evaluating the Perceived Social Impacts of Hosting Large-Scale Sport Tourism Events: Scale Development and Validation, *Tourism Management* 48, 21–32.

Laketa, S. (2016), Geopolitics of Affect and Emotions in a Post-Conflict City, *Geopolitics* 21(3), 661–685.

Lin, W. (2015), "Cabin Pressure": Designing Affective Atmospheres in Airline Travel, *Transactions of the Institute of British Geographers* 40(2), 287–299.

Lindblom, J., Vogt, C., and Andereck, K. (2020), Construal Level Theory as a Framework for Navigating Community Contexts in Tourism Planning, *Tourism Planning and Development*, www.tandfonline.com/doi/abs/10.1080/21568316.2020.1855238.

Loureiro, S.M.C., Stylos, N., and Bellou, V. (2020), Destination Atmospheric Cues as Key Influencers of Tourists' Word-of-Mouth Communication: Tourist Visitation at Two Mediterranean Capital Cities, *Tourism Recreation Research*, 1–24.

McCarthy, W. (2019), "Meet Me on Main Street": Disneyland as Place Attachment for Southern Californians, *Tourism Geographies* 21(4), 586–612.

McGillivray, D. (2019), Sport Events, Space and the "Live City," *Cities* 85, 196–202.

Ohmann, S., Jones, I., and Wilkes, K. (2006), The Perceived Social Impacts of the 2006 Football World Cup on Munich Residents, *Journal of Sport and Tourism* 11(2), 129–152.

Royo-Vela, M. (2009), Rural-Cultural Excursion Conceptualization: A Local Tourism Marketing Management Model Based on Tourist Destination Image Measurement, *Tourism Management* 30(3), 419–428.

San Martín, H., and Del Bosque, I.A.R. (2008), Exploring the Cognitive-Affective Nature of Destination Image and the Role of Psychological Factors in Its Formation, *Tourism Management* 29(2), 263–277.

Schlegel, A., Pfitzner, R., and Koenigstorfer, J. (2017), The Impact of Atmosphere in the City on Subjective Well-Being of Rio de Janeiro Residents During (vs. Before) the 2014 FIFA World Cup, *Journal of Sport Management* 31(6), 605–619.

Sobecka, K. (2018), Atmospheric Turn, in Clingerman, F.J., and Bergmann, S. (eds), *Arts, Religion, and the Environment: Exploring Nature's Texture*. Brill, Boston, 43–58.

Stefansdottir, H. (2018), The Role of Urban Atmosphere for Non-Work Activity Locations, *Journal of Urban Design* 23(3), 319–335.

Stewart, K. (2011), Atmospheric Attunements, *Environment and Planning D: Society and Space* 29(3), 445–453.

Sulek, J., and Hensley, R. (2004), The Relative Importance of Food, Atmosphere, and Fairness of Wait: The Case of a Full-Service Restaurant, *Cornell Hotel and Restaurant Administration Quarterly* 43(3), 235–247.

Taks, M., Chalip, L., and Green, B.C. (2015), Impacts and Strategic Outcomes from Non-Mega Sport Events for Local Communities, *European Sport Management Quarterly* 15(1), 1–6.

Uhrich, S., and Benkenstein, M. (2010), Sport Stadium Atmosphere: Formative and Reflective Indicators for Operationalizing the Construct, *Journal of Sport Management* 24(2), 211–237.

Uhrich, S., and Koenigstorfer, J. (2009), Effects of Atmosphere at Major Sports Events: A Perspective from Environmental Psychology, *International Journal of Sports Marketing and Sponsorship* 10(4).

Volgger, M., and Pfister, D. (2020), *Atmospheric Turn in Culture and Tourism: Place, Design and Process Impacts on Customer Behaviour, Marketing and Branding.* Emerald Publishing, Bingley.

Wise, N. (2020), (Re) Building a Bridge: Landscape, Imagination and Memory in Mostar, in Wise, N., and Jimura, T. (eds), *Tourism, Cultural Heritage and Urban Regeneration.* Springer, Cham, 157–171.

Wise, N., and Harris, J. (2017), Introduction: Framing Sport, Events, Tourism and Regeneration, in Wise, N., and Harris, J. (eds), *Sport, Events, Tourism and Regeneration.* Taylor & Francis, Abingdon, 1–8.

Wise, N., and Perić, M. (2017), Sports Tourism, Regeneration and Social Impacts: New Opportunities and Directions for Research, the Case of Medulin, Croatia, in Bellini, N., and Pasquinelli, C. (eds), *Tourism in the City.* Springer, Cham, 311–320.

10. Rural events and social development

Lucia Aquilino

Rural events

This chapter focuses on the case of the World Alternative Games (WAG) and provides a critical overview of how events as human experiences and social practices boost social development in rural communities. This focus is important because human experiences play a key role in community development (Richardson, 1991). Social and cultural practices constitute the first matters of community development, which make use of all the values embedded in a place and its community (Chalip, 2006a; Jepson and Clarke, 2015; Smith, 2012). In particular, leisure and tourism activities can play a leading role in the process of community development itself (Crouch, 2000; Hanrahan et al., 2017; Hassan, 2014; Koski and Lämsä, 2015). Also, the renegotiation and reconfiguration of cultural and social meanings can be boosted by tourism and leisure activities through which changes in communities may occur (Crouch, 2000; Hassan, 2014).

Generally speaking, leisure and tourism practices offer a space in which individuals can experience encounters with different people and different places (Lamont and McKay, 2012; Wise and Harris, 2019). By engaging in this space and in its related activities, individuals tend to develop feelings, values and lenses to make sense of the world (Crouch, 2000; Lamont and McKay, 2012). Leisure and tourism practices such as those promoted in sports tourism and events provide individuals with the opportunity to develop knowledge through which the ways of thinking of and connecting with places and other people are renegotiated (Crouch, 2000). The renegotiation of meanings can also be observed in leisure activities (e.g. sport) as they work not only as a vehicle of social categorisation and identity development but also as a device of social cohesion and/or reconstruction of a sense of community (Dallaire, 2015;

Harris and Parker, 2009). Based on this, tourism and leisure practices can enable the development of a space in which a sense of community is manifested and/or reconfigured (Ramshaw and Hinch, 2006; Silk and Amis, 2005). In this particular context, the utilisation of physical space does make its own part in the process discussed. Indeed, on the one hand, its peculiarities may characterise forms of affiliation of a given activity with the local and/or tourist groups (Lamont and McKay, 2012; Ramshaw and Hinch, 2006). On the other, however, changes imposed by external forces (e.g. tourism development, urban regeneration) may affect meanings embedded in local groups (Silk and Amis, 2005). Thus, it is based on these perspectives that tourism and event activities can be seen as vehicles of social development whereby community identities are staged and opportunities for social and cultural encounters multiply (Chalip, 2006b; Misener and Mason, 2006; Schulenkorf et al., 2011; Wise and Harris, 2017).

The motivations which justify participation or attendance in general in tourism events can be diverse. One of these is represented by a particular bond linking people to a certain place, also identified in the event tourism literature, which may become a good reason for attending or participating in an event held in a particular geographical area (Kirkup and Sutherland, 2015; Urry, 2002). Small-scale events taking place in rural landscapes, for example, may offer a learning experience, which, through the engagement of all the senses boosted by the peculiarities of the natural setting and of the event activities, tend to shape perceptions of the natural environment and its relative values (cultural and others). Arguably, then, all the people involved in the same event context may bring about senses of place and community (Bertella, 2014). Forms of identification and engagement not only with the natural setting of the event but also with other attendees or participants (local or not) are shaped through interactions with the surrounding environment and with people within the event context (Kirkup and Sutherland, 2015).

Other forms of identification arise when interactions occurring in tourism and event contexts are scrutinised from different perspectives. As tourism practices, such as sport, are activities involving people and stimulating social encounters and interactions, events can be viewed as a sort of space where these social exchanges take place (see Coaffee, 2008; Jepson and Clarke, 2015; Zhou and Kaplanidou, 2017). In this particular context, interactions are enabled by spirit of celebration, event themes and common and shared values which define or bring about specific identities (see Green and Jones, 2005; Shipway and Jones, 2007). Thus, event tourism enacts a process of identification to a given community, such as a sports community (Fairley and O'Brien, 2017; Wichmann, 2017), and the expression of sense of belonging to it (Kim

et al., 2013; Snelgrove et al., 2008). Here, the same social processes and constructs (e.g. language, body language, clothes, icons, etc.) defining social and
cultural identities in everyday life are used, for example, in a sports tourism
dimension where they are converted into particular processes and constructs
used to exhibit sport identities (see Fairley and O'Brien, 2017; Rickly-Boyd,
2012, 2013). This process of identification may turn an event into a place where
a sense of community develops.

These reflections provide a valid explanation of how active and passive tourists and eventgoers, who decide to elude roles that they have to fulfil in daily
social interactions (e.g. family, work, friends), develop a specific identity in
order to interact with those who share the same or similar ones (Green and
Jones, 2005; Kim et al., 2013; Rickly-Boyd, 2012, 2013). Although Shipway
and Jones (2007) provided empirical evidence of the fact that this process of
identification explains mainly the tourist experience of active participants in
sports tourism events, their study offers an insight into how to understand
the experience of all participants, both locals and tourists in tourism events,
regardless of the level of involvement. An event is viewed here as an entangled
tourism and social process which enables and affects a complex group of
people involved in tourism activities, regardless of economic, social, cultural
or other discrepancies.

Insights from the World Alternative Games in rural Wales

The community of Llanwrtyd Wells is the town that hosts the WAG, a bi-annual
event hosted since 2012. This case example is used in this chapter to provide
scope and context for a study on community development to describe how
events are vehicles of social development in rural areas. The dramatic rural
landscape, the vast green lands crowded with sheep and rabbits which sur-
round Llanwrtyd Wells, offer a picturesque setting to the community activities.
The WAG are enjoyable competitions which take place every two years in
the smallest town in Britain (Aquilino et al., 2020; World Alternative Games,
2016a, 2016b). The small-scale event preserves its focus on people and participation which makes it an ideal case for scrutinising communities. It promises
and gives any individuals, regardless of boundaries or differences and, mostly,
sports skills, the opportunity to engage in quirky activities so as to take part
in a sort of 'celebration' of people, whether they are winners or not (Aquilino
et al., 2020, 2021). Peculiar games, rural shows and night gatherings are features which support the idea of considering the WAG as a community-based

event. The utilisation of local natural resources and the endeavours of the host community in planning the event itself seem to be very important. The local community, a population of 600, is an essential resource. It plays a leading role in the organisation of the event and provides further support through volunteering activities showing a positive attitude toward tourism developments.

This chapter presents part of the findings of a research project which focused on developing an understanding of how a small-scale event affects a rural community. A combination of formal semi-structured interviews and observations were performed to provide relevant insights into community meanings which were not necessarily the product of verbal interactions between the researcher and the participants (see also Angrosino, 2005; Fontana and Frey, 2005; Tedlock, 2005; Yin, 2014). Many groups of stakeholders were involved in this study: event organisers, volunteers, media people, owners of local businesses and lands, councillors, participants and spectators and other community members. A purposive sampling technique was used to identify key informants at the beginning of the sampling process. In fact, when a few organisers or other key stakeholders were approached, they would recommend other key informants to address based on a snowballing activity (Devers and Frenkel, 2000; Marshall, 1996).

Key findings show that, in the WAG space, many different sub-groups experienced their own communal moments at the same time. The event activities, from the organisation to the game performances, were interactions enabling people to strengthen their ties within their own very intimate idea of community which seemed to be encompassed in family, friendship or camaraderie. These findings seem to echo Chalip's (2006b) arguments related to sense of celebration and camaraderie emerging from getting involved in event activities. Furthermore, in light of Delanty (2009) and Falassi's (1987) reflections on the interruption of everyday life into festivals and events contexts, time seemed to slow down to a different pace within the WAG space. It seemed that people gave themselves time to linger on something that ordinary life took away from them. Within this particular temporal space, the sub-groups of the WAG community tended to revive the traditional forms of community (e.g. family, friendship) through engaging in activities which had no relation whatsoever with those that they usually performed on a daily basis.

The co-creation of a related memory was perceived as the production of long-term benefits which would fill the gaps in everyday life. Thus, by engaging in event activities enacting processes of socialisation and shared moments, people would make time. By investing their time, which was thought to produce a positive outcome during the events and in the future as well, this helped to unite people through hosting and participating. In other words, within the event space, the time interruption created an opportunity to dwell on and perform the idea of community that all the WAG sub-groups had in mind with the aim of projecting it on future activities not necessarily related to event activities.

'Taking part is more important than winning' is the motto of the WAG and the message engraved on the medals that all participants (winners or losers) gain at the end of each game. Beyond its power in blurring boundaries, its strength is in encompassing and projecting the desire of embracing and performing certain values. Indeed, the games were crowded with symbols and rituals on which people purposively relied in order to develop further meanings while embodying them through their performances. Certain peculiar dresses and attitudes seemed to dominate the WAG scenario.

In reflecting a sort of viral enjoyment and inciting a desire to touch or swim in a pit despite its unpleasant appearance, the water of the bog as other peculiar elements of the games (e.g. hay bales, shopping trolleys) seemed to represent meaningful assets (see Figures 10.1 and 10.2 from the bog snorkelling event). It seemed to symbolise the equality of all people standing on its edges and of all performers as anybody could aspire to plunge into it free from restrictions and judgements and any snorkellers received a medal, regardless of the scores recorded. As such, inclusiveness and equality are meanings which tend to be constructed and projected on people in first place, and tend to be embraced and performed when spectators turn into competitors and directly engage in the games. Cohen's (1985) arguments pertaining to the symbolic process fuelling connectedness among a group of people come to mind as the act of taking part in the games acts as a ritual and certain elements of the event activities like the water of the bog or the participants' comments could be seen as symbols. Swimming in the bog or the mere act of competing in any games was a sort of ritual through which people showed their equality and performed their inclusiveness in an inclusive community, the WAG community, despite their differences and the diversity of the performance approaches.

The meaningful process boosted by such symbols make the development of the WAG community quite visible. Several authors, including Berger and Luckmann (1966) and Delanty (2010), explain how community development hinges upon the social consensus of a group of people. However, these findings tend to tease the equality and inclusiveness meanings outlined above revealing a sort of intersection and friction between meanings of equality and inclusiveness and meanings of diversity within the WAG. In other words, the act of competing in a game as a practice enabling the construction of meanings of

Source: Photograph by Nicolas Wise.

Figure 10.1   Bog snorkelling venue in the countryside just outside of
Llanwrtyd Wells

equality, inclusiveness, and sense of belonging also created the conditions for other meanings to emerge and which defined the inner peculiarity of the subjects involved in the games. Thus, inclusiveness of the WAG community was such that it was within it that people were free to act and be different beyond any kind of kinship, affiliation or rules. Here is the great peculiarity of a community which presented more diverse traits than common ones. Certainly, the mere act of participating embodied meanings of inclusiveness of people into the WAG group.

Source: Photograph by Nicholas Wise.

Figure 10.2   Bog snorkelling competitor at the World Alternative Games in rural Wales

In addition, it was also a stimulus for the variety of diverse traits (e.g. age, nationality, able-bodied/disabled, attitude, dresses) to stand out without marking boundaries. This seems to reflect the characteristics of a postmodern community which Delanty (2010, 109) defines communication community as those whose experiences are characterised by 'a certain unity in diversity and the absence of a foundational point of reference'. The sense of belonging to the WAG community was performed through communicating one's diversity and expressing peculiar traits while enjoying the event experience in a rural locale. Based on these findings, the triple function of practice of event activities tends to emerge. The active engagement generated interactions and relationships thus boosting a sense of belonging. However, it was also in itself a process through which values were embraced and embodied and individual peculiarities unleashed. In light of this, the WAG became a space of freedom and of belonging at the same time, a space wherein social development could be easily perceived.

Research directions

This study provides further perspectives in the understanding of event impacts on community development and participation. It sheds light on how social interactions boosted by events enhance community well-being (see Zhao and Wise, 2019). The findings emerging from the research on the WAG in rural Wales represents a valuable foundation for the developing body of knowledge related to those interdisciplinary threads of meanings linking society and events (see Patterson and Getz, 2013). Indeed, this chapter showed how communal moments, boosted by event experiences, helps us to understand the wacky or unusual physical assets during certain events. It shows how funny dress codes and gestures of participants and organisers can ultimately blur social distance and differences and instil meanings of inclusiveness in the minds of people taking part in the quirky events of Llanwrtyd Wells. A sense of shared belonging amongst communities emerged as a result of participation and social interactions. Memories created across communal interactions reinforce community ties and inspire the development of new ones. These memories are then preserved and re-experienced by event participants in Llanwrtyd Wells or in other places. Participants bring in and take away event activities as memories, and this helps reinforce their collections and feelings of community – which grounds social development and feelings of belonging and well-being.

Future research needs to continue putting emphasis on co-creating and attributing meanings within the event space. This means that researchers need to be directly involved and interact with people to fully understand how people develop community meanings and find ways to enhance their well-being. In so doing, a further understanding of how they contribute to building up the event and the community that they like in the moment when this happens, regardless of the nature of their participation, can be developed. Bearing in mind that perceptions contribute to shaping event experiences, this study provides tools to move forward the exploration of connections between events and society.

As a wacky event, the WAG provide people with the opportunity to create their own meanings and values of the event from scratch by unleashing their inner feelings and creativity. In other words, an uncontrolled event crowd could create their own event experience based on their desired outcomes. This discussion tends to challenge Chalip's (2006a) arguments related to the necessity to develop more accurate strategies to shape event experiences which can enhance their social leverage and contribute to community development. It does align with Đurkin and Wise (2018) because it puts the needs of the participants first, but this can cause local conflicts. Indeed, eventgoers were able or willing to create themselves social values and belongings through shaping and engaging in activities whose design was quite rudimentary. As such, more advanced management or marketing strategies seem to not be needed in designing or managing social leveraging events as eventgoers desire to be the creators of their own community development.

References

Angrosino, M.V., 2005. Recontextualising observation. In: Denzin, N.K. and Lincoln, Y.S., ed. *The SAGE handbook of qualitative research*. 3rd ed. London: SAGE Publications, 729–745.

Aquilino, L., Wise, N., and Harris, J., 2020. Wackiness and event management: The case of the World Alternative Games. *Event Management*, 24(5), 567–577.

Aquilino, L., Harris, J., and Wise, N., 2021. A sense of rurality: Events, placemaking and community participation in a small Welsh town. *Journal of Rural Studies*, 83, 138–145.

Berger, P. and Luckmann, T., 1966. *The social construction of reality: A treatise in the sociology of knowledge*. London: Penguin.

Bertella, G., 2014. Designing small-scale sport events in the countryside. *International Journal of Event and Festival Management*, 5(2), 132–145.

Chalip, L., 2006a. Toward a distinctive sport management discipline. *Journal of Sport Management*, 20(1), 1–21.

Chalip, L., 2006b. Towards social leverage of sport events. *Journal of Sport and Tourism*, 11(2), 109–127.

Coaffee, J., 2008. Sport, culture and the modern state: Emerging themes in stimulating urban regeneration in the UK. *International Journal of Cultural Policy*, 14(4), 377–397.

Cohen, A., 1985. *The symbolic construction of community*. London: Tavistock.

Crouch, D., 2000. Places around us: Embodied lay geographies in leisure and tourism. *Leisure Studies*, 19(2), 63–76.

Dallaire, C., 2015. Assessing the sociology of sport: On national and ethnocultural communities in Canada. *International Review for the Sociology of Sport*, 50(4–5), 375–379.

Delanty, G., 2010. *Community*. London: Routledge.

Devers, K.J. and Frankel, R.M., 2000. Study design in qualitative research: Sampling and data collection strategies. *Education for Health*, 13(2), 263–271.

Ðurkin, J. and Wise, W. 2018. Managing community stakeholders in rural areas: Assessing the organisation of local sports events in Gorski kotar, Croatia. In: Jepson, A. and Clarke, A., ed. *Power, construction and meaning in festivals and events*. London: Routledge, 185–200.

Fairley, S. and O'Brien, D., 2017. Accumulating subcultural capital through sport event participation: The AFL International Cup. *Sport Management Review*, 21(3), 1–12.

Falassi, A., 1987. Festival: Definition and morphology. In: Falassi, A., ed. *Time out of time: Essays on the festival*. New Mexico: University of New Mexico Press, 1–10.

Fontana, A. and Frey, J.H., 2005. The interview: From neutral stance to political involvement. In: Denzin, N.K. and Lincoln, Y.S., ed. *The SAGE handbook of qualitative research*. 3rd ed. London: SAGE Publications, 695–728.

Green, B.C. and Jones, I., 2005. Serious leisure, social identity and sport tourism. *Sport in Society*, 8(2), 164–181.

Hanrahan, J., Maguire, K. and Boyd, S (2017), Community engagement in drive tourism in Ireland: Case study of the Wild Atlantic Way, *Journal of Heritage Tourism*, 12(5), 509–525.

Harris, J. and Parker, A., 2009. *Sport and social identities*. Basingstoke: Palgrave Macmillan.

Hassan, D., 2014. Sport and communities: An introduction. *Sport in Society*, 17(1), 1–5.

Jepson, A. and Clarke, A., 2015. *Exploring community festivals and events*. Abingdon: Routledge.

Kim, J.W., James, J.D. and Kim, Y.K., 2013. A model of the relationship among sport consumer motives, spectator commitment, and behavioral intentions. *Sport Management Review*, 16(2), 173–185.

Kirkup, N. and Sutherland, M., 2015. Exploring the relationships between motivation, attachment and loyalty within sport event tourism. *Current Issues in Tourism*, 20(1), 1–8.

Koski, P. and Lämsä, J., 2015. Finland as a small sports nation: Socio-historical perspectives on the development of national sport policy. *International Journal of Sport Policy and Politics*, 7(3), 421–441.

Lamont, M. and McKay, J., 2012. Intimations of postmodernity in sports tourism at the Tour de France. *Journal of Sport and Tourism*, 17(4), 313–331.

Marshall, M.N., 1996. Sampling for qualitative research. *Family Practice*, 13(6), 522–525.

Misener, L. and Mason, D.S., 2006. Creating community networks: Can sporting events offer meaningful sources of social capital? *Managing Leisure*, 11(1), 39–56.

Patterson, I. and Getz, D., 2013. At the nexus of leisure and event studies. *Event Management*, 17(3), 227–240.

Ramshaw, G. and Hinch, T., 2006. Place identity and sport tourism: The case of the Heritage Classic Ice Hockey Event. *Current Issues in Tourism*, 9(4), 399–418.

Richardson, L., 1991. Postmodern social theory: Representational practices. *Sociological Theory*, 9(2), 173–179.

Rickly-Boyd, J.M., 2012. Lifestyle climbing: Toward existential authenticity. *Journal of Sport and Tourism*, 17, 85–104.

Rickly-Boyd, J.M., 2013. Existential authenticity: Place matters. *Tourism Geographies*, 15(4), 680–686.

Schulenkorf, N., Thomson, A. and Schlenker, K., 2011. Intercommunity sport events: Vehicles and catalysts for social capital in divided societies. *Event Management*, 15(2), 105–119.

Shipway, R. and Jones, I., 2007. Running away from home: Understanding visitor experiences and behaviour at sport tourism events. *International Journal of Tourism Research*, 9, 373–383.

Silk, M. and Amis, J., 2005. Sport tourism, cityscapes and cultural politics. *Sport in Society*, 8(2), 280–301.

Smith, A., 2012. *Events and urban regeneration: The strategic use of events to revitalise cities.* New York: Routledge.

Snelgrove, R., Taks, M., Chalip, L. and Green, B.C., 2008. How visitors and locals at a sport event differ in motives and identity. *Journal of Sport and Tourism*, 13(3), 165–180.

Tedlock B., 2005, The observation of participation and the emergence of public ethnography. In: Denzin, N.K. and Lincoln, Y.S., ed. *The SAGE handbook of qualitative research.* 3rd ed. London: SAGE Publications, 467–481.

Urry, J., 2002. *The tourist gaze.* London: SAGE Publications.

Wichmann, A., 2017. Participating in the World Gymnaestrada: An expression and experience of community. *Leisure Studies*, 36(1), 21–38.

Wise, N. and Harris, J., eds. 2017. *Sport, events, tourism and regeneration.* London: Routledge.

Wise, N. and Harris, J., eds. 2019. *Events, places and societies.* London: Routledge.

World Alternative Games, 2016a. *Llanwrtyd Wells: Events and activities.* Llanwrtyd Wells: Welsh Country Magazine.

World Alternative Games, 2016b. *World Alternative Games 2016.* Assessed January 2016 at www.worldalternativegames.co.uk/about/

Yin, R.K., 2014. *Case study research: Design and methods.* London: SAGE Publications.

Zhao, Y. and Wise, N., 2019. Evaluating the intersection between 'green events' and sense of community at Liverpool's Lark Lane Farmers Market. *Journal of Community Psychology*, 47(5), 1118–1130.

Zhou, R. and Kaplanidou, K., 2017. Building social capital from sport event participation: An exploration of the social impacts of participatory sport events on the community. *Sport Management Review*, 1–13.

11. Local Authority planning, sustainability, and event governance

Kelly Maguire

Local Authority planning and event governance

Local Authorities according to the Republic of Ireland's Department of the Environment Community and Local Government are 'the main vehicle of governance and public service delivery at local level – leading economic, social and community development, delivering efficient and good value services and representing citizens and local communities effectively and accountably' (DECLG, 2012). Planning events at the local level in Ireland is predominantly governed by the Planning and Development Regulations 2001–2015 (licensing of outdoor events). This legislation places a statutory onus on Local Authorities throughout Ireland to play a key role in the approval or disapproval of large-scale outdoor public events through the process of event licensing (Maguire, 2019). Through the process of event licensing and regulation, Local Authorities in Ireland have a remit to control the overall process of planning for event management. They also have the ability to control the delivery of public services necessary for event management in Ireland (Maguire, 2019). This provides Local Authorities with a statutory obligation to perform a wide and rather complex variety of roles in the arena of large-scale outdoor public events. However, Wood (2005) mentions that the extent of government involvement varies according to event size and type and, indeed, the level of Local Authority interest, resources and commitment to events. The significant functions held by Local Authorities in relation to event planning at local level in Ireland can be seen in Box 11.1.

Box 11.1 Scope of Local Authority involvement in events at local level in Ireland

There are 31 Local Authorities involved in events in Ireland, County Councils and City Councils, and their main area of involvement is:

- Event licensing.
- Event regulations.
- Infrastructure provision (roads and traffic management, water supply and sewage, waste management, food safety, environmental protection, health and welfare, signage, car parks, planning).
- Service providers (fire and emergency services, housing, land use planning, grants, community development, enterprise support, motor taxation).
- Resource management (water, energy, waste).
- Air and noise pollution control.
- Granting temporary trading licenses.
- Provision of supporting materials and conditions to be complied with for event developments.
- Support for tourism and event development and planning.
- Funding for local tourism event activities.
- Promoting event tourism initiatives at local level.
- Building control.
- Venue and attraction ownership and management.
- Providing advice and guidance.
- Consulting authority and regulatory body.
- Policy development and City/County Development Plan implementation.
- Implementation and oversight of legislation.

Source: Adapted and modified from DECLG (2012); LGMA (2012); DEHLG (2014); DTTAS (2015); Maguire (2018).

Local Authorities are responsible for overseeing the application of state laws through event licensing which governs the preparation and sale of food, street closures, environmental protection, water supply and sewage, waste management and removal, road closures, health and welfare and the creation of temporary structures at local level (Maguire, 2020). The responsibility of such diverse functions however falls to a number of departments within Local Authorities which can at times complicate the process of planning for event management (Maguire, 2019). The management of each of these services is detrimental to the quality and health of the environment, society and economy and also to the quality of the event itself. Page (2015) states that effective planning functions lie in a functional planning system within Local Authorities. Hence, it is important to highlight that the above Local Authority functions can vary and not all Local Authorities implement the same planning processes with regards to planning for event management. For example, the level of planning required for events in Dublin City may be different to the needs and requirements of the industry in County Roscommon (Maguire and Hanrahan, 2017).

The roles, responsibilities and functions of Local Authorities in Ireland have advanced over the last decade (Boyle and O'Riordan, 2013; NPF, 2018). Previously, Local Authorities had a key responsibility for tourism development and promotion; however, the expansion of the national event industry has altered this function to incorporate a more progressive approach towards events. Their involvement was established principally through the provision of local tourism infrastructure, the maintenance of an attractive environment through planning and development control and the development of proactive policies to stimulate the private sector and promotion and marketing of tourism (Charlton and Essex, 1996). While these functions are still important today, the scope of their involvement in the delivery of public services has been expanded to include a variety of sectors including events and a heightened range of services in relation to events, tourism, climate change, economic development and enterprise and heritage protection. It is at a local level where the impacts of events are most strongly felt. Therefore, with the rate at which the profiles of events are growing at a local level in Ireland, it is vital that events are planned and managed sustainably.

The growth of the event tourism industry and its potential to contribute positively to the economic and social fabric of host destinations has affected the way in which events are governed and how planning processes are undertaken. There is a clear need to control developments to ensure they do not impact negatively upon the economic, social and environmental resource base at destination level in Ireland. By controlling event developments in a sustainable manner, Local Authorities have the ability to cater for the growing number of events and their visitors. However, there exists a clear debate within academic literature in relation to the ability of Local Authorities to govern at a local level. The role of governance and particularly its capacity for directing and shaping change has been questioned (Whitford et al., 2014). Boyle and O'Riordan (2013, 3) question 'whether Local Authorities in Ireland are fit for purpose, whether they have the ability to address challenges, adapt to new roles, follow through on commitments and achieve valued outcomes for citizens'.

Others have claimed that the challenge for Local Authorities in fulfilling their statutory functions is down to a lack of adequate resources, particularly in terms of funding and staffing (Hogan, 2017), and have pointed out that 'Local Authorities are in need of major reform' (Quinn, 2017). In order for a collective commitment amongst Local Authorities in governing event activities towards sustainable thresholds to be achieved, effective local governance is needed.

Thomas and Wood (2004) discuss how the public-sector departments responsible for event provision and planning tend to have limited resources in terms of funding, time, staff and expertise. Nevertheless, the provision of staff with adequate training and expertise within Local Authorities for events is necessary to guide the process of planning for event management. While Local Authorities in Ireland are experiencing shortfalls in terms of financing and staffing, the functions of Local Authorities in relation to the process of planning for event management are crucial to sustaining the competitiveness of the event industry in Ireland. Getz and Page (2016) discuss how events must secure tangible resources and political support to become sustainable. Thus, given the role of Local Authorities and their commitment in committing to sustainable development through the National Planning Framework (NPF) for Ireland (2018), Local Authorities are in an ideal position to shape the sustainable development of tourism and event industries. However, Quinn (2017) states that for effective local governance, adequate resources are needed at local level.

Local Authority planning in Ireland

The Government of Ireland launched Project Ireland 2040, the National Planning Framework (NPF) (2018), which articulated further the government's commitment to achieving sustainable development. Aligned to the United Nations Sustainable Development Goals set out in the 2030 Agenda for Sustainable Development, the vision of the NPF is to shape the future growth and development of the country:

> We have a responsibility to plan for the changes that we face, to manage our future growth in a planned, productive and sustainable way. If we fail to plan for growth and for the demand it will place on our built and natural environment as well as on our social and economic fabric, then we will certainly fail in our responsibility to future generations of Irish men and women. (NPF, 2018: 10)

Therefore, to support this vision, there is a need to develop new approaches to anticipate and prepare for the future (Maguire, 2019). As such, Local Authorities are tasked with strengthening more environmentally focused planning at local level. This is essential if government wishes to meet the needs of the climate change mitigation plan for Ireland (DCCAE, 2017), which outlines a clear focus on transitioning to a low-carbon, climate-resilient and environmentally sustainable economy by 2050. There is also a clear emphasis on the sustainable management of water and waste, the protection of biodiversity, cultural heritage and landscapes as well as air quality and noise management (NPF, 2018). In light of this government commitment, there is a fundamental need for Local Authorities to plan for such issues in the context of planning for event management, considering that such issues are pertinent within the event industry (Maguire, 2020). This is essential to ensure event developments occur within environmental limits, having regard to host communities and to the requirements of national legislation, especially since it has been reported that events are expected to play a fundamental role in the recovery of economies and societies post-Covid-19 (Hambleton, 2020; OECD, 2020). Thus, the added role of events to host destinations and the role of the government's plans to develop, grow and recover tourism industries at a national and local level in Ireland is essential to leverage benefits and secure the future competitiveness of the industry.

The aim of this research is to contribute to new knowledge on whether or not Local Authorities are placing environmental sustainability at the forefront of their event management planning agenda in Ireland. In order to accomplish this, it will be necessary to establish whether planning guidelines for event management are being provided by Local Authorities as part of the event planning and licensing process to aid event managers in the process of ensuring environmental protection and preservation from the impacts of events in Ireland.

The study presented in this chapter sets forth to examine the priority placed on monitoring environmental sustainability performance by Local Authorities for events with a specific focus on the Republic of Ireland. In Ireland, Local Authorities have a legal responsibility to license events and to facilitate and regulate the process of planning for large-scale outdoor public events (in excess of 5000 people) under the Planning and Development Regulations 2001–2015. Furthermore, under the NPF for Ireland (2018), Local Authorities have legal obligations to plan for the economic, social, cultural and environmental development of respective counties (Maguire and Hanrahan, 2016). A quantitative content analysis of Local Authority event management planning guidelines aims to paint a picture on the topic in question.

To examine the level of environmental sustainability and performance within the legal local government agenda for event management planning in Ireland, a content analysis of Local Authority event management planning guidelines was applied. The content analysis approach allowed for direct comparisons to be made between Local Authorities throughout the research process. This enabled the identification of variations and gaps in relation to Local Authority planning for environmental sustainability and performance when planning for event management in Ireland. Having identified published Local Authority event management planning guidelines, the content analysis framework that was developed allowed for a comparable examination of results in relation to the provision of core guidelines to manage the impacts and issues of events by Local Authorities. This permitted the authors to determine the current level of sustainable planning for the environmental impacts of events by the legally obligated Local Authorities.

The findings presented in Table 11.1 illustrate how planning for the environmental sustainability of events by the legally required Local Authorities in Ireland is absent, despite the legal frameworks in place to govern environmental sustainability at national and local levels. The research has found that just 10 per cent of Local Authorities are planning ahead to address the issues of litter and waste generation at events. However, the management of litter and waste is pivotal at events given that the vast accumulation of waste is regarded as inevitable at all events (Maguire and Hanrahan, 2016). Irrespective of size and type, Jones (2014) details how this issue has the potential to cause long-term damage and degradation to the natural environment. Hence, managing event litter and waste is critical for event sustainability and should thus form a core part of all Local Authority event management plans and guidelines, particularly since Local Authorities through the NPF (2018) have a commitment to sustainably manage waste, and in light of the EPA (2020) recognising that it is an area in need of attention.

No Local Authority addressed issues of energy and water consumption at events, as outlined in Table 11.1. However, the mindless consumption of energy and water at events can produce undesirable impacts, contribute to resource depletion and toxicity (Maguire and Hanrahan, 2016) and produce large quantities of carbon emissions (Mair, 2011). With events being identified as major contributors of carbon emissions (McKercher et al., 2013), such issues could be integrated in all Local Authorities' plans and guidelines for event management. Yet, despite an international political consensus on climate change being agreed by 196 countries, including Ireland (EC, 2017), no Local Authority included climate change responsiveness as an important consideration for event management planning. Ireland's first national plan containing

Table 11.1   Assessment matrix of the level of environmental planning for events in Ireland

Criteria to assess Local Authorities' sustainable planning for events management in Ireland

Local Authorities in Ireland (abbreviated by first and last letter, e.g. DL = Donegal)

Local Authority	Provision of planning guidelines for event management	Provisions for monitoring environmental impacts	Management of litter and waste at events	Energy consumption/ conservation	Water consumption/ conservation
WW					
WX	×		×		
WH					
WD					
TY					
SO					
RN					
OY					
MN					
MO					
MH	×				
LD					
LH	×		×		
LK	×				
LM					
LS					
KY					
KK					
KE					
GC					
GY					
FL					
Ds					
Dr					
Dc	×		×		
DL					
Cc					
CK					
CE					
CN					
CW					

Local Authorities in Ireland (abbreviated by first and last letter, e.g. DL = Donegal)

Criteria to assess Local Authorities' sustainable planning for events management in Ireland	CW	CN	CE	CK	Cc	DL	Dc	Dr	Ds	FL	GY	GC	KE	KK	KY	LS	LM	LK	LH	LD	MH	MO	MN	OY	RN	SO	TY	WD	WH	WX	WW
Minimising carbon emissions																															
Climate change responsiveness																															
Provision of drinking water																															
Protection of water quality							✕												✕												
Management of catering and food services identified							✕												✕												
Provision of sanitary facilities/ accommodation							✕												✕												

Local Authorities in Ireland (abbreviated by first and last letter, e.g. DL = Donegal)

Criteria to assess Local Authorities' sustainable planning for events management in Ireland	WW	WX	WH	WD	TY	SO	RN	OY	MN	MO	MH	LD	LH	LK	LM	LS	KY	KK	KE	GC	GY	FL	Ds	Dr	Dc	DL	Cc	CK	CE	CN	CW
Sewage treatment measures identified													×												×						
Measures for the treatment of wastewater identified																															
Reducing air and soil pollution at events identified																															
Reducing light pollution at events identified																															
Reducing noise pollution at events identified													×	×											×						
Reducing transport impact at events identified																															

Local Authorities in Ireland (abbreviated by first and last letter, e.g. DL = Donegal)

Criteria to assess Local Authorities' sustainable planning for events management in Ireland	CW	CN	CE	CK	Cc	DL	Dc	Dr	Ds	FL	GY	GC	KE	KK	KY	LS	LM	LK	LH	LD	MH	MO	MN	OY	RN	SO	TY	WD	WH	WX	WW
Biodiversity conservation/protection identified																															
Measures to prevent the abandonment of tents																															
Environmental landscape protection																															
Environmental clean-up and remedial woks identified							×												×												

a series of mitigation measures and actions to address Ireland's carbon issue and commitment to tackling climate change was published in July 2017 (DCCAE, 2017). This was followed with the inclusion of 'transitioning to a low carbon climate resilient society by 2030', with a commitment of €22 billion to achieve this (NPF, 2018). The Environmental Protection Agency (2020) questions if Ireland is on track for achieving this. This plan outlines the need to appoint climate change teams within Local Authorities. As such, managing the areas of waste, water, energy and climate change can facilitate optimum resource recovery and minimal environmental degradation and should be a priority for Local Authorities when planning for event management.

The provision of drinking water is an incremental requirement at events for reasons of public health. It is critical that water quality be maintained and monitored to sustain the quality and health of the environment (Jones, 2014) while also protecting public health. This too was recommended in the NPF (2018). However, just 6 per cent of Local Authorities recognised the importance of providing drinking water at events and protecting water quality. This finding is concerning and needs to be addressed by Local Authorities. Without the provision of clear plans and guidelines for ensuring the provision of water and protection of water quality, it will be more difficult for Local Authorities to ensure public safety. This could open Local Authorities up to potential litigation from the public.

Furthermore, only 6 per cent of Local Authorities identified the need to maintain sanitary accommodation. Jones (2014) highlights the fundamental need to manage wastewater and sewage as a result of the impacts that can be created due to the mismanagement of sanitary facilities, including pollution of ecosystems and damage to habitats and biodiversity. In this regard, the NPF (2018) has an objective to implement European Union directives to protect Ireland's environment, biodiversity and wildlife. The maintenance of sanitary facilities at events should be a primary concern for Local Authorities and could be integrated within Local Authority event management plans and guidelines.

Local Authorities in Ireland have a statutory role to play through granting casual trading licenses to facilitate catering and food services at events (DECLG, 2007). Therefore, it is astounding that just 6 per cent of Local Authorities have prioritised catering and food safety in their plans and guidelines for event management. Given the statutory role of Local Authorities to grant casual trading licenses and ensure compliance with food safety standards (EPA, 2014), it is vital that the provision of catering and food services be prioritised by all Local Authorities when planning for event management.

Transport has a huge impact on the environment, being acknowledged as the largest carbon contributor for events (Mair, 2011). No Local Authority addressed the need to reduce traffic impacts at events, even though by 2030, according to the NPF for Ireland, it is proposed that no non-zero emission vehicles will be sold in Ireland. Furthermore, the importance of biodiversity and the authenticity of nature (Holden, 2008) are currently being completely overlooked by Local Authorities. This is worrying given the existence of the directives relating to the conservation of natural habitats and of wild fauna and flora (Directive 92/43/ECC), which have assisted in protecting the biodiversity of tourism destinations in Ireland. Ireland's natural biodiversity has created breathtaking landscapes for tourists and visitors to explore (Fáilte Ireland, 2016). Indeed, Fáilte Ireland acknowledges the importance of biodiversity and has developed a set of general principles for the protection of biodiversity, which should be adhered to across the sector (Fáilte Ireland, 2016). Thus, the importance of planning for such impacts will help safeguard and enhance the destinations' natural assets upon which the tourism and event industry is so dependent; so far this has not yet been recognised.

Jones (2014) discusses how pollution can occur and be caused by not managing water, waste, food, sanitary facilities and transport impacts. Local Authorities have a role in monitoring and enforcing statutory controls on pollution in certain areas as outlined in the Water Pollution Act 1977. Light pollution has been suggested to impact host community members of events (Case, 2013). Yet, these issues are currently not receiving any attention from Local Authorities. Similarly, noise pollution is an incremental element at events, which can adversely impact general health and cause community hostility toward the event (David, 2009). Just 10 per cent of Local Authorities made provisions for the prevention of noise pollution at events. Under environmental noise regulations 2006 (SI NO 140) Local Authorities must ensure noise levels are kept at a reasonable level. Ensuring the proactive management of noise is a fundamental requirement of Local Authorities under the NPF for Ireland. The importance of managing pollution clearly needs to be communicated to all Local Authorities in Ireland.

Future research directions

An increasingly important consideration at events is the issue of tents being left behind (Maguire and Hanrahan, 2016). This is a major problem at festivals and events in Ireland and has become a very familiar sight at the end of music festivals but the issue is being overlooked by Local Authorities. However, it is indeed an issue that needs to be tackled in light of the physical and visual impacts it can cause (Maguire, 2020). Furthermore, the environmental clean-up and remedial works at events, which form a core part of the Local Authority event management planning process (Planning and Development Act 2015), are vital for the protection of the environment and the quality of the event (Maguire, 2020). Yet, it was found that just 6 per cent of Local Authorities acknowledged the importance of clean-up and remedial works, despite the issue of thousands of tents being abandoned at events each year in Ireland. Local Authorities need to place a fundamental onus on protecting the environment and reducing the environmental impacts events can often have on natural resources. As a result of environmental impacts created by events, some large-scale events do not take place every year, for example Glastonbury takes a fallow year every six years (*The Guardian*, 2016) to prevent excessive damage to the event site. Perhaps this is a technique that could be followed for large-scale public events in Ireland.

As part of the process of planning for event management, referring back to Chapter 3, Local Authorities require an environmental monitoring pro-gramme for before, during and after the proposed event. However, according to national standards (Planning and Development regulations 2001–2015), this only applies when the event exceeds a capacity of 5000 people. This gives Local Authorities a fundamental role to ensure events are planned in an environmen-tally appropriate way. Yet, just 27 per cent of Local Authorities reported that they required an environmental monitoring programme for events. Clearly, there is little emphasis placed on monitoring the environmental impacts of events by Local Authorities, despite their legal requirement to request an environmental monitoring programme as part of the event management plan-ning process. With the reputation of events to create negative environmental impacts (Case, 2013; Collins and Cooper, 2016), there is a fundamental need for Local Authorities to approach planning with a primary focus on the envi-ronment. Regardless of the number of planning solutions available to Local Authorities to assist in monitoring the environmental consequences of events, it is evident from the analysis that a significant number of Local Authorities do not provide guidance in conducting an environmental impact assessment or strategic environmental assessment on event activities. Although the need for an environmental assessment and monitoring process has been advocated to safeguard the environment from event activities (Getz and Page, 2016), results confirmed that very few Local Authorities provide guidance on environmental monitoring. However, to ensure event developments do not negatively impact the natural environment and considering the environment is a key reason for choosing Ireland as a destination to visit, it is important that Local Authorities recognise the need to protect that environment from the direct impacts of event activities. This can be achieved through the application of indicator systems such as the Euopean Tourism Indicator System and detailed policies and plans within their respective County Development Plans, an event planning tool-kit and a functional Local Authority event manager and dedicated staff.

Given the complicated relationship between events and the environment, the issues identified in Table 11.1 should form a key agenda of Local Authorities when planning for event management and environmental event sustainability. However, the evidence is overwhelming and clearly identifies that the environmental impacts of events, which have been identified from international best practice guidelines, have been largely overlooked by Local Authorities. This is despite Local Authorities having a legal responsibility through LA Agenda 21, the 2030 Agenda for Sustainable Development and the NPF 2018 to plan for environmental sustainability. Without effective plans and guidelines on how to better manage the interactions between the environment and events, Local Authorities will not be able to plan for or address the environmental impacts that events are capable of creating. Hence, there is a clear need for nationwide improvements and a consistent state-wide sustainable approach to planning for event management with comprehensive guidelines to manage the environmental impacts of events as previously recommended by Maguire (2020). The NPF for Ireland 2040 stated how the avoidance of unnecessary impacts is the preferred mitigation strategy for the NPF. As part of the wider implementation of the NPF, the Department of Housing, Local Government and Heritage will develop updated statutory guidelines to assist planning authorities in making sustainable planning decisions which fully integrate the relevant environmental requirements and support the delivery of national policy objectives of the framework (NPF, 2018). Therefore, with the Department of Transport, Tourism and Sport (2015) acknowledging that the economic viability and competitiveness of the Irish tourism industry can only be sustained if the quality of the environment is maintained, it is essential that Local Authorities recognise this, abide by their legal obligations and respond to the environmental impacts generated by event activities (Maguire, 2019). This is essential to the long-term success of the event industry.

References

Boyle, R. and O'Riordan, J. (2013), Capacity and Competencies Requirements in Local Government, accessed 1 February 2021 at www.ipa.ie/_fileUpload/Documents/C APACITYandCOMPETENCY_SEPT2013.pdf

Case, R. (2013), *Events and the Environment*. Routledge, London.

Charlton, C. and Essex, S. (1996), The Involvement of District Councils in Tourism in England and Wales, *Geoforum*, 27(2), 175–192.

Collins, A. and Cooper, C. (2016), Measuring and Managing the Environmental Impacts of Festivals: The Contribution of the Ecological Footprint, *Journal of Sustainable Tourism*, 25(1), 1–15.

David, L. (2009), Events and Tourism: An Environmental Approach and Impact Assessment, *Journal of Tourism, Challenges and Trends*, 2(2), 66–75.

Department of Communication, Climate Action and Environment (DCCAE) (2017), National Mitigation Plan, accessed 13 January 2021 at www.dccae.gov.ie

Department of the Environment Community and Local Government (DECLG) (2007), Planning Acts, accessed 14 January 2021 at www.environ.ie/en/DevelopmentHousing/ PlanningDevelopment/Planning/PlanningLegisla tion-Overview/PlanningActs

Department of the Environment Community and Local Government (DECLG) (2012), A Guide to Planning Enforcement in Ireland, accessed 13 January 2021 at www .environ.ie/en/Publications/DevelopmentandHousing/Planning/FIleDownLoad ,31564, en.pdf

Department of Environment Heritage and Local Government (DEHLG) (2014), Implementation of Regional Planning Guidelines: Best Practice Guidelines, accessed 4 September 2020 at www.housing.gov.ie/sites/default/files/migrated-files/en/ Publications/DevelopmentandHousing/Planning/FileDownLoad,1605,en.pdf

Department of Transport, Tourism and Sport (DTTAS) (2015), People, Place and Policy: Growing Tourism to 2025, accessed 4 January 2021 at www.dttas.ie/sites/ defaulta/files/publications/tourism/english/people-place-and-policygrowing -tourism-2025/people-place-and-policy-growing-tourism-2025.pdf

European Commission (EC) (2017), Sustainable Tourism: Agenda for a Sustainable and Competitive European Tourism, accessed 4 February 2021 at http://eur-lex .europa.eu/legalcontent/EN/TXT/?uri=legissum:l10132

Environmental Protection Agency (EPA) (2014), Reducing Toxic Air Pollutants. Wexford, Ireland, accessed 1 January 2021 at www.epa.gov/airquality/peg_caa/ toxics.html

Environmental Protection Agency (EPA) (2020), Irelands Environment: An Integrated Assessment, accessed 5 January 2021 at www.epa.ie/media/EPA-Ireland%27s -Environment-2020-Summary.pdf

Fáilte Ireland (2016), Minister Ring Announces Funding of over €1m for Major Festivals and Events, accessed 4 January 2021 at www.failteireland.ie/Footer/MediaCentre/ Minister-Ring-announces-funding-of-over-%E2%82%AC1m-for-ma.aspx

Getz, D. and Page, S. (2016), *Event Studies: Theory, Research and Policy for Planned Events*, 3rd edn. Routledge, New York.

Hambleton, R. (2020), The Bristol One City Approach to City Governance: New Civic Leadership in Action. *Urban Research and Practice*, 13(2), 228–237.

Hogan, P. (2017), *Local Government to Provide Social and Economic Development*. McGill Summer School, Donegal.

Holden, A. (2008), *Environment and Tourism*. Routledge, New York.

Jones, M. (2014), *Sustainable Event Management: A Practical Guide*, 2nd edn. Routledge, London.

Local Government Management Agency (LGMA) (2012), Local Government in Ireland, accessed 3 October 2020 at www.lgma.ie/en/

Maguire, K. (2018) An Examination of the Local Authority Sustainable Planning for Events Management in Ireland. Accessed 13 September 2021 at www.itsligo.ie

Maguire, K. (2019), Examining the Power Role of Local Authorities in Planning for Socio-Economic Event Impacts, *Local Economy*, 34, 657–679.

Maguire, K. (2020), An Examination of the Level of Local Authority Sustainable Planning for Event Management: A Case Study of Ireland, *Journal of Sustainable Tourism*, 1–25.

Maguire, K. and Hanrahan, J. (2016), Local Authority Provision of Environmental Planning Guidelines for Event Management in Ireland, *European Journal of Tourism Research*, 12, 54–81.

Maguire, K. and Hanrahan, J. (2017), Assessing the Economic Impact of Event Management in Ireland: A Local Authority Perspective, *Event Management: An International Journal*, 21, 333–346.

Mair, J. (2011), Events and Climate Change: An Australian Perspective, *International Journal of Event and Festival Management*, 2(3), 245–253.

McKercher, B., Prideaux, B. and Pang, S. (2013), Attitudes of Tourism Students to the Environment and Climate Change, *Asia Pacific Journal of Tourism Research*, 18(1–2), 108–143.

National Planning Framework (NPF) (2018), *Project Ireland 2040: National Planning Framework*. Government of Ireland, Dublin, accessed 7 January 2021 at http://npf.ie/

OECD (2020), OECD Policy Responses to Coronavirus (COVID-19): Social Economy and the Covid-19 Crisis: Current and Future Roles, accessed 8 January 2021 at www.oecd.org/coronavirus/policy-responses/social-economy-and-the-covid-19-crisis-current-and-future-roles-f904b89f/

Page, S. (2015), *Tourism Management*, 5th edn. Routledge, Abingdon.

Quinn, B. (2017), *Local Government: Ripe for Central Reform*. McGill Summer School, Donegal.

The Guardian (2016), Glastonbury Festival Confirms Fallow Year for 2018, accessed 20 September 2020 at www.theguardian.com/music/2016/sep/12/glastonbury-festival-fallow-year-2018-2017-ticket-sale-dates

Thomas, R. and Wood, E.H. (2004), Event Based Tourism: A Survey of Local Authority Strategies in the UK, *Local Governance*, 29(2), 127–136.

Whitford, M., Phi, G.T. and Dredge, D. (2014), Principles and Practice: Indicators for Measuring Event Governance Performance, *Event Management*, 18(3), 387–403.

Wood, E. (2005), Measuring the Economic and Social Impacts of Local Authority Events, *International Journal of Public Sector Management*, 18(1), 37–53.

12. The impact of events on place branding

Waldemar Cudny

Place branding

Recent decades have brought the rise of the number and diversity of events and the development of event-related research interest (Getz and Page 2016; Wise and Harris 2019). Events are today meaningful factors influencing local and regional growth, thus they are often used in event-led development strategies (García 2004; Cudny 2016). Some of them (i.e. mega- or hallmark events) are also successful in promoting and branding the spaces in which they are held (Cudny 2020b). According to Getz (2012, 37), "events by definition, have a beginning and an end. They are temporal phenomena, and with planned events, the event program or schedule is generally planned in detail and well-publicised in advance." The variety of planned events includes cultural celebrations, political and state events, arts and entertainment, business and trade, educational and scientific events, as well as sports competitions, recreational and private events (Getz 2013). The number and variety of events continue to rise and have an impact on place branding. This is confirmed by scholars and the growth in the number of festivals or sports events will continue to increase event tourism opportunities (Alexandris and Kaplanidou 2014; Ballico 2018; Cudny 2016; Faulkner et al. 2000; Getz and Page 2016; Long et al. 2004; Quinn 2005; Singh and Zhou 2016).

The growing event sector and the development of event tourism create numerous impacts (legacies) for host destinations (cities, regions, countries) (García 2004; Cudny 2020b). Types of event impacts, according to Prayag and Savalli (2020), include economic, socio-cultural and environmental impacts. Events exert positive legacies (e.g. income from tourism) but they also have negatives (like organizational costs or conflicts between residents and tourists) (Chappelet 2012). We can distinguish tangible (measurable, physically visible) and intangible (hard to measure or unmeasured) impacts of events (Dwyer et al. 2000). Tangible impacts encompass, for instance, the construction of facilities and infrastructure (Preuss 2015). Intangible impacts include among others social and cultural legacies but also promotional and branding effects of event organization (Chappelet 2012; Cudny 2016). Dwyer et al. (2000) state that marketing communication and promotion evoked by an event organized in a specific location may create favorable images in the minds of potential tourists. The promotional and branding role of events to host areas has also been noted in many other scientific publications (Boisen et al. 2018; Broudehoux 2017; Cudny 2016, 2020b; Smith 2005).

The aim of this chapter is to define the role that events play in creating the brand of a specific location. The analysis also aims to determine what role in this process is played by various types of geographical space, as well as the human perception of this space. Another research aim is to present a selected case study to confirm the model. Therefore, this chapter comprises two sections: a theoretical section explaining the model, and an analytical section with a presentation of a case study. The case study encompasses the analysis of the legacies of the EURO 2012 mega-sports event on the brand of the Polish city of Gdańsk.

In working towards a conceptual understanding and model that relates space, events and brand perceptions, it is first worth outlining these interconnected areas of inquiry. Space, according to Harvey (1973), is distinguished based on three main understandings in modern geography: absolute space, relative space and relational space. Absolute space is an external framework existing beyond the influence of humans and their activities. Relative space is different because it represents space as a complex dimension defined and formed by the interactions between space and different entities inhabiting it in time. The relative space exists only because of the objects within existing and relating to each other. Relational space is presented by Harvey (1973, 13) "as being contained in objects in the sense that an object can be said to exist only insofar as it contains and represents within itself relationships to other objects". Henri Lefebvre argued that space is a creation of people's daily practice and their design of space, which expresses the imperatives of economics and ideology (Lefebvre and Nicholson-Smith 1991). Beyond doubt, space is a complex and very complicated notion and a fundamental issue for social sciences, including human geography. Therefore, the simplistic view of absolute space has been replaced with the current relative interpretation of space (Massey 1999).

Analyzing relational space, Thrift (2003) distinguished four types of geographical space. First is a space of empirical constructions (tangible, physical space) encompassing all objects present physically in our surroundings (e.g. buildings, infrastructure, cars, trains). The second is the unblocking space including all connections (flaws) through what we know as the world interacts. It includes the local and global flows of people, goods, information and money. The third kind of space includes various types of images representing different aspects of our world, i.e. paintings, photographs, graphs, animations, etc. As Thrift wrote:

> images are a key element of space because it is so often through them that we register the spaces around us and imagine how they might turn up in the future ... Increasingly we live in a world in which pictures of things like news events can be as or more important than the things themselves, or can be a large part of how a thing is constituted (as in the case of a brand or a media celebrity). (Thrift 2003, 100)

The fourth type is place space presented by Thrift (2003, 103) as "resources of many different kinds (for example, spatial layouts which may allow certain kinds of interaction rather than others) but they also provide cues to memory and behavior. In a very real sense, places are a part of the interaction." Place, then, is shaped by the location, and depending on the scale of a place, it can be shaped by changing relations with other places and by human behaviors affecting the environment. This is important when considering events and what is possible in each location. Moreover, a place has a certain meaning attached to it, and depending on perceptions and meanings that people associated with a place will play a role in branding, imaginations and associations (see Hahm and Severt 2018; Wise and Mulec 2015). Ultimately, a place is labile and is co-created by the environment, cultural pressure and human perception.

Regarding the analysis given in this chapter, the second notion of unblocking space as well as the third image space of are important. These two types of space identified by Thrift (2003) are included in the of place brand creation with the use of events. However, before proceeding to the model a few additional notions should be explained. First is the concept of place branding. According to Kotler and Armstrong (2010), a brand is a complex notion encompassing a name, term, sign, symbol or design. A composition of these elements is typical to support and help people relate to a specific product. The purpose of brand creation is to identify a product delivered by a certain producer and distinguish it from the products offered by others to get people involved and interested (Cudny 2020b; Hereźniak and Florek 2018; Richards 2017).

Places also offer their products (e.g. residential and investment areas, tourist assets) to different groups of people as their consumers (Cudny 2020a). However, place branding is not about giving a name or a symbol to a place, it is about identity, recognition, reputation and destination positioning (Getz, 2013). Most places already have their names and symbols. Therefore, place branding is more about doing something to enhance the brand image of places and making them famous (Anholt 2010). As mentioned by Zenker and Beckmann (2013, 7) place brand should be defined as "a network of associations in the consumers' mind based on the visual, verbal, and behavioral expression of a place, which is embodied through the aims, communication, values, behavior and the general culture of the place's stakeholders and the overall place design". The result of place brand creation is the image of the place evoked in people's minds thanks to the application of place-branding strategies (Deffner and Metaxas 2010).

The fundamental question of place branding is how to create the highly anticipated positive associations of places in the minds of place product consumers. Here the notions of Thrift's (2003) unblocking and image spaces come into question. Both of these spaces participate in creating human imaginations and behaviors that form the basis for place branding. Here we have to refer to the concept of behavioral geography concerning the interaction between a human being and the surrounding space. Behavioral geography focuses on how the human mind knows and processes information about the surrounding environment (Walmsley and Lewis 1997). Gold (1980) presents the concept whereby environmental information perceived with senses passes through the perception filter of personality and creates two types of cognitive representations. The first type encompasses images of reality evoked by the imagination. The second includes mental schemata representing the environment constructed based on memory and information obtained experimentally.

As Gold (2019) later explained, images are the mental pictures called to mind from memory when objects, people and places are not part of current sensory observation, whereas spatial schemata are frameworks within which people organize their knowledge of the environment, encompassing a mix of past experience and current sensory information. Both elements (i.e. images and spatial schemata) are affected by cognitive processes, personality and socio-cultural variables. Thanks to the above-presented process, a kind of cognitive map is created in the minds of the recipients, representing the environment (Walmsley and Lewis 1997). Considering the aforementioned information on space and its types, the issues of place branding and the theory of creating environmental representations in the human mind, a model of the impact of events on the place brand (Figure 12.1) was proposed.

Events organized in a specific location induce two types of branding effects influencing the human perception filter. The first is an event marketing

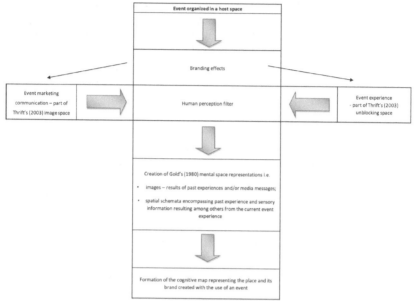

Source: Author's elaboration.

Figure 12.1   Model presenting the role of events, space and mental
representations in the creation of place brand

communication and the second is event experience. They influence mental
space representations and form cognitive maps in human minds representing
the place and its brand created with the use of an event (Figure 12.1). Event
marketing communication aims to promote the event and/or the host area,
and it encompasses media coverage, promotional materials and social media
messages. Moreover, event marketing communication today mainly consists
of images because this helps detail a particular imagination of a place, and such
coverage may be treated as part of Thrift's (2003) image space. As a result of
event-related marketing communication, human minds (including those of
event-goers) are subjected to various stimuli (commercials, media relations,
Facebook posts, tweets). They modify the human perception filter and influence two types of Gold's (1980) mental space representations (i.e. images and
spatial schemata).

The second type of effect influencing the human perception filter includes
event experience. It requires participation in an event as a spectator and allows
the event-goer to see the visited space through a prism of event experience.
Going to events is part of tourism and, therefore, it is part of the flows of

people forming Thrift's (2003) unblocking space. If a person takes part in an event, the event experience co-creates Gold's (1980) spatial schemata reflecting the sensory information resulting from it. For example, a person may visit different spaces in a city that are indicated in a cultural festival or sports event program and may perceive the visited spaces through the prism of the current event experience (Figure 12.1).

Of course, Gold's (1980) images, except media coverage, may also be a relic of previous event participation. For example, if a person participated in an event in a given city a few years ago, then this person's perception of that city is also based on images of that visit recalled from memory. Moreover, Gold's (1980) spatial schemata are also co-created by the images reflected from memory and they are not solely based on current sensory information. However, in each of the above conceptual directions discussed, events play an important role in the perception and creation of the image of the host place. Moreover, in the afore-mentioned cases, the creation of mental space representations takes place with the participation of Thrift's (2003) unblocking and image space. Finally, the result of organizing an event in a host destination includes a variety of influences on the event-goers' perception. The changes in perception are created by the interaction of Thrift's (2003) image space and unblocking space. The result of these changes is the generation of Gold's (1980) mental images and spatial schemata, which in turn create a cognitive map representing the host place and its brand formed with the use of an event (Figure 12.1).

Euro 2012 in Gdańsk

This section will present a case example to illustrate the model described in Figure 12.1. UEFA EURO 2012 organized in Poland was selected for the purpose of this chapter. It was the only sports mega-event organized in Poland over the last two decades. The European Football Championship organized by UEFA is considered to be the third-largest sports event in the world. Based on a decision made by UEFA the tournament in 2012 was jointly organized by Ukraine and Poland. The event lasted from June 8 to July 1 in Poland and the host cities were Gdańsk, Poznań, Warsaw and Wrocław. Thirty-one matches were played at stadiums in Poland, and over 600,000 spectators attended these events. To add to the experience outside the stadiums, fan zones were organized in Polish cities (visited by over 3 million people). Four of these matches were held in Gdańsk, involving the national teams of Spain, Greece, Italy, Germany, Ireland and Croatia. Gdańsk was visited by approximately

160,000 foreign fans, mainly from Germany, Spain, Ireland and Croatia. For the event, many investments were made, including a new football stadium (Podsumowanie kosztów i oszacowanie korzyści z organizacji turnieju UEFA EURO 2012™ Gdańsk, 2012).

The case study discussed in this chapter concerns the impact of organizing UEFA EURO 2012 on the image of the city of Gdańsk. Gdańsk is a large port city (approx. 470,000 inhabitants) located on the Gdańsk Bay, at the mouth of the Motława River to Vistula River, and it is one of the most important Polish tourist centers. The data presented here come from the detailed report elaborated by the consulting company Deloitte Polska (Podsumowanie kosztów i oszacowanie korzyści z organizacji turnieju UEFA EURO 2012™ Gdańsk, 2012). The report presents the costs of organizing the event, income from event tourism and the social, administrative and organizational benefits. Moreover, it includes the presentation of the image benefits obtained by Gdańsk as a result of the UEFA EURO 2012 organization. The image-related research presented in the report was based on media analytics and a questionnaire survey was conducted with a representative group of foreign spectators participating in the event.

The image-related benefits for Gdańsk will be presented in this chapter in two dimensions. The first is the media dimension covering event-related messages presenting Gdańsk. According to the previously described model (Figure 12.1), media messages should be treated as part of Thrift's (2003) image space. The media information included press articles, television broadcasts and posts in social media about UEFA EURO 2012, and referring to Gdańsk. The second dimension of the analysis presented here is the event experience dimension, which encompassed direct participation in the UEFA EURO 2012 in Gdańsk. In this case, we are dealing with Thrift's (2003) unblocking space because participation in the event evoked the flow of people arriving for a football match, often from another city, region or from abroad.

Media messages and event experience create Gold's (1980) mental space representations (i.e. images and spatial schemata). These, in turn, influence recipients' cognitive maps representing the place and its brand created with the use of an event (see, again, Figure 12.1). According to the Deloitte report, about 60,000 event-related mentions of Gdańsk were identified on Polish television and radio. In 2012, the number of mentions of Gdańsk in the context of the event in the press and online media exceeded 35,000. During the event, Gdańsk's presence on social media increased tenfold compared to 2011. In total, tens of thousands of photos and over 2,000 videos from Gdańsk were published in them, and hundreds of reports were posted on blogs, in over 30 languages.

Regarding foreign media, a lot of mentions appeared in Spain, whose national team played all its matches in Gdańsk. The Deloitte report presented an analysis of the Spanish media for the time between May 15 and July 17, 2012. During that time, 13,700 mentions of Gdańsk in the context of UEFA EURO 2012 were published there. Except for the media coverage described above, the Gdańsk authorities organized their promotional campaign aimed at foreign tourists. During this campaign, from April to June 2012, 160 spots were broadcast on CNN, BBC and Eurosport. Online promotion activities were carried out in May 2012 in Spain, Ireland and Italy. As a result, over 60 million views of materials promoting Gdańsk were received. These activities were supplemented by campaigns in the foreign press and participation in tourism fairs. Additionally, 120 foreign journalists were invited to Gdańsk, and a paperback guide for tourists was published (with 100,000 copies distributed).

According to the Deloitte report, the organization of UEFA EURO 2012 also resulted in an improvement in the city's image in the eyes of tourists. This improvement was possible thanks to the images and event experience which influenced people's mental space representations and led to the creation of a cognitive map representing Gdańsk and its brand created with the use of the event (Figure 12.1). The data presented in the Delloite report are based on a questionnaire survey conducted among foreign tourists staying in Gdańsk during the event. The respondents positively assessed the atmosphere in the city (95 percent), the work of volunteers (93 percent), a fan zone prepared for spectators (87 percent), the organization of the event (82 percent) and public transport (76 percent). Around 60 percent of the respondents in total considered their stay and experience in Gdańsk positive, exceeding previous expectations. Around 36 percent of tourists assessed their stay as expected, and 3 percent expressed disappointment with their visit. The Spaniards were the most positively surprised by the stay, and 67.6 percent found it exceeding expectations. As many as 57 percent of all respondents expressed their willingness to revisit Gdańsk in the next three years, and 89 percent declared that they would recommend the city to their friends as worth visiting (Podsumowanie kosztów i oszacowanie korzyści z organizacji turnieju UEFA EURO 2012™ Gdańsk, 2012). Overall these results suggest that the impact of the event was positively viewed among those who visited Gdańsk for the event.

Research directions

The first section of this chapter presented the theoretical model explaining the relationship between the organization of an event and the creation of the place image. The model presented the impact of an event on the two types of geographic space delimited by Thrift (2003) (i.e. image and unblocking space) and explained the event's impacts on Gold's (1980) mental space representations (i.e. images and spatial schemata) and on the creation of a cognitive map representing the place and its brand (as displayed in Figure 12.1).

The second section of the chapter included a case study analyzing the impacts of UEFA EURO 2012 on the image of the city of Gdańsk. The presented case study confirmed the above-mentioned model. It turned out that the organization of a sports mega-event influences two types of geographical space, i.e. image and unblocking space. Thanks to the event, media representations (part of image space) and the event experience (part of unblocking space) are evoked. As a result, the human mind is subjected to a series of interactions generated by Gold's (1980) images and spatial schemata that create a positive cognitive map representing Gdańsk.

However, it has to be noted that the analysis presented here has its limitations. It refers to one event of a specific type and does not include research on the image effects over a longer time. Therefore, to fully confirm the model presented here, it is necessary to undertake further research with its use. The model should be tested at events of a different type and size and in different countries. To fully confirm the model it is also necessary to undertake the research on image-related effects over a longer time, e.g. several years after the organization of the event under study.

The future research directions encompassing the impact of events on place branding should include research on how tourists and residents perceive urban brands in relation to events organized in host cities and towns. Moreover, future research should investigate which events are advantageous to these brands and why. The focus should be on media coverage and event experience (Wise et al. 2015). Very important is the in-depth analysis of event-related media relations, with a special focus on social media. The latter is the most important channel of information and brand creation in our contemporary world, therefore it should receive special attention. Future research should also focus on the motivations of cities and event organizers driving the events. Why are events organized, what do the managers and city authorities want to achieve in terms of urban branding and how could their endeavors be merged in order to increase positive image-related results? These are up-to-date topics that should be analyzed. The research on the impacts of the Covid-19 pandemic on event organization must be considered as well. Research issues should encompass how events can be staged online, what safety measures should be applied and how they may influence an urban brand and its perception.

References

Alexandris, K. and Kaplanidou, K. (2014) Marketing sport event tourism: Sport tourist behaviors and destination provisions, *Sport Marketing Quarterly*, 23(3), 125–127.

Anholt, S. (2010) Definitions of place branding: Working towards a resolution. *Place Brand and Public Diplomacy*, 6, 1–10.

Ballico, C. (2018) Everyone wants a festival: The growth and development of Western Australia's contemporary live music festival sector, *Event Management*, 22(2), 111–121.

Boisen, M., Terlouw, K., Groote, P. and Couwenberg, O. (2018) Reframing place promotion, place marketing, and place branding-moving beyond conceptual confusion, *Cities*, 80, 4–11.

Broudehoux, A.M. (2017) *Mega-events and urban image construction: Beijing and Rio de Janeiro*. Routledge, London.

Chappelet, J.L. (2012) Mega sporting event legacies: A multifaceted concept, *Papeles de Europa*, 25, 76–86.

Cudny, W. (2016) *Festivalisation of urban spaces: Factors, processes and effects*. Springer, Cham.

Cudny, W. (2020a) *City branding and promotion: The strategic approach*. Routledge, London.

Cudny, W. (2020b) The concept of place event marketing: Setting the agenda, in: W. Cudny (ed.), *Urban events, place branding and promotion: Place event marketing*, pp. 1–24. Routledge, London.

Deffner, A. and Metaxas, T. (2010) Place marketing, local identity and branding cultural images in Southern Europe: Nea Ionia, Greece and Pafos, Cyprus, in: G.J. Ashworth and M.M. Kavaratzis (eds), *Towards effective place brand management-branding European cities and regions*, pp. 49–68. Edward Elgar Publishing, Cheltenham, UK and Northampton, MA, USA.

Dwyer, L., Mellor, R., Mistilis, N. and Mules, T. (2000) A framework for assessing "tangible" and "intangible" impacts of events and conventions, *Event Management*, 6(3), 175–189.

Faulkner, B., Chalip, L., Brown, G., Jago, L., March, R. and Woodside, A. (2000) Monitoring the tourism impacts of the Sydney 2000 Olympics, *Event Management*, 6(4), 231–246.

García, B. (2004) Urban regeneration, arts programming and major events: Glasgow 1990, Sydney 2000 and Barcelona 2004, *International Journal of Cultural Policy*, 10(1), 103–118.

Getz, D. (2012) *Event studies: Theory research and policy for planned events*. Routledge, London.

Getz, D. (2013) *Event tourism: Concepts, international case studies, and research.* Cognizant Communication, Putnam Valley, NY.

Getz, D. and Page, S.J. (2016) *Event studies: Theory, research and policy for planned events.* Routledge, London.

Gold, J.R. (1980) *An introduction to behavioral geography.* Oxford University Press, London.

Gold, J.R. (2019) Behavioural geography, in A. Kobayashi (ed.), *International encyclopedia of human geography,* second edition, vol. 1, pp. 283–292. Elsevier, Oxford.

Hahm, J. and Severt, K. (2018) Importance of destination marketing on image and familiarity, *Journal of Hospitality and Tourism Insights,* 1(1), 37–53.

Harvey, D. (1973) *Social justice and the city.* Edward Arnold, London.

Hereźniak, M. and Florek, M. (2018) Citizen involvement, place branding and mega events: Insights from Expo host cities. *Place Branding and Public Diplomacy,* 14, 89–100.

Kotler, P. and Armstrong, G. (2020) *Principles of marketing.* Prentice, Upper Saddle River, NJ.

Lefebvre, H. and Nicholson-Smith, D. (1991) *The production of space.* Blackwell, Oxford.

Long, P., Robinson, M. and Picard, D. (2004) Festivals and tourism: Links and developments, in P. Long and M. Robinson (eds), *Festivals and tourism: Marketing, management and evaluation,* pp. 1–14. Centre for Tourism and Cultural Change, Doxford.

Massey, D. (1999) Space-time, "science" and the relationship between physical geography and human geography, *Transactions of the Institute of British Geographers,* 24(3), 261–276.

Podsumowanie kosztów i oszacowanie korzyści z organizacji turnieju UEFA EURO 2012™ Gdańsk (2012) Report presenting the costs and benefits from organizing the UEFA EURO 2012 event in Gdańsk, available at: https://gdansk.xgcmy.pl/s1/d/20121244118/Raport-Korzysci-Euro-Gdansk.pdf

Prayag, G. and Savalli, M. (2020) Residents' perceptions of event impacts and support for the 2012 Formula One Grand Prix in Monaco, in: D. Gursoy, R. Nunkoo and M. Yolal (eds), *Festival and event tourism impacts,* pp. 139–153. Routledge, London.

Preuss, H. (2015) A framework for identifying the legacies of a mega sport event, *Leisure Studies,* 34(6), 643–664.

Quinn, B. (2005) Arts festivals and the city, *Urban Studies,* 42(5–6), 927–943.

Richards, G. (2017) From place branding to placemaking: The role of events, *International Journal of Event and Festival Management,* 8(1), 8–23.

Singh, N. and Zhou, H. (2016) Transformation of tourism in Beijing after the 2008 Summer Olympics: An analysis of the impacts in 2014, *International Journal of Tourism Research,* 18(4), 277–285.

Smith, M.F. (2005) Spotlight events, media relations, and place promotion: A case study, *Journal of Hospitality and Leisure Marketing,* 12(1–2), 115–134.

Thrift, N. (2003) Space: The fundamental stuff of geography, in: S. Rice and G. Valentine (eds), *Key concepts in geography,* pp. 95–108. Sage, London.

Walmsley, D.J. and Lewis, G.J. (1997) *Geografia człowieka. Podejście behawioralne,* PWN, Warsaw.

Wise, N. and Harris, J. (2019) Events, places and societies: Introducing cases, perspectives and research directions, in N. Wise and J. Harris (eds), *Events, places and societies,* pp. 1–9. London: Routledge.

Wise, N. and Mulec, I. (2015) Aesthetic awareness and spectacle: Communicated images of Novi Sad (Serbia), the exit festival, and the Petrovaradin Fortress. *Tourism Review International*, 19(4), 193–205.

Wise, N., Flinn, J. and Mulec, I. (2015) Exit festival: Contesting political pasts, impacts on youth culture and regenerating the image of Serbia and Novi Sad, in O. Moufakkir and T. Pernecky (eds), *Ideological, social and cultural aspects of events*, pp. 60–73. CABI, Wallingford.

Zenker, S. and Beckmann, S.C. (2013) My place is not your place: Different place brand knowledge by different target groups. *Journal of Place Management and Development*, 6(1), 6–17.

13. Mega-event trends and impacts

Tara Fitzgerald and Brij Maharaj

Mega-events

Events are resulting in a wide range of social impacts on people, places, and society (Richards et al., 2013; Wise and Harris, 2019). There is an increasing trend of declining bids for, and contestations against, hosting mega-sporting events in global North (western) cities (Lauermann, 2016). Concomitantly, there has been an increase in successful bids from global South cities, especially BRICS countries intent on enhancing their geopolitical aspirations, image, and destination appeal (Wise, 2019). BRIC was an acronym developed by Goldman Sachs in 2001, advising investors that Brazil, Russia, India, and China would be countries that would experience rapid growth as emerging market economies. South Africa joined in 2011, hence the name change to BRICS (Mielniczuk, 2013).

Generally, authoritarian governments like China and Russia do not have to take cognizance of public opinion when bidding for mega-sports events (Caffrey, 2013; Orttung and Zhemukhov, 2017). Hence, events like the Olympics can 'become propaganda showcases for authoritarian regimes, as happened with the 2008 Olympics in China, and the 2014 Winter Olympics in Sochi, Russia' (Somin, 2016, 1). If the escalating costs of hosting these mega-sports events are not controlled, 'expect to see a lot more Chinas, Russias, Qatars, and Kazakhstans hosting them in the future' (Keating, 2014, 1). All the BRICS countries have hosted at least one mega-sporting event over the past 15 years: Beijing hosted the 2008 Summer Olympics; South Africa hosted FIFA 2010; India hosted the Commonwealth Games in Delhi in 2010; Russia hosted the 2014 Winter Olympics in Sochi and FIFA 2018; and Brazil hosted FIFA 2014 and the Rio Summer Olympics in 2016. Even in more liberal democracies like India, South Africa, and Brazil, some civil rights were curtailed for the duration of the mega-event. This chapter presents an overview of mega-event trends and impacts in BRICS countries, drawing from a review of published literature and research reports.

A major public concern is that the money that is spent on infrastructure development could alternatively be used to address the social challenges in the host city and country. The focus is on the following themes, and the chapter is structured accordingly: cost–benefit analysis; event seizure: capturing the host nation; violation of human rights; and resistance from below.

BRICS nations as hosts

In the global South, mega-events are used as neoliberal strategies as cities compete for world-class status. From a cost–benefit analysis standpoint, the result is the socio-spatial and political reconfiguration of host cities, which overestimate benefits and underestimate costs. Such transformations are fraught with social, political, and sustainability challenges (Othman and Ahmed, 2013). Despite these challenges, nations in the global South continue to bid for the chance to host mega-events due to the perceived socio-economic benefits – economic expansion, international investor confidence, increased gross domestic product, and tourism expenditure. However, economic benefits are often exaggerated, and so intangible benefits such as nation (re)branding and social cohesion are overemphasized. Conversely, the misappropriation of scarce resources in the global South resulted in mass demonstrations and xenophobic attacks in Brazil and South Africa, respectively, in the lead up to the FIFA World Cup (Desai and Vahed, 2010; Nunes, 2014; Zimbalist, 2016). Hence, scholars have questioned why governments continue to bid for the right to host mega-sporting events (de Nooij and van den Berg, 2018).

Cost overruns are inherent in mega-sports events (Müller, 2015a). Funds are typically generated from the public purse and spent on tourism facilities, security, organizational costs, and transport and sports infrastructure (Müller, 2015b). Müller (2015a) provided six reasons as to why the real cost of hosting mega-events remain hidden. These include: (1) fixed deadlines; (2) corruption; (3) long project implementation period; (4) the impending threat of contingencies; (5) deliberately misrepresenting the real cost of the event; and (6) the non-divisible nature of such projects.

Russia hosted both the Olympic Games (2014) and the FIFA World Cup (2018) and experienced the most significant cost overruns in mega-event history (Müller, 2017a). Cost overruns and time constraints compromise the integrity of mega-event construction projects. Poorly constructed facilities for mega-events caused safety concerns at the 2016 Summer Olympics in Rio de Janeiro, the 2014 Winter Olympics in Sochi, the 2014 FIFA World Cup in Brazil, and the 2010 Commonwealth Games in New Delhi (Chakrabarti, 2010; Foxall, 2014; Segal, 2014; Warkins, 2014).

Such oversized and overpriced construction projects are mostly underutilized post-event, and mega-event facilities become expensive white elephants. As a result, many nations have fallen victim to the 'winner's curse' (Müller, 2017b). The winner's curse is arguably the most severe implication that arises when hosting costs are underestimated in the bidding process. This concept was first introduced in 1971 and described the outcome of overbidding for an auction product that yielded little value (Capen et al., 1971). To be selected as a mega-event host, bidders must present a positive economic impact that the event will generate. Private financial consultants are encouraged to present a report with grandiose economic benefits that the mega-event is said to elicit (Andreff, 2012).

The result is a winning bidder who is cursed with high hosting costs and exaggerated benefits (de Nooij and van den Berg, 2018). A cost–benefit analysis reveals mega-sporting events to be the riskiest and most expensive mega-project on a global scale (Flyvbjerg et al., 2016). Thus, although better equipped to host mega-events, nations in the global North have mostly withdrawn from the bidding process. International sporting institutions (ISIs) continue to award mega-events to countries in the global South where the 'developing' status results in reduced leverage, allowing ISIs to capture and seize host nations (Müller, 2017a).

It has become commonplace for mega-events to displace the development priorities of the host country. Instead, a 'state of exception' is created (Vainer, 2016). In such instances, democratic governance is mostly substituted with authoritarianism, where public oversight is reduced, participation is selective, regular laws are bypassed, corruption is certain, ethical responsibilities are neglected, and new legislation is introduced, which accelerates the development process and guarantees capital accumulation to event owners (Broudehoux and Sánchez, 2016; Gaffney, 2016b; Broudehoux, 2017). Furthermore, seizure of the host nation by the international event mostly entails the capture of prime urban locations where the Summer Olympic Games, for example, generally require an area of 700 hectares (1,734 acres) to meet the infrastructural needs of the event.

Brazil is a prime example of misplaced development priorities, where politically connected elite and corporate interests drove the urban development agenda to suit the needs of the 2016 Olympic Games, 2014 FIFA World Cup, and the 2007 Pan American Games (Müller, 2015a). However, such elite-centred priorities, which drove the development agenda of the events, is not unique to the Brazilian experience nor the global South. Instead, many host nations have fallen prey to the development façade that is flaunted as being in the public's interest but instead displaces the needs of the poor (Maharaj, 2015; Müller, 2017a).

Brazil had operated as a state of exception for several years as the nation was host to both the 2014 FIFA World Cup and the 2016 Summer Olympic Games. This state of exception was also evident in Russia, which hosted the 2014 Winter Olympic Games and the 2018 FIFA World Cup (Müller, 2017a). Both nations introduced several legislative changes that were required by either the International Olympics Committee (IOC) or FIFA. This is also a requirement for single-event hosts such as South Africa, which hosted the 2010 FIFA World Cup. The adoption of such legislation ensured:

1. a zone of exclusion (typically 1 km radius around the event venues) where exclusive branding and advertising rights were owned and distributed by FIFA or the IOC;
2. a suspension of basic rights where individual equality was bypassed, and elite stakeholders and property rights were prioritized over that of the citizenry;
3. the voice of civil society was weakened; and
4. the events were sites of rent extraction where future economic growth and the long-term sustainability of the countries were diminished (Broudehoux and Sánchez, 2016; Broudehoux, 2017; Müller, 2017a).

The state of exception has become the *modus operandi* of both the IOC and FIFA (Nunes, 2014). Hence, Gotham (2016) borrowed the term 'creative destruction' to describe how mega-events seize host nations, resulting in volatile and uneven development across the built environment. Therefore, in creating elite urban spaces, mega-events perpetuate 'accumulation by dispossession' by using event projects to facilitate capital accumulation while dispossessing vulnerable communities and violating their human rights (Harvey, 2003; Gotham, 2016).

Violation of human rights has been a pressing issue, notwithstanding the numerous urban challenges in BRICS countries, cities offer refuge and livelihood opportunities for poor communities (McGranahan and Martine, 2014). However, when hosting mega-sporting events, many cities have been redeveloped to produce a world-class spectacle for the elite, in which poverty is an embarrassment. The state of exception discussed above provides conditions for a sense of emergency, and there have been many cases of the violation of human rights, most notably through the repression of free speech and mobility, forced removal, threats to livelihoods, and exclusion (Corrarino, 2014; Adams and Piekarz, 2015). Within these considerations are two critical directions: (1) reduced freedoms (through media repression, police harassment, and protest restrictions); and (2) disempowerment, dispossession, and displacement.

Concerning reduced freedoms, and although Brazil, India, and South Africa present more liberal democracies, when hosting a mega-event, the media is controlled in a manner that manufactures consent for the event and related developments and subsequently creates 'the illusion of freedom of the press and a democratic society' (Lenskyj, 2000, 173). Such actions violate democratic freedoms and instead enforce an authoritarian regime to produce 'staged cities' (Green, 2003, 163). In creating unequal cities of spectacle (Shin, 2012), host governments legitimize the militarization of populations under the guise of 'national security' (Rekow, 2015, 119). This was most evident in Brazil when the state implemented the *Unidades Pacificadores Policiais* (Police Pacification Units) in various favelas across the state (Gaffney, 2016a). In 2008 the pacification unit began infiltrating 107 of the 1000 favelas to tackle gang violence and drug trafficking in what was promoted as a campaign to bridge the gap between the police and the public (Saborio, 2013). However, the units have since been criticized for militarizing and neutralizing marginalized groups through actions that restricted their right to mobilize, their right to freedom of expression, and their right to a safe environment (Saborio, 2013; Rekow, 2015).

Peaceful protests were met with excessive force and violent tactics from the police and the military, including grenades, tear gas, rubber bullets, batons, and arbitrary detentions (Amnesty International, 2014). The repression of the right to protest was a violation of the Brazilian Constitution, and resistance resulted in the death of 8000 people between 2006 and 2015 (Amnesty International, 2016a, 2016b). Protest repression, police brutality, and media censorship were experienced in several mega-event host nations, including Russia (Halchin et al., 2014), China (Human Rights Watch, 2008), and South Africa (Bond, 2010). Media censorship suppressed acts of police brutality and the forced displacement of the poor.

The experiences of those who become disempowered, dispossessed, and displaced in the lead up to the event also require consideration. This is necessary to address because cities undergo urban image reconstructions, which influences how a place is branded and marketed as a modern-day entrepreneurial city (see Cudny, 2020). The political and corporate elite seeks to create a *space of illusion* that showcases the best of what the city offers. Hence, realities of inequality, poverty, and social divisions are deliberately concealed to protect and enhance the city's image (Broudehoux, 2017). City redevelopments and clean-up campaigns reconfigure urban space while simultaneously disempowering, dispossessing, and displacing vulnerable communities.

Urban lands acquired for FIFA- or IOC-related infrastructure resulted in the forced removal of countless people in the emerging economies of Beijing (COHRE, 2007), New Delhi (Bhan, 2009), South Africa (Newton, 2009), Russia (Foxall, 2014), and Brazil (Talbot and Carter, 2018). In BRICS countries, forced evictions linked with mega-events violated human rights through:

1. evictions without consultation or community participation;
2. poor planning (no relocation option or compensation for loss);
3. the tactics used to remove people (harassment, brutality, and violence);
4. the conditions under which eviction occurs (weather, respect for person and belongings); and
5. the consequences of eviction (disruption in work and education, trauma, lost belongings, impoverishment, homelessness, no provision of basic services, loss of livelihoods) (UN-HABITAT, 2014; Maharaj, 2015; Gaffney, 2016a, 2016b).

The exact number of forced evictions in Brazil is unknown. However, reports indicated that those displaced amounted to hundreds of thousands for the 2014 World Cup alone, many of whom were given less than 30 minutes to leave their residences (Corrarino, 2014; Butler and Aicher, 2015). The Housing and Land Rights Network (2011) concluded that at least 200,000 New Delhi residents were evicted ahead of the 2010 Commonwealth Games.

Ahead of FIFA 2010, countless South Africans were evicted and removed to make way for development. Many were forcibly resettled to Temporary Relocation Areas. However, these areas became *de facto* permanent housing for those resettled (Doherty, 2013). Arguably the most severe case of forced evictions was in Beijing, China, where authorities forcibly removed 1.5 million people to make way for Olympic-related infrastructure. The urban poor were displaced from thriving central areas to the periphery, losing access to resources and livelihoods (Corrarino, 2014). In India and Brazil, informal settlements that could not be removed were rendered invisible to international visitors by using various visual filters, including screen walls, acoustic barriers, and hedges (Broudehoux, 2017). In New Delhi, those who could not be removed ahead of the 2010 Commonwealth Games were concealed by 'curtains' made from bamboo (Nelson, 2009). Rio de Janeiro's 'Wall of Shame' concealed a collection of favelas referred to as the Maré, which could previously be viewed from the motorway. The erection of the wall disrupted the livelihoods of countless individuals, specifically street vendors who once sold snacks to those stuck in traffic along the motorway. Brazilians viewed the wall as a product of exclusion, concealment, and containment and likened this segregation tactic to the apartheid regime in South Africa (Broudehoux, 2017; Martins, 2017).

Those who could not be forcibly removed or concealed were instead filtered out by exclusion zones, clean-up campaigns, and security measures, which resulted in displacement and lost livelihoods in South Africa (Maharaj, 2015), Brazil (Corrarino, 2014), and India (Uppal, 2009). Security measures and clean-up campaigns were also used to remove undesirable populations ahead of the 2008 Beijing Summer Olympics (Yu et al., 2009). Such exclusionary tactics were decried as 'social cleansing', 'social genocide', and a 'war on the poor' (Broudehoux, 2017) and were met with resistance.

Results and reactions have been resistance tactics, which have varied from actions of violence to responses that are more in line with 'soft resistance'. The extent of the response has depended on: (1) the geopolitical conditions of the host nation; or (2) the severity of the offences (Broudehoux, 2017). For instance, soft resistance mostly included campaigns that focused on exclusion and labour rights abuses. In South Africa, the World Cup Cities for All campaign connected FIFA 2010 with inequality, dispossession, and loss of livelihoods. The campaign involved the mobilization of street vendors, hawkers, sex workers, labour unions, and social movements, which contested the impacts of the event on poor and vulnerable urban communities (Ngonyama, 2010).

Another significant drive was the Play Fair campaign which focused on child labour ahead of the 2008 Beijing Olympics and labour rights abuses before the South African 2010 FIFA World Cup (Pedrina and Merz, 2011; Institute for Human Rights and Business, 2013). Other campaigns include Red Card to Child Labour Programme, Building and Wood Workers' International, Clean Clothes Campaign, War on Want, Human Rights Watch, COHRE, Amnesty International, and the Olympic Resistance Network (Boykoff, 2011; Timms, 2012). These campaigners opposed and resisted top-down, exclusionary tactics and human rights violations (Broudehoux, 2017; Horne, 2017). In Brazil, mass demonstrations denounced the billions misused on FIFA-required infrastructure when most of the poor lacked essential resources (Saad-Filho, 2013). In Rio, a diverse alliance comprising residents, scholars, students, lawyers, and activists coalesced to successfully resist the eviction of Vila Autódromo (Ivester, 2017).

In the lead up to the 2010 FIFA World Cup in South Africa, 3000 people from 26 civil society organizations protested against exorbitant spending, the misappropriation of scarce resources, corruption, and the exclusion of, and attack on, the poor (Pillay, 2010; Veith, 2010). For example, in Durban, an alliance of traders, vendors, researchers, academics, architects, planners, non-governmental organizations, and unions successfully mobilized against the destruction of the century-old Early Morning Market, a strategy to 'clean up' the inner city in preparation to host FIFA 2010 matches (Maharaj, 2020).

Future directions

There has been an increasing shift to global South countries, especially BRICS, successfully bidding for and hosting mega-sports events – which reflects the geopolitical ambitions of these emerging economies. Although mega-sporting events do produce benefits such as infrastructural developments, the experience across all BRICS countries has shown that the privileged benefit at the expense of the poor. Similar to the global North experience, the costs of mega-events in BRICS countries were underestimated, benefits were exaggerated, and international sporting organizations like FIFA and the IOC captured host cities. There were also significant human rights violations, especially forced removals, threats to livelihoods, and exclusion, which were especially serious in authoritarian states like China and Russia.

Despite restrictions on the right to protest, mass mobilization and demonstrations in Brazil and South Africa denounced acts of forced removal, loss of livelihoods, and the attacks on the poor. In BRICS, the creative destruction of low-income communities deepened socio-economic inequalities, and neoliberal cities became a product of human sacrifice where the rights to participate, to be seen, to transparency, to privacy, to livelihoods, and to inclusion were eroded. Instead, 'undesirable' residents of shantytowns, favelas, and informal settlements were concealed or removed to produce 'staged cities', and the right to the city was reserved for the elite.

Given the negative socio-economic repercussions of mega-sporting events, it is necessary for future host nations, especially BRICS, to consider sustainability challenges before committing to the bidding process. There should be more research on the environmental consequences of mega-sports events. The implications for climate change should be a priority. Also, there has to be more research on how the negative impacts on poor communities can be minimized. For example, rather than displacement and relocation, there should be research recommendations on how urban transformation projects can incorporate and empower the poor.

References

Adams, A. and Piekarz, M. (2015), Sport Events and Human Rights: Positive Promotion or Negative Erosion?, *Journal of Policy Research in Tourism, Leisure and Events*, 7(3), 220–236.

Amnesty International (2014), *They Use a Strategy of Fear: Protecting the Right to Protest*, London: Amnesty International.

Amnesty International (2016a), Brazil: Police Repression Mars Peaceful Protest in São Paulo, accessed 16 May 2019 at www.amnesty.org/en/latest/news/2016/01/brazil -police-repression-mars-peaceful-protest-in-sao-paulo/.

Amnesty International (2016b), *Violence Has No Place in These Games! Risk of Human Rights Violations at the 2016 Olympic Games*, London: Amnesty International.

Andreff, W. (2012), The Winner's Curse: Why Is the Cost of Sports Mega-Events So Often Underestimated?, in Maening, W. and Zimbalist, A. (eds), *International Handbook on the Economics of Mega Sporting Events*, Cheltenham, UK and Northampton, MA, USA: Edward Elgar Publishing, 37–69.

Bhan, G. (2009), 'This Is No longer the City I Once Knew': Evictions, the Urban Poor and the Right to the City in Millennial Delhi, *Environment and Urbanization*, 21(1), 127–142.

Bond, P. (2010), Six Red Cards for FIFA, accessed 3 July 2019 at www.cetri.be/Six-red -cards-for-Fifa?lang=fr.

Boykoff, J. (2011), The Anti-Olympics, *New Left Review*, 67(1), 41–59.

Broudehoux, A. (2017), *Mega-Events and Urban Image Construction: Beijing and Rio de Janeiro*, Abingdon: Routledge.

Broudehoux, A. and Sánchez, F. (2016), The Politics of Mega-Event Planning in Rio de Janeiro: Contesting the Olympic City of Exception, in Viehoff, V. and Poynter, G. (eds), *Mega-Event Cities: Urban Legacies of Global Sports Events*, Routledge, Abingdon, 109–119.

Butler, B. and Aicher, T. (2015), Demonstrations and Displacement: Social Impact and the 2014 FIFA World Cup, *Journal of Policy Research in Tourism, Leisure and Events*, 7(3), 299–313.

Caffrey, K. (2013), *The Beijing Olympics: Promoting China: Soft and Hard Power in Global Politics*, New York: Routledge.

Capen, E., Clapp, R., and Campbell, W. (1971), Competitive Bidding in High-Risk Situations, *Journal of Petroleum Technology*, 23(6), 641–653.

Chakrabarti, S.K. (2010), *Will India Be Ready to Host the Commonwealth Games?*, accessed 1 April 2019 at http://content.time.com/time/world/article/0,8599,2007643 ,00.html.

COHRE (2007), *Fair Play for Housing Rights: Mega-Events, Olympic Games and Housing Rights*, Geneva: Centre on Housing Rights and Eviction.

Corrarino, M. (2014), Law Exclusion Zones: Mega-Events as Sites of Procedural and Substantive Human Rights Violations, *Yale Human Rights and Development Law Journal*, 17(1), 180–204.

Cudny, W. (ed.) (2020), *Urban Events, Place Branding and Promotion*, London: Routledge.

de Nooij, M. and van den Berg, M. (2018), The Bidding Paradox: Why Politicians Favor Hosting Mega Sports Events Despite the Bleak Economic Prospects, *Journal of Sport and Social Issues*, 42(1), 68–92.

Desai, A. and Vahed, G. (2010), World Cup 2010: Africa's Turn or the Turn on Africa?, *Soccer and Society*, 11(1–2), 154–167.

Doherty, K. (2013), Cape Town, the City Without and Within White Lines, in Alegi, P. and Bolsmann, C. (eds), *Africa's World Cup Critical Reflections on Play, Patriotism, Spectatorship, and Space*, Ann Arbor, MI: University of Michigan Press, 52–58.

Flyvbjerg, B., Stewart, A., and Budzier, A. (2016), *The Oxford Olympics Study 2016: Cost and Cost Overrun at the Games*, accessed 21 March 2019 at https://arxiv.org/ftp/ arxiv/papers/1607/1607.04484.pdf.

Foxall, A. (2014), *Russia's Olympic Shame: Corruption, Human Rights and Security at 'Sochi 2014'*, London: Henry Jackson Society.

Gaffney, C. (2016a), Gentrifications in Pre-Olympic Rio de Janeiro, *Urban Geography*, 37(8), 1132–1153.

Gaffney, C. (2016b), The Urban Impacts of the 2014 World Cup in Brazil, in Gruneau, R. and Horne, J. (eds), *Mega-Events and Globalization: Capital and Spectacle in a Changing World Order*, Abingdon: Routledge, 167–185.

Gotham, K. (2016), Beyond Bread and Circuses: Mega-Events as Forces of Creative Destruction, in Gruneau, R. and Horne, J. (eds), *Mega-Events and Globalization: Capital and Spectacle in a Changing World Order*, Abingdon: Routledge, 43–59.

Green, S.J. (2003), Staged Cities: Mega-Events, Slum Clearance, and Global Capital, *Yale Human Rights and Development Law Journal*, 6(1), 161–187.

Halchin, E., Rollins, J., Tiersky, A., and Woehrel, S. (2014), *The 2014 Sochi Winter Olympics: Security and Human Rights Issues*, Congressional Research Service, accessed 15 November 2020 at https://fas.org/sgp/crs/misc/R43383.pdf.

Harvey, D. (2003), *The New Imperialism*, Oxford: Oxford University Press.

Horne, J. (2017), Sports Mega-Events Three Sites of Contemporary Political Contestation, *Sport in Society*, 20(3), 328–340.

Housing and Land Rights Network (2011), *Planned Dispossession: Forced Evictions and the 2010 Common Wealth Games*, New Delhi: Housing and Land Rights Network.

Human Rights Watch (2008), *China: Olympics Media Freedom Commitments Violated*, accessed 17 February 2021 at www.hrw.org/news/2008/07/07/china-olympics-media -freedom-commitments-violated.

Institute for Human Rights and Business (2013), *Striving for Excellence: Mega Sporting Event and Human Rights*, London: Institute for Human Rights and Business.

Ivester, S. (2017), Removal, Resistance and the Right to the Olympic City: The Case of Vila Autódromo in Rio de Janeiro, *Journal of Urban Affairs*, 39(7), 970–985.

Keating, S. (2014), Nobody Wants to Host the Winter Olympics, accessed 12 November 2020 at https://archive.sltrib.com/article.php?id=57996793&itype=CMSID.

Lauermann, J. (2016), Boston's Olympic Bid and the Evolving Urban Politics of Event-Led Development, *Urban Geography*, 37(2), 313–321.

Lenskyj, H. (2000), *Inside the Olympic Industry: Power, Politics, and Activism*, New York: SUNY Press.

Maharaj, B. (2015), The Turn of the South? Social and Economic Impacts of Mega-Events in India, Brazil and South Africa, *Local Economy*, 30(8), 983–999.

Maharaj, B. (2020), Contesting Violent Displacement: The Case of Warwick Market in Durban, South Africa, *International Development Planning Review*, 42(1), 13–33.

Martins, G. (2017), 'Wall of Shame' in the Maré (Brazil): Apartheid in a So-Called Democratic Country, accessed 23 May 2019 at www.stopthewall.org/2017/11/13/wall-shame-mar-brazil-apartheid-so-called-democratic-country.

McGranahan, G. and Martine, G. (2014), *Urban Growth in Emerging Economies: Lessons from the BRICS*, New York: Routledge.

Mielniczuk, F. (2013), BRICS in the Contemporary World: Changing Identities, Converging Interests, *Third World Quarterly*, 34(6), 1075–1090.

Müller, M. (2015a), The Mega-Event Syndrome: Why So Much Goes Wrong in Mega-Event Planning and What to Do about It, *Journal of the American Planning Association*, 81(1), 6–17.

Müller, M. (2015b), What Makes an Event a Mega-Event? Definitions and Sizes, *Leisure Studies*, 34(6), 627–642.

Müller, M. (2017a), How Mega-Events Capture Their Hosts: Event Seizure and the World Cup 2018 in Russia, *Urban Geography*, 38(8), 1113–1132.

Müller, M. (2017b), Approaching Paradox: Loving and Hating Mega-Events, *Tourism Management*, 63, 234–241.

Nelson, D. (2009), *New Delhi to Hide Slums with 'Bamboo Curtains' during 2010 Commonwealth Games*, accessed 22 May 2019 at www.telegraph.co.uk/sport/othersports/commonwealthgames/6043719/New-Delhi-to-hide-slums-with-bamboo-curtains-during-2010-Commonwealth-Games.html.

Newton, C. (2009), The Reverse Side of the Medal: About the 2010 FIFA World Cup and the Beautification of the N2 in Cape Town, *Urban Forum*, 20(1), 93–108.

Ngonyama, P. (2010), The 2010 FIFA World Cup: Critical Voices from Below, *Soccer and Society*, 11(1–2), 168–180.

Nunes, R. (2014), There Will Have Been No World Cup, accessed 30 April 2019 at www.aljazeera.com/indepth/opinion/2014/05/brazil-world-cup-protests-201452910299437439.html.

Orttung, R.W. and Zhemukhov, S.N. (2017), *Putin's Olympics: The Sochi Games and the Evolution of Twenty-First Century Russia*, New York: Routledge.

Othman, E. and Ahmed, A. (2013), Challenges of Mega Construction Projects in Developing Countries, *Organization, Technology and Management in Construction: An International Journal*, 5(1), 730–746.

Pedrina, V. and Merz, J. (2011), The Trade Union Legacy of the World Cup: International Solidarity Revitalised, in Cottle, E. (ed.), *South Africa's World Cup: A Legacy for Whom?*, Scottsville: University of KwaZulu-Natal Press, 117–132.

Pillay, K. (2010), South Africa: 'World Cup for All!' 'People before Profit!', accessed 10 July 2019 at http://links.org.au/node/1747.

Rekow, L. (2015), Police, Protests, and Policy in Rio de Janeiro: Mega-Events, Networked Culture, and the Right to the City, in Foth, M., Brynekov, M., and Ojala, T. (eds), *Citizen's Right to the Digital City*, Singapore: Springer, 119–135.

Richards, G., de Brito, M., and Wilks, L. (2013), *Exploring the Social Impacts of Events*, London: Routledge.

Saad-Filho, A. (2013), Mass Protests under 'Left Neoliberalism': Brazil, June–July 2013, *Critical Sociology*, 39(5), 657–669.

Saborio, S. (2013), The Pacification of the Favelas: Mega-Events, Global Competitiveness, and the Neutralization of Marginality, *Socialist Studies*, 9(2), 130–145.

Segal, D. (2014), Now What? A City Fears a Flameout, accessed 15 February 2021 at   www.nytimes.com/2014/02/24/sports/olympics/sochi-olympics-construction -weighs-on-citys-future.html.

Shin, H. (2012), Unequal Cities of Spectacle and Mega-Events in China, *City*, 16(6), 728–744.

Somin, I. (2016), *How to Put an End to the Dark Side of the Olympics*, accessed 20 November 2020 at www.washingtonpost.com/news/volokh-conspiracy/wp/2016/ 08/07/how-to-put-an-end-to-the-dark-side-of-the-olympics/.

Talbot, A. and Carter, T. (2018), Human Rights Abuses at the Rio 2016 Olympics: Activism and the Media, *Leisure Studies*, 37(1), 77–88.

Timms, J. (2012), The Olympics as a Platform for Protest: A Case Study of the London 2012 'Ethical' Games and the Play Fair Campaign for Workers' Rights, *Leisure Studies*, 31(3), 355–372.

UN-HABITAT (2014), *Forced Evictions*, New York: United Nations Human Rights Office of the High Commissioner.

Uppal, V. (2009), The Impact of the Commonwealth Games 2010 on Urban Development of Delhi, *Theoretical and Empirical Researches in Urban Management*, 4(10), 7–29.

Vainer, C. (2016), Mega-Events and the City of Exception: Theoretical Explorations of the Brazilian Experience, in Gruneau, R. and Horne, J. (eds), *Mega-Events and Globalization*, Abingdon: Routledge, 109–124.

Veith, M. (2010), *Thousands Protest against World Cup Spending*, accessed 10 July at   https://mg.co.za/article/2010-06-16-thousands-protest-against-world-cup -spending.

Warkins, P. (2014), *The 2014 World Cup and 2016 Olympics Highlight the Need for Project Turnaround Considerations*, accessed 1 April 2019 at https://blog .westmonroepartners.com/the-2014-world-cup-and-2016-olympics-highlight-the -need-for-project-turnaround-considerations/.

Wise, N. (2019), Eventful Futures and Triple Bottom Line Impacts: BRICS, Image Regeneration and Competitiveness, *Journal of Place Management and Development*, 13, 89–100.

Wise, N. and Harris, J. (eds) (2019), *Events Places and Societies*, London: Routledge.

Yu, Y., Klauser, F., and Chan, G. (2009), Governing Security at the 2008 Beijing Olympics, *International Journal of the History of Sport*, 26(3), 390–405.

Zimbalist, A. (2016), *Circus Maximus: The Economic Gamble behind Hosting the Olympics and the World Cup*, Washington, DC: Brookings Institute.

14. Postponement of events

Alexander Bond, Daniel Parnell, and Jan Andre Lee Ludvigsen

Postponements

The Union of European Football Associations (UEFA) 2016 European Championship in men's football took place whilst France was still formally in a state of emergency following the terrorist attacks in Paris in November 2015 (Goldblatt, 2019). Subsequently, questions were asked around what it would take to see an event of this size postponed when this in itself seemingly was not enough. Four years later, in light of the global outbreak of COVID-19, some of these questions re-emerged, though in relation to a different type of threat. Ultimately, the COVID-19 crisis became synonymous with a large number of postponed events where mass gatherings were expected to be present (Parnell et al., 2020).

Postponements are inherent risks to managing events and must be con-textualised within the responsibility of event organisers and authorities to provide basic public safety at events and for the general public (Roche, 2017). Consequently, postponements are mainly unavoidable, representing the only viable option, and are not always consequences of pandemic or epidemic threats or realities. For example, events staged outdoors are occasionally postponed as a result of extreme weather or temperatures risking the health or safety of spectators and athletes (Rutty et al., 2015). Indeed, there are several other factors that may result in event postponement, including (but not limited to) natural disasters, floods, political turmoil, stadium disasters or incomplete stadium projects.

Additionally, postponements may occur with varying amounts of prior warning. To illustrate, in May 2016, Manchester United's English Premier League match versus Bournemouth was postponed after a 'suspect package' was found inside the stadium only minutes before kick-off. However, the package was later found to be a 'bomb replica', and the game could be played only days after its postponement (Ludvigsen and Millward, 2020). Thus, the causes of event postponements are complex and difficult to account for in risk management strategies. More recently, in the early months of 2020, event postponements were caused mainly by the aforementioned COVID-19 pandemic, which this chapter primarily focuses on concerning mega-events.

Unlike the *cancellation* of events, the decision to postpone – for whichever reason –implies that efforts are made to reschedule the relevant event to a different time, date or location. Naturally, postponements of large-scale events are a double-edged sword; while they protect the integrity of the event, there are potential sizeable negative impacts. First, they may impact the number of attendees and their availability, which may prevent them from attending the rescheduled event. Second, postponements will have economic consequences for all stakeholders – event owners, organisers, sponsors and spectators – creating ripples across the sports ecosystem and sometimes further. For example, as a result of the postponement of the 2020 Olympic and Paralympic Games in Tokyo, athletes from the United Kingdom requested £53.4 million exceptional funding due to the postponement (BBC, 2020a). So, while postponements often allow event owners to protect revenue from sponsorship and broadcasting agreements, the financial costs run much deeper and wider than immediate stakeholders. Third, the new rescheduled event may coincide with other events in the sporting calendar or events occurring in the same city or region. This may translate into extra strain on public and emergency services, and also incur higher costs for spectators than originally anticipated. Further, attempts to reschedule may be complex and politicised processes, as illustrated by the attempts to resume the English Premier League under the banner of 'Project Restart' following COVID-19 (*The Guardian*, 2020). Thus, postponements have wide-reaching consequences for the various stakeholders in event organisation and management.

This chapter will focus specifically on the postponements of 'mega-events'. Whilst accepting the many existing definitions of this term (see Müller, 2015), it is defined here as 'large-scale cultural (including commercial and sporting) events which have a dramatic character, mass popular appeal and international significance' (Roche, 2000, 1). The study of mega-events has grown into a manifold of avenues in recent years (Grix and Lee, 2013 Müller, 2015; Roche, 2017;), including a growing literature base examining mega-event risk management and responses to security and safety threats (Boyle and Haggerty, 2009; Giulianotti and Klauser, 2010; Ludvigsen, 2018, 2019; Cleland, 2019; Ludvigsen and Hayton, 2020).

However, the impact of mega-event postponement and the subsequent crisis management remains underexplored. This, of course, is related to the fact that mega-event postponements are rare, although, as Müller and Gaffney (2018, 245) acknowledge, mega-events are 'inherently risky undertakings' and postponements pose a fundamental risk to mega-event organisation, planning and execution. A study by Ludvigsen and Millward (2020) examined football spectators' perceptions of the aforementioned postponement of the English Premier League match between Manchester United and Bournemouth. Responding to the decision to postpone, a number of fans highlighted that this was not merely the correct decision, but the only justifiable option. Ultimately, it was appreciated that event and safety managers prioritised spectators' health and safety over allowing the game to be played as planned. While this study is important, furthering our understanding of responses to postponement, there is little known about the broader implications associated with postponement, especially mega-events. Therefore, mega-event postponement presents an area for examination from a wide range of disciplines and practitioners. This chapter will provide some important directions for researchers within events and sports management.

The COVID-19 pandemic in 2020 is not the first infectious disease to threaten mega-events. Previous epidemics include SARS (prior to the 2002 FIFA men's World Cup), the Ebola virus (ahead of the 2015 Africa Cup of Nations) and the Zika virus (prior to the 2016 Olympic Games in Brazil) (see McCloskey et al., 2020; Parnell et al., 2020). The widespread impact of the COVID-19 pandemic however underscores the extraordinarily unprecedented situation. As mega-events and mass gatherings were faced by COVID-19, McCloskey et al. (2020) argued that events should be postponed subject to risk assessments based on the specific context in which the event was to take place. Contrarily, Memish et al. (2020) argued that, in light of the pandemic uncertainties, the only justifiable option on health grounds was to suspend events that expected mass gatherings. As such, this yields insight into some of those consideration points that event managers must follow before the decision to postpone or not postpone a mega-event is made.

Given the unprecedented impacts on mass gatherings, the sports industry, the world of events and human life in general, it is to be expected that COVID-19 will be synonymous with more attention being given to the examination of postponed events (Parnell et al., 2020). Ultimately, COVID-19 saw two of the largest sport mega-events of 2020 postponed: the 2020 European Championships in men's football (Euro 2020) and the 2020 Olympic and Paralympic Games in Tokyo that originally was due to take place during the summer of 2020. In March 2020, these events were provisionally postponed for 12 months by the events' respective owners; UEFA and the International Olympic Committee. Other tournaments owned by UEFA were also postponed, including the Champions League and Europa League. The volume of postponed football events led Tovar (2020) to argue that the effects of COVID-19 in sports was truly generational and had more disrupting effects on sport than the Second World War. The next section uses the case of the Euro 2020 postponement to highlight important impacts and areas for future events and sports management research. However, it is also important to emphasise that whereas a postponement may initially provide a window of time to reorganise or reschedule, there are not always guarantees that postponed events can be rescheduled, consequently requiring organisers to cancel or innovate.

The postponement of UEFA Euro 2020

As Horne (2010) asserts, the European Football Championship (or the 'Euros') represents a highly important tournament, especially when considering both its material and representational legacies across Europe and European communities. Commonly considered one of UEFA's flagship tournaments, the Euros take place quadrennially, usually in the same year as the Summer Olympics. However, as was confirmed in 2012, Euro 2020 would depart from the tournament's traditional hosting format consisting of one or two host countries. Instead, in order to celebrate the tournament's 60th anniversary, it was announced that Euro 2020 would be staged across 12 host cities in 12 different European countries. The Euro 2020 host cities included London, Glasgow, Dublin, St Petersburg, Bucharest, Bilbao, Copenhagen, Amsterdam, Budapest, Rome, Baku and, finally, Munich.

This was a historical shift in the world of mega-events. Indeed, it was also believed to be a one-off occasion. Regardless, this extraordinary hosting format naturally gave life to a number of new questions speaking to event tourism, security management and event organisation and impacts (Ludvigsen, 2019). Ultimately, Euro 2020's host cities, fixture lists and the movement of players, fans and images that would have followed were marked by a pronounced interconnectivity in the event's design and structure.

Originally, Euro 2020 was scheduled for 12 June to 12 July 2020. The tournament's opening fixture was due to be staged at Rome's *Stadio Olimpico*. The semi-finals and final were assigned to London's Wembley Stadium. As already mentioned, however, events are seldom isolated from their wider global, regional or local contexts. Such a claim is particularly well demonstrated by the case of Euro 2020.

In March 2020 – just three months prior to the original kick-off – it was confirmed that Euro 2020 had to be postponed because of the COVID-19 pandemic (Parnell et al., 2020). This decision was made on 17 March 2020, and UEFA (2020a) issued the following statement:

> UEFA today announced the postponement of its flagship national team competition, UEFA EURO 2020, due to be played in June and July this year. The health of all those involved in the game is the priority, as well as to avoid placing any unnecessary pressure on national public services involved in staging matches. The move will help all domestic competitions, currently on hold due to the COVID-19 emergency, to be completed.

Here, we may see that the postponement is framed in terms of health and safety and in order not to place any additional pressure on public and emergency services throughout an unprecedented crisis. The new provisional dates for Euro 2020 were set to be 11 June to 11 July 2021. Interestingly, it was confirmed that the event would keep 'UEFA Euro 2020' as its formal title, despite being staged in 2021. This was a decision made in the name of sustainability, given the large amounts of branded material that had already been produced prior to the postponement (UEFA, 2020b). Having placed the postponement of Euro 2020 in context, this chapter now zooms in on some of the social, economic and organisational impacts of the Euro 2020 postponement.

As stated, postponements impact the organisation of sporting events. For example, questions emerge around whether fans can safely attend stadiums and fan zones. Also, stakeholders – including sports bodies, sponsors, partners and broadcasters –question whether they will still get the anticipated return. The latter question is important since mega-events involve a large and diverse body of stakeholders, which for Euro 2020 is 12-fold as hosting rights were assigned to 12 different European countries. Consequently, the organisational uncertainties related to the staging and delivery of the event are amplified when facing a pandemic. Firstly, there was the issue of national and regional outbreaks. The 12 host countries of Euro 2020 were affected differently by COVID-19, adapting different strategies in order to contain the virus and subsequently reopen societies following periods of lockdown. Although the 12-nation format is expected to still be employed for the rearranged event, UEFA acknowledged possible changes given the unclear COVID-19 situation in each country. However, possible changes may also be necessary as some host cities may already be committed to other events, concerts or occasions on the same dates, in the same stadiums or areas, as the new Euro 2020 dates. For example, the rescheduling of Euro 2020 to 2021 saw the UEFA Women's Euro 2021 (in England) moved to July 2022, to avoid a clash between the two UEFA competitions (BBC, 2020b).

Regarding the hosting format, UEFA President Aleksander Čeferin stated in an interview in May 2020: 'We've had conversations with nine [host] cities and everything is set', but as he continued, he noted that 'with three cities, we have some issues. So, we will discuss further' (quoted in Standard, 2020). In the same interview, Čeferin also announced: 'In principle, we will do it [host Euro 2020] in 12 cities but if not, we are ready to do it in 10, nine or eight'. This statement accurately demonstrates how the event owner, organisers and stakeholders had to remain flexible in a time of much uncertainty. Indeed, at the time of writing, the global situation with COVID-19 is still uncertain and society remains in a state of flexibility when planning ahead.

Event owners need to be flexible with regards to host cities that possibly *could not* commit to the new event dates. Subsequently, this may require some host cities committing to stage a higher volume of games than originally planned if other host cities were withdrawn in light of the COVID-19 situation or other commitments on the new event dates. Thus, local organisers, authorities and stakeholders had to be flexible in adapting to any additional fixtures and, faced with COVID-19, the geographies of Euro 2020 called for particularly anticipatory stances which could flexibly adapt to local and national contexts.

As has been argued elsewhere, Euro 2020's networked strength became one of its organisational vulnerabilities when faced with the pandemic threat (Parnell et al., 2020). And although UEFA (2020c) confirmed on 17 June 2020 that the original 12 stadiums would remain the same, there was little doubt that, with an inherently unpredictable situation, each host (including public health organisations, local authorities and law enforcement) would have to carefully assess up until the event's commencement whether it would be justifiable on health and safety grounds to stage Euro 2020. Further, they would have to assess whether all host cities or only a select few would be able to welcome fans into stadiums in socially distant ways, depending largely on local outbreaks and lockdown restrictions in the respective host city/country.

Indeed, the host countries/cities had to balance the health and safety risk against the economic returns of hosting part of the event. As the pandemic continues and tourism is depleted, both cities and countries around the globe are looking for an economic boost. The negative economic impact of postponing the Euro 2020 event is not limited to the proposed 12 host cities, it is felt across the football world (Parnell et al., 2020). For example, 84 broadcasters

(UEFA, 2020d) across the globe were relying on the Euro 2020 event for content, which in turn would drive subscriptions and/or advertising revenue. Similarly, sponsors at all levels from national teams to global partners who have strategically aligned Euro 2020 to deliver key organisation objectives (part of which is also contingent on broadcasters) have also been negatively impacted. This highlights that these decisions to postponement events are nuanced and networked decisions, scrutinised at every level of society, from pub owners to multinational conglomerates. While UEFA was set to lose €300 million due to postponing, it potentially saved €100 million compared to totally cancelling the event (Statista, 2020). Therefore, postponement in this situation represents a double-edged sword, protecting the integrity of the sport – financially and fan interest – but also creates many other issues, such as timetabling, scheduling and logistics.

Research directions

As argued already, and shown by the case of Euro 2020, postponements raise a host of questions for researchers to engage with in future scholarship. Hence, we will pose a number of tentative postponement-related topics that researchers and students can engage with. This does not comprise an all-inclusive list, yet engagement with the following directions would significantly enhance the evidence base on event postponements and their (in)visible impacts. However, this remains particularly important in the context of the global health crisis caused by COVID-19, where the pandemic's early impacts on sports economics (Drewes et al., 2021) and the national and sporting responses to the crisis (Clarkson et al., 2020; Begović, 2020) have been highlighted in the growing scholarship. Ultimately, event postponements and their impacts tie firmly into these broader themes.

Firstly, we need a better understanding of decision-making processes. Indeed, mega-events are economic beasts not only for the organising body and host region, but also for sponsors, athletes, broadcasters and media who are all interconnected and interdependent. The networked financial model, coupled with fan interest, creates an exceptionally difficult management situation attracting an abundance of pressure from a range of stakeholders. This creates an extraordinary setting for scrutiny, especially from fans who have an unprecedented emotional connection with the event, which creates a managing-in-a-fishbowl scenario (Smith and Stewart, 2010). Consequently, research should focus on how the network of stakeholders impacts the decision-making process and trade-off between ensuring stakeholder satisfaction and the duty of event owners to ensure a safety-first approach.

Secondly, we propose that there is a pressing need now to engage with how COVID-19 related postponements impact event spectators and their willingness to attend the postponed events and their stadiums, fan zones and host cities in general. To date, the existing research on spectators' perceptions of risks and security issues has primarily examined this in relation to perceived terrorism threats (Toohey et al., 2003; Cleland, 2019; Ludvigsen and Millward, 2020). Questions remain around how the pandemic has impacted the way mega-events are attended and consumed, or if the heightened awareness of biological threats to mega-events has generated scepticism among sports fans and tourists. Furthermore, it remains crucial for researchers to examine how attendees who *do* attend future events respond to new measures and facilities provided to ensure, for example, hand hygiene or social distancing. Essentially, as Perić et al. (2021) find, sports event consumers display a willingness to return to sporting events when COVID-19 restrictions are lifted or eased. The study also points towards the importance of safety-related protective measures. Empirical findings related to event spectators' perceptions can assist event organisers.

Finally, given that security and risk management compose a key part of mega-event organisation and pre-planning, it is necessary to examine how future postponements may alter the risk and security management for specific upcoming events. For example, how exactly will postponements prolong the planned security and policing operations? Researchers are thus encouraged to consider the different ways in which COVID-19 (or future epidemics or pandemics) impacts security and risk management before and during mega-events and represents another element that must be accounted for by organisers, authorities and stakeholder groups. Ultimately, there is always a risk of postponement in the realm of event and sports management, and this chapter and its avenues for research can help us understand the diverse and (un)intended impacts of event postponements better, in order to create a knowledge base for practitioners, stakeholders and researchers.

References

BBC (2020a), Tokyo 2020 Olympics and Paralympics: UK Sport asks government for exceptional funding. Available at: www.bbc.co.uk/sport/52544576.

BBC (2020b), Women's European Championship: Tournament to be moved back a year. Available at: www.bbc.co.uk/sport/football/52128646.

Begović, M. (2020), Effects of COVID-19 on society and sport a national response, *Managing Sport and Leisure*, 1–6.

Boyle, P. and Haggerty, K.D. (2009), Spectacular security: Mega-events and the security complex, *International Political Sociology* 3(3), 57–74.

Clarkson, B.G., Culvin, A., Pope, S. and Parry, K.D. (2020), Covid-19: Reflections on threat and uncertainty for the future of elite women's football in England, *Managing Sport and Leisure*, 1–12.

Cleland, J. (2019), Sports fandom in the risk society: Analyzing perceptions and experiences of risk, security and terrorism at elite sports events, *Sociology of Sport Journal* 36(2), 144–151.

Drewes, M., Dauman, F. and Follert, F. (2021), Exploring the sports economic impact of COVID-19 on professional soccer, *Soccer and Society* 22(1–2), 125–137.

Giulianotti, R. and Klauser, F. (2010), Security governance and sport mega-events: Toward an interdisciplinary research agenda, *Journal of Sport and Social Issues* 34(1), 48–60.

Goldblatt, D. (2019), *The Age of Football: The Global Game in the Twenty-First Century*, Macmillan, London.

Grix, J. and Lee, D. (2013), Soft power, sports mega-events and emerging states: The lure of the politics of attraction, *Global Society* 27(4), 521–536.

Horne, J. (2010), Material and representational legacies of sports mega-events: The case of the UEFA EURO™ football championships from 1996 to 2008, *Soccer and Society* 11(6), 854–866.

Ludvigsen, J.A.L. (2018), Sport mega-events and security: The 2018 World Cup as an extraordinarily securitized event, *Soccer and Society* 19(7), 1058–1071.

Ludvigsen, J.A.L. (2019), 'Continent-wide' sports spectacles: The 'multiple host format' of Euro 2020 and United 2026 and its implications, *Journal of Convention and Event Tourism* 20(2), 163–181.

Ludvigsen, J.A.L. and Hayton, J.W. (2020), Toward COVID-19 secure events: Considerations for organizing the safe resumption of major sporting events, *Managing Sport and Leisure*, 1–11.

Ludvigsen, J.A.L. and Millward, P. (2020), A security theater of dreams: Supporters' responses to 'safety' and 'security' following the Old Trafford 'fake bomb' evacuation, *Journal of Sport and Social Issues* 44(1), 3–21.

McCloskey, B., Zumla, A., Ippolito, G., Blumberg, L., Arbon, P., Cicero, A., Endericks, T., Lim, P.L. and Borodina, M. (2020) Mass gathering events and reducing further global spread of COVID-19: A political and public health dilemma, *The Lancet* 395(10230), 1096–1099.

Memish, Z.A., Ahmed, Q.A., Schlagenhauf, P., Doumbia, S. and Khan, A. (2020), No time for dilemma: Mass gatherings must be suspended, *The Lancet*, 1–2.

Müller, M. (2015), What makes an event a mega-event? Definitions and sizes, *Leisure Studies* 34(6), 627–642.

Müller, M. and Gaffney, C. (2018), Comparing the urban impacts of the FIFA World Cup and Olympic Games from 2010 to 2016, *Journal of Sport and Social Issues* 42(2), 247–269.

Parnell, D., Widdop, P., Bond, A. and Wilson, R. (2020), COVID-19, Networks and sport, *Managing Sport and Leisure*, 1–7.

Perić, M., Wise, N., Heydari, R., Keshtidar, M. and Mekinc, J. (2021), Getting back to the event: Attendance and perceived importance of protective measures, *Kinesiology* 53(1), 12–19.

Roche, M. (2000), *Mega-Events and Modernity: Olympics and Expos in the Growth of Global Culture*, Routledge, London.

Roche, M. (2017), *Mega-Events and Social Change: Spectacle, Legacy and Public Culture*, Manchester University Press, Manchester.

Rutty, M., Scott, D., Steiger, R. and Johnson P. (2015), Weather risk-management at the Olympic Winter Games, *Current Issues in Tourism* 18(10), 931–946.

Smith, A.C. and Stewart, B. (2010), The special features of sport: A critical revisit, *Sport Management Review* 13(1), 1–13.

Standard (2020), UEFA willing to hold rescheduled Euro 2020 in fewer cities amid 'issues', says Aleksander Ceferin. Available at: www.standard.co.uk/sport/football/ uefa-willing-hold-euro-2020-fewer-cities-issues-aleksander-ceferin-a4442781.html.

Statista (2020), Potential loss of revenue for UEFA for postponing or cancelling Euro 2020 due to the coronavirus (COVID-19) pandemic as of March 2020. Available at: www.statista.com/statistics/1105619/covid-euro-2020-revenue-loss/.

The Guardian (2020), Premier League's restart plan 'needs Commons debate' to allay safety fears. Available at: www.theguardian.com/football/2020/may/12/premier -leagues-restart-plan-needs-public-scrutiny-says-shadow-minister.

Toohey, K., Taylor, T. and Lee, C.K. (2003), The FIFA World Cup 2002: The effects of terrorism on sports tourists, *Journal of Sport and Tourism* 8(3), 186–196.

Tovar, J. (2020), Soccer, World War II and coronavirus: A comparative analysis of how the sport shut down, *Soccer and Society* 22(1–2), 66–74.

UEFA (2020a), UEFA postpones EURO 2020 by 12 months. Available at: www.uefa .com/insideuefa/about-uefa/news/025b-0f8e76aef315-8506a9de10aa-1000--uefa -postpones-euro-2020-by-12-months/?referrer=%2Finsideuefa%2Fabout-uefa %2Fnews%2Fnewsid%3D2641071.

UEFA (2020b), Executive Committee approves guidelines on eligibility for participation in UEFA competitions. Available at: www.uefa.com/insideuefa/about-uefa/news/ 025c-0f8e77ff99c2-6827588aa119-1000--executive-committee-approves-guidelines -on-eligibility-for-part/?referrer=%2Finsideuefa%2Fnews%2Fnewsid%3D2641715.

UEFA (2020c), Venues confirmed for EURO 2020. Available at: www.uefa.com/ uefaeuro-2020/news/025e-0fac6d3ee9e4-85b1a76389ea-1000/.

UEFA (2020d), Where to watch UEFA EURO 2020. Available at: www.uefa.com/ uefaeuro-2020/news/025a-0ec0d02154c8-5fa71e862f15-1000--where-to-watch-euro -2020/?iv=true.

15. Disability, access, and inclusion

Erin Pearson and Laura Misener

Parasport events

The growth of interest in disability sport (hereafter parasport) is demonstrated through the many different advances of mainstreaming sport, from the mainstreaming of extreme sports (i.e., para climbing and para surfing), to the highlighting of Paralympic athletes in media and popular press (i.e., Nike, the *Sports Illustrated* Body Issue), to the exciting event of the Paralympic Games which has become a mega-event in its own right. The growth of parasport is significant but does not, however, come without its tensions visible in its language, representation, opportunity, access, inclusion which is evident in the events industry.

In 2006, the United Nations introduced the Convention on the Rights of Persons with Disabilities (CRPD) which required nations that adopted this protocol to guarantee the rights of persons with disabilities in all spheres of life. The CRPD suggests that "disability is an evolving concept and that disability results from the interaction between persons with impairments, and attitudinal and environmental barriers that hinders their full and effective participation in society on an equal basis with others" (United Nations, 2006, p. 1). Article 30 of the CRPD specifically recognizes the rights of persons with disabilities in cultural life, recreation, leisure, sport, and tourism. Persons with disabilities should therefore have the right to participate on an equal basis. Yet, there remain significant barriers to participation including inaccessible facilities, lack of assistance and transportation, the need for specialized equipment, and community attitudinal misperceptions about disability.

Large-scale sports events that include parasport must now adhere to strict guidelines around broad-based accessibility and inclusion (McGillivray et al., 2017). These guidelines are set by the international governing bodies including the International Paralympic Committee. Moreover, the inclusion of athletes with disabilities in large-scale sports events has been regarded as a means of creating social legacies for those who are often marginalized in their communities (Cashman and Darcy, 2008; Misener et al., 2013). For example, event hosts make bold promises about using the event to enhance accessibility of venues, transport, public spaces, and other urban infrastructures. Despite this, an ableist perspective of events and legacy (i.e., the viewpoints of the non-disabled) remain central and dominant within the events industry (Misener et al., 2019). This creates a challenge for achieving positive social impacts through parasport events when able-bodiedness is the starting point and thus viewed as a "normal" experience.

The majority of sports event impact research has focused on examining event legacies, predominantly for able-bodied sports events (Brown and Pappous, 2018; Misener et al., 2013). Event legacy has, however, been a highly debated term for both its conceptualization and use within events literature. Event legacy is typically understood by scholars as the enduring outcomes that remain after an event has ended (Preuss, 2007). Leveraging, while concerned with an event's potential impact, is different from legacy with respect to its focus and strategic approach. Chalip (2004, 2017) suggested that a leveraging approach is often more appropriate for strategically embedding impacts in local community agendas, versus legacy which relies heavily on the organizers and event itself to produce positive impacts. Further, leveraging offers an active, embedded, *ex ante* approach. Leveraging focuses on the process in which impacts are planned and strategically utilized to achieve desired outcomes for local communities through hosting an event (Chalip, 2006). This revised focus on leveraging allows scholars to identify which specific strategies and tactics can be implemented and/or were effective in generating specific event impacts (Chalip, 2006; Misener, 2015).

Smith (2014) extends Chalip's (2006) conceptualization of leveraging by making the distinction between two main types of leveraging: event-led and event-themed. According to Smith (2014), event-led leveraging aims to manipulate and regulate the impacts of events in order to optimize outcomes. For example, this may include using the event as a mechanism for creating new programs, strategies, and/or policies in the host city. Event-led leveraging is directly tied to the organizing committees' (OC) objectives and funding which leaves less room for flexibility and a more top-down execution by event organizers, as opposed to community members. In comparison, event-themed leveraging focuses on outcomes that would not normally be expected to occur from hosting an event (Smith, 2014). These outcomes are a result of creative leveraging strategies that are often built upon existing programs, strategies, and/or policies in the host city (Smith, 2014).

Few scholars have investigated parasport events in general and even fewer have applied a leveraging lens to understand the opportunities and potential impacts from hosting these events. Darcy (2001, 2003) was one of the first scholars to consider the role of parasport in creating a legacy, but also recognized the need for planning and resource allocation in the events agenda. Misener et al.'s (2013) synthesis of disability legacy research revealed that there is little empirical evidence on Paralympic legacies and event leverage considerations were entirely absent. Since then, Misener (2015) has developed a parasport leveraging framework for small to medium-sized parasport events. This research demonstrated how leveraging strategies need to be clearly aligned with the access and inclusion goals of a community and at the same time recognize that the event does not occur in isolation (i.e., it must also fit within the broader policy agenda). Misener et al. (2019) further explored the value of large-sized parasport events as being an effective source of social and public policy change for enhancing the lives of marginalized populations. Similarly, the scholars found that opportunity exists for parasport events to enable social change for people with disabilities, if the right conditions are in place to support that change. These conditions exist, for example, if there is an effective leveraging of governmental resources and enhanced communication between those who organize parasport events with policy makers and those who represent the disability community (McPherson et al., 2017).

What remains a challenge in event leveraging literature, however, is the lack of clarity around the ways in which event impacts may be developed. Taks et al.'s (2015) research on event leveraging in medium-sized participatory events highlighted the need to consider what mechanisms are in place for leveraging and how host communities can consider partnerships as a new strategy for enhancing a leveraging approach. Here we use a case example to demonstrate how a collaborative partnership (i.e., between the OC and key disability community members) was able to effectively leverage a large-scale parasport event in order to achieve positive impacts for the host community. We present the case of the Ontario Parasport Legacy Group (OPLG) as an example for future cities seeking to leverage parasport events in order to achieve broader community objectives.

The Ontario Parasport Legacy Group

The Pan/Parapan American Games are an international multisport event with the Parapan American Games specifically involving athletes with disabilities. The Pan/Parapan American Games occurs in the year preceding the Olympic and Paralympic Games and includes athletes from North, Central, and South America. The sporting event functions similarly to the Olympic and Paralympic Games where the able-bodied event precedes the parasport event. The 2015 Pan/Parapan American Games were hosted by Toronto and the Greater Golden Horseshoe region of Ontario, Canada from August 7 to 15, 2015. The Games were awarded to the city of Toronto in 2009 by the Pan American Sports Organizations and Americas Paralympic Committee. The Toronto 2015 Pan/Parapan American Games marked the first time that the Pan American and Parapan American Games were held simultaneously by one OC.

Our focus here is on the Parapan component of the Toronto 2015 Pan/Parapan American Games as this event led to the establishment of the OPLG. In the bid document for the Games, the Toronto 2015 OC (TO2015), with input from the National Parasport Governing Body (NPGB), outlined four key areas for parasport legacy: (1) accessible facilities; (2) training and development; (3) grassroots parasport development; and (4) volunteer recruitment (TO2015 Bid Committee, 2009). The NPGB determined that the legacy plans of the OC were insufficient to create the desired outcomes, and that strong linkages between the parasport community at the national, provincial, and municipal levels were required in order to achieve these potential impacts.

In December 2012, the NPGB took initiatives to catalyze these efforts. They hosted the provincial Parasport Summit which brought together over 50 members of the parasport community. The summit allowed for discussions which outlined the strengths of the parasport system and areas for improvement. The outcome of the summit resulted in a number of targeted projects with the most crucial being the creation of the OPLG as a critical piece of the current parasport system in Ontario. There was a unanimous realization at the summit that a leadership group was required to create enhanced opportunities for parasport in Ontario through stronger linkages between stakeholders in the provincial parasport system leading up to the Games. Shortly after the summit, the NPGB invited key individuals and organizations representing a diversity of interests (i.e., coaching, grassroots, high performance parasport) and sectors (i.e., disability sport organizations, municipal sport organizations, provincial parasport governing bodies, government bodies) to be part of the OPLG (Misener and Carlisi, 2015). The NPGB chose these individuals and organizations based on their perceived capacity to secure and mobilize resources in order to capitalize on the Games through current and new parasport initiatives.

In 2013, a Municipal Forum was held in order to engage representatives from municipalities in the host region. The main message to the municipalities was to create opportunities for leveraging around the Games in order to create positive impacts for parasport in their communities (i.e., create their own strategic plans). Ultimately, municipalities were empowered to develop their own leveraging agenda that would be supported by the OPLG. A number of opportunities were identified and considered as potential outcomes capitalizing on the Games at the Municipal Forum. Municipalities were asked to frame their plans around the following four objectives:

1. Increased participation of persons with a disability in sport in the province of Ontario.
2. Increased number of coaches involved in parasport in the province.
3. Increased level of awareness of parasport and parasport opportunities across the province.
4. Increased implementation of accessibility standards in sport and recreation facilities across the province (Misener, 2016).

When the OPLG became more formalized in 2014, the objectives were refined (for more on the development of the OPLG, see Misener et al., 2020). The OPLG recognized that an event held in the Greater Toronto Area involving 14 municipalities would not necessarily have impacts broadly across such a large province. Thus, the focus of the planning centered upon the municipalities that were hosting parasport events during the Games. In December 2014, seven municipalities submitted Parasport Legacy Plans to the OPLG for review. Members of the OPLG were then assigned to work with each municipality to support their efforts. The leveraging plans from each municipality evolved over time in order to support their specific needs and interests. The goals from the plans were to be completed by the end of 2017 (i.e., two years after the Games). A brief overview of each municipality's objectives and leveraging strategies are displayed in Table 15.1. Importantly, each municipality chose a different approach based on their localized desired outcomes.

Numerous strategies and tactics were implemented as part of the strategic leveraging agenda. As a result of the plans, there was an overall increase in awareness about parasport throughout the sports community, attitudes

Table 15.1 Summary of municipalities' Parasport Legacy Plan objectives and leveraging strategies

Municipality	Legacy Plan objectives	Type of leveraging
Hamilton	Excite and engage people in the community through demonstrations and opportunities during the event. Connect local partners for shared opportunities, space, and cross-promotion. Develop new trial program through City Recreation department for introduction to parasports.	Event-led leveraging leading up to the Games, but their post-Games parasport programming can be seen as event-themed.
Markham	Expansion of existing programs (wheelchair basketball, wheelchair tennis, and sledge hockey). Pursue hosting of parasport events at Markham Pan Am Centre – swimming, water polo, synchro, table tennis, basketball, volleyball, etc. Working with local synchronized swimming club to develop para synchronized swimming program.	Event-led and tied mainly to the Markham Pan Am Centre.
Milton	Maximize use of the velodrome (Mattamy National Cycling Centre) in legacy mode for Parapan recreation and sport activities. Coordination of Parapan sport in the community; improved understanding of system gaps and opportunities to build developmental programs based upon Canadian Sport for Life principles. Establishment of a coaching network to deliver programs and provide coaching support in legacy mode. Heightened community awareness of access to sport and recreation programs for persons with disabilities.	Event-led and directly tied to the new velodrome.

Municipality	Legacy Plan objectives	Type of leveraging
Mississauga	To ensure that there is the opportunity to develop direct parasport grassroots recreation programming at the community level that meets the needs of persons with physical disabilities. To ensure that the Hershey Centre is adaptable and identified as parasport friendly moving forward. To develop an equipment legacy for Mississauga facilities by having the ability to purchase equipment or develop legacy funding to help support parasport equipment inventory following the Parapan Games to put us in a position to host future events. To supply the equipment for individuals to participate in parasports being integrated in our recreation program offerings. To develop and roll out both an instructional and recreational sport league with a focus on wheelchair basketball. To develop and roll out a Parapan Camp or Parasport Camp during the summer months in Mississauga allowing children with or without disability the opportunity to be exposed to various parasports.	Event themed – centralized existing programs and augmented marketing approaches.
Niagara	Increase participation of persons with a disability in sport in Niagara. Create/promote new opportunities for participation in sport for persons with a disability. Foster a stronger network of coaches involved in parasport. Increase the level of awareness of parasport in Niagara.	Event-themed approach offering opportunity to push forward the Niagara Accessible Sports Council.
Toronto	Increase the number of coaches involved in parasport in Ontario. Increase the number of participants involved in parasport. Increase awareness of parasport. Develop capacity of partners to work towards legacy objectives for 2015 and beyond.	Event-led approach with sustainability as a concern as resources from city and organizing committee key in success leading up to Games.
Whitby	Increase awareness and understanding of parasport. Capitalize on Abilities Centre to increase parasport opportunities. Connect with education sector on training and awareness opportunities.	Event-led and event-themed approaches utilizing the Abilities Centre.

towards parasport improved, and more opportunities for participation for parasport became available (Paradis et al., 2017). By including municipalities early on in the development process, specific and achievable projects were developed that aligned with local development agendas. This resulted in local ownership of the initiatives which was key to the sustainability of opportunities and the ongoing efforts toward increasing parasport participation and reach in the host region of the event. The collaborative partnership allowed for individuals and organizations to capitalize on the accessible infrastructure, parasport awareness, and augment some existing programs rather than attempting to reinvent new approaches. The OPLG also involved a research group with sport legacy specific expertise in order to oversee, analyze, and support the process. This ensured evidence-based decision making going forward. However, the greatest legacy of all is that the OPLG (now called the Ontario Parasport Collective) continues to work together to this day on projects related to creating enhanced opportunities and awareness for parasport across Ontario (Misener et al., 2020).

The key learning from the OPLG's work for TO2015 was that legacy plans need to be developed at the beginning of the bid process and be complemented by locally developed policies and resources. This would allow for municipalities to have concrete plans and a clear idea of what resources are needed to achieve their specific legacy plans. The majority of plans developed were event-led which resulted in difficulties trying to accomplish the municipalities' diverse ideas and negotiate the resources required to effectively leverage the opportunity presented by the Games. This was particularly evident for the city of Hamilton, which had strong ideas and potential for event-led strategies at the outset. The city, however, failed to deliver on any of their promises by the end of the Games due to challenges with their leadership, limited personnel, and overall lack of knowledge about parasport (Misener, 2016). Having resources secured from the outset would have allowed for an effective leveraging of resources rather than trying to acquire already stretched resources during the implementation of the Games. For example, the city of Niagara focused on event-themed strategies that would create relationships among organizations and support broader parasport development in the Niagara region (Misener, 2016). The city of Whitby additionally focused on capitalizing on their world-class accessibility facility (i.e., the Abilities Centre), already positioned to offer programming for parasports (Misener, 2016). Therefore, having plans from the outset of the planning process for the Games, or even better from the bid stage, can help to provide municipalities with ownership of their plans. This is critical to achieving sustainable event outcomes as host communities are the ones who have the capacity to support their plans after the lifecycle of the Games (Misener, 2015).

Future directions

A key question that remains relatively absent from the scholarly literature is who and/or what groups are responsible for delivering the impacts and outcomes from events. The OC is often tasked with delivering legacy surrounding the hosting of large-scale events, however, it has become an accepted perspective that the OC cannot be responsible for all legacy delivery because its primary objective is the hosting of the event itself (Misener et al., 2019). A number of scholars have addressed this issue determining that other groups should be responsible for event leverage. For example, Taks et al. (2015, 2018) determined that sport participation outcomes should be the responsibility of community sport organizations, but there remain significant capacity challenges in delivering these outcomes. Similar to the work that we have presented here, the key elements of embedding the leveraging tactics within existing programs and policies (i.e., event-themed strategies) have tended to be more sustainable opportunities. Certainly, greater understanding and engagement with organizational capacity (e.g., Girginov et al., 2017) and capabilities research is needed to understand how these groups might use an event to achieve their desired outcomes. However, there remain numerous gaps in understanding how different groups can take responsibility for delivering these impacts and how they are managed. Understanding the institutional complexity (e.g., Gillett and Tennent, 2020) of these often temporary organizations is key to considering how event impact strategies become embedded in the socio-political architecture of host regions. Our case example demonstrates that some municipalities with the appropriate mix of personnel and programs can take advantage of these opportunities if appropriately positioned from the outset. Thus, future research should focus on the locus of responsibility in delivering legacy and leveraging plans to determine the most appropriate plans for different sizes, scales, social, and political contexts for events.

The work we have presented here has focused on communities that were part of the hosting process. Thus, it was natural for them to consider leveraging strategies linked to the event that would be sustainable and benefit the local communities. Far less scholarly attention has been paid to non-host cities/municipalities/groups that might also consider the opportunity presented by the event. Part of the work that was done with the OPLG was to get the group to focus on understanding the scope and reach of possible event impacts. To assume that an event hosted in one specific region can have far-reaching impacts is problematic. The only way that the event can have those impacts is if specific regionalized strategies are developed. Researchers that have focused on non-host regions have emphasized the importance of the necessary social, cultural, and political conditions for event leveraging well in advance of the event (Beesley and Chalip, 2011) and the critical nature of strategic partnerships in shaping the ideas of leveraging (Chen and Misener, 2019). Yet, there remain lots of opportunity to consider the value of events for non-host communities that might engage in event-themed strategies. Embedded within this opportunity is also the space for greater consideration of the power dynamics of event legacies and how leveraging might help empower groups who are typically marginalized in the event-hosting landscape. This type of research will require engagement with different theoretical approaches that value and place previously marginal groups at the center of the research agenda (see for example Chen et al., 2018).

References

Beesley, L.G., and Chalip, L. (2011). Seeking (and not seeking) to leverage mega-sport events in non-host destinations: The case of Shanghai and the Beijing Olympics. *Journal of Sport and Tourism, 16*(4), 323–344.

Brown, C., and Pappous, A. (2018). "The legacy element … it just felt more woolly": Exploring the reasons for the decline in people with disabilities' sport participation in England 5 years after the London 2012 Paralympic Games. *Journal of Sport and Social Issues, 42*(5), 343–368.

Cashman, R., and Darcy, S. (2008). *Benchmark games: The Sydney 2000 Paralympic Games.* Petersham: Walla Walla Press.

Chalip, L. (2004). Beyond impact: A general model for sport event leverage. In B. Ritchie and D. Adair (Eds), *Sport tourism: Interrelationships, impacts and issues* (pp. 226–252). Bristol: Channel View Publications.

Chalip, L. (2006). Towards social leverage of sport events. *Journal of Sport and Tourism, 11*(2), 109–127.

Chalip, L. (2017). Trading legacy for leverage. In I. Brittain, J. Bocarro, T. Byers, and K. Swart (Eds), *Legacies and mega events* (pp. 25–41). Abingdon: Routledge.

Chen, C., Mason, D.S., and Misener, L. (2018). Exploring media coverage of the 2017 World Indigenous Nations Games and North American Indigenous Games: A critical discourse analysis. *Event Management, 22*(6), 1009–1025.

Chen, S., and Misener, L. (2019). Event leveraging in a nonhost region: Challenges and opportunities. *Journal of Sport Management, 33*(4).

Darcy, S. (2001). The games for everyone? Planning for disability and access at the Sydney 2000 Paralympic and Olympic Games. *Disability Studies Quarterly, 21*(4), 70–84.

Darcy, S. (2003). The politics of disability and access: The Sydney 2000 Games experience. *Disability and Society, 18*(6), 737–757.

Gillett, A.G., and Tennent, K.D. (2020). Hybrid goals: Institutional complexity and "legacy" in a global sporting mega-event. *Public Management Review,* 1–26.

Girginov, V., Peshin, N., and Belousov, L. (2017). Leveraging mega events for capacity building in voluntary sport organisations. *VOLUNTAS: International Journal of Voluntary and Nonprofit Organizations, 28*(5), 2081–2102.

McGillivray, D., McPherson, G., and Misener, L. (2017). Major sporting events and geographies of disability. *Urban Geography, 39*(3), 329–344.

McPherson, G., Misener, L., McGillivray, D., and Legg, D. (2017). Creating public value through parasport events. *Event Management, 21*(2), 185–199.

Misener, L. (2015). Leveraging parasport events for community participation: Development of a theoretical framework. *European Sport Management Quarterly, 15*(1), 132–153.

Misener, L. (2016). *Municipal case studies: Leveraging 2015 Parapan American Games*. London, ON: Western University.

Misener, L., and Carlisi, R. (2015). *Accessibility Directorate of Ontario Report – Canadian Paralympic Committee ENABLING CHANGE*. London, ON: Western University.

Misener, L., Darcy, S., Legg, D., and Gilbert, K. (2013). Beyond Olympic legacy: Understanding Paralympic legacy through a thematic analysis. *Journal of Sport Management, 27*, 329–341.

Misener, L., Lu, L., and Carlisi, R. (2020). Leveraging events to develop collaborative partnerships: Examining the formation and collaborative dynamics of the Ontario Parasport Legacy Group. *Journal of Sport Management, 34*(5), 447–461.

Misener, L., McPherson, G., McGillivray, D., and Legg, D. (2019). *Leveraging disability sport events: Impacts, promises, and possibilities*. Abingdon: Routledge.

Paradis, K., Misener, L., McPherson, G., McGillivray, D., and Legg, D. (2017). Examining the impact of integrated and non-integrated parasport events on volunteer attitudes towards disability. *Sport in Society, 20*(11), 1724–1744.

Preuss, H. (2007). The conceptualisation of measurement of mega sport event legacies. *Journal of Sport Tourism, 12*(3), 207–228.

Smith, A. (2014). Leveraging sport mega-events: New model or convenient justification? *Journal of Policy Research in Tourism, Leisure and Events, 6*(1), 15–30.

Taks, M., Chalip, L., and Green, B.C. (2015). Impacts and strategic outcomes from non-mega sport events for local communities. *European Sport Management Quarterly, 15*(1), 1–6.

Taks, M., Green, B.C., Misener, L., and Chalip, L. (2018). Sport participation from sport events: Why it doesn't happen? *Marketing Intelligence and Planning, 36*(2), 185–198.

TO2015 Bid Committee (2009). *Toronto 2015: Your moment is here*. Retrieved from https://images.toronto2015.org/system/asset_pdfs/ 906/original/bid-book.pdf.

United Nations (2006). *Convention on the rights of persons with disabilities*. Retrieved from www. un.org/esa/socdev/enable/rights/convtexte.htm.

16. Events and climate change

Judith Mair

Climate change

According to the United Nations Development Programme, 'the climate is in crisis' (United Nations Environmental Programme, 2019, 175). The Intergovernmental Panel on Climate Change (IPCC) has explicitly stated that 'warming of the climate system is unequivocal' and has consistently provided strong confirmation of the scientific basis for this phenomenon (IPCC, 2014, 4), demonstrating that our current climate change is a direct result of increasing emissions of greenhouse gases (GHGs) into the atmosphere from the Industrial Revolution onwards and through human actions such as burning fossil fuels, agricultural activities and slash and burn deforestation (IPCC, 2014). The effects of climate change include increased global temperatures, drought or conversely flooding, periods of extreme heat, sea level rise and an increase in the frequency and intensity of severe weather events such as hurricanes, typhoons and cyclones (IPCC, 2014). A range of other secondary impacts are also predicted by the IPCC (2014) to include increased likelihood of wildfires, increased mobility of disease, pests and weeds, changes in water availability, biodiversity loss and damage to vulnerable ecosystems such as coral reefs. Perhaps one of the most concerning aspects of climate change is the fact that even if we are able to stabilise global emissions of GHGs at 2014 levels, a general warming of the Earth and sea level rise will continue (IPCC, 2014).

It is usual to take a systems approach to understanding climate change because of the extent and variability associated with its impacts. A social ecological system is defined as a system that includes societal and ecological subsystems in mutual interaction (Gallopín, 2006). Examples include communities and tourist destinations. One of the key aspects to understanding how climate change may affect a system is to examine its vulnerability to a number of potential climate change impacts. Vulnerability is defined as a function of exposure to climate factors, sensitivity to change and capacity to adapt to that change (Adger and Vincent, 2005). Exposure reflects the interaction of the individual, community or society with a particular change or disturbance, whereas sensitivity is how affected a system is after being exposed to stress (Adger, 2006). Adaptive capacity relates to the ability of a system to make changes to cope with the consequences of climate change (IPCC, 2007). Another important and associated concept is resilience. Resilience refers to the amount of disturbance that a system can absorb while remaining functional – 'the ability of a social or ecological system to absorb disturbances while retaining the same basic structure and ways of functioning, the capacity for self-organisation, and the capacity to adapt to stress and change' (IPCC, 2007, 878). The significance of resilience for a socio-ecological context is that people within the system can learn and adapt to changing circumstances, meaning that resilience can be enhanced over time (Folke, 2006). This leads to two interrelated concepts which are essential for managing the impacts of climate change – adaptation and mitigation (IPCC, 2007). Mitigation aims to slow or prevent climate change, whereas adaptation aims to reduce vulnerability to the ongoing impacts of climate change (Sanderson and Islam, 2007).

Mitigation, defined by the IPCC (2007, 878) as 'anthropogenic intervention to reduce the anthropogenic forcing of the climate system including strategies to reduce greenhouse gas sources and emissions and enhancing greenhouse gas sinks', places significant emphasis on the creation of technical solutions, such as the development of clean energy options or processes to reduce energy use. However, economic strategies can also be used, such as carbon emissions regulations, or carbon emissions trading schemes (Stern and Great Britain Treasury, 2007). In the context of tourism, examples of mitigation may include efforts by the airline industry to find fuel options that emit fewer GHGs, or the use of alternative energy sources (such as solar power, wind power or the purchase of 'green' energy) by resorts and attractions.

Adaptation is defined by the IPCC (2007, 869) as 'adjustment in natural or human systems in response to actual or expected climatic stimuli or their effects, which moderates harm or exploits beneficial opportunities'. It is a way to manage risk and improve business certainty in a complex and dynamic world. Adaptation places the emphasis firmly on how we can adjust our behaviour to cope with the impacts of climate change that are already occurring. As Smit and Wandel (2006) point out, all business and societal planning and decision making, globally and across all economic and social sectors, will need to be adjusted to adapt to changes posed by climate change. A well-known example in the tourism context is the use of artificial snow to extend the ski season in destinations reliant on winter sports.

Both mitigation and adaptation are vital to efforts to manage climate change. Mitigation is key to attempting to prevent any worsening of the current levels of climate change (and to rehabilitate the environment in response to existing negative climate change impacts), but adaptation at the community, regional, national and global levels is imperative to help cope with existing and predicted future climate-related risks. However, the ability of individuals, organisations and countries to adapt varies according to demographic, social, cultural and geopolitical factors – their so-called adaptive capacity.

The IPCC defines adaptive capacity in relation to climate change impacts as 'the ability of a system to adjust to climate change (including climate variability and extremes), to moderate potential damages, to take advantage of opportunities, or to cope with the consequences' (IPCC, 2007, 869). Broadly speaking, those socio-ecological systems with higher levels of adaptive capacity will be more resilient and able to cope better with the impacts of climate change, with the opposite being true for those with low levels of adaptive capacity (Smit and Wandel, 2006). Adaptive capacity can be characterised as relating to having sufficient economic resources; suitably skilled and qualified people; the ability and willingness to access climate change information; methods for identifying adaptation strategies; access to the required technologies; and governance and institutional systems with sufficient flexibility to permit the necessary changes (IPCC, 2014).

Events and climate change

There is a complex relationship between events and climate change. On the one hand, events are significant emitters of GHGs, particularly through their transport and energy use (Collins and Potoglou, 2019). On the other hand, events offer an opportunity to showcase best practice in mitigation and adaptation and have the potential to educate, inform and influence behaviour among attendees (Mair, 2014). There has been a significant amount of research into environmental sustainability at events and festivals, investigating both supply and demand issues (see, for example, work by Jones, 2017); however, a full review of event sustainability is beyond the scope of this chapter, which focuses solely on climate change adaptation and mitigation. Prior research has demonstrated that weather conditions play a role in event attendance, with wet weather reducing attendance numbers for outdoor events, and unexpectedly mild weather inconveniencing events celebrating the start of the ski season (Jones et al., 2006). Further, increasing uncertainty around weather and climate conditions is predicted to continue to affect the success of events in future, with those events with low levels of adaptive capacity the most vulnerable (Jones et al., 2006). Additionally, there has been a limited stream of research outside the events management field on the impacts of climate change on specific events, for example the timings of the Japanese cherry blossom festivals (Sakurai et al., 2011) and Daffodil Weekend in the United Kingdom (Sparks, 2014).

In 2011, Mair published one of the first papers to systematically examine the potential impacts of climate change on a variety of event types and host locations, pointing out that the vulnerability of each event will be different – it will depend on its venue, location, date/season, number of attendees and other factors – and concluding that different types of events are therefore likely to be impacted in different ways by climate change (Mair, 2011). However, since then, there have been few advances in terms of event-specific climate change research. For such an important economic sector, academic knowledge of the impacts of climate change for events and event management is startlingly scarce.

Following on from Mair (2011), it is useful to consider those types of events which are most affected by the impacts of climate change, as well as examining what action the organisers have chosen to take. One framework which provides a conceptual underpinning to this is that proposed by Smit and Wandel (2006), which contains four elements: (1) adapt to what?; (2) who or what adapts?; (3) how does adaptation occur?; and (4) how good is adaptation?

Regarding the first question – *adapt to what?* – it is helpful to differentiate between two major types of climate change impacts. These are biophysical impacts (changes in rainfall and temperature patterns, sea level rise, storm surges, drought, wildfire/bushfire risk and water quality/accessibility) and socio-economic impacts (impacts on settlements, altered destination image, changing consumer behaviour and demands and national and international policy responses) (Mair, 2011). Table 16.1 identifies the types of events that are most affected by each of these climate change impacts. Naturally, outdoor events will broadly speaking be more vulnerable to the biophysical impacts of the changing climate than those held indoors; however, there are still potentially significant socio-economic impacts that will affect a wide range of event types.

The second question in Smit and Wandel's framework is *who or what adapts?* This relates to the adaptive capacity of an event, which depends on a number of factors, including the size of the event, the event governance structures, the

Table 16.1   Types of events most affected by each climate change impact

Type of climate change impact		Type of event impact
Biophysical impacts		
Rainfall	Decreased rainfall – difficulties with water shortages; affects the image of event	All events, but particularly those held outdoors
	Increased rainfall – reduction in event attractiveness leading to lower attendance, and resulting in potential financial difficulties	
Temperature	Many cities are expected to become warmer, with more hot days and fewer cold nights	Outdoor events, particularly in vulnerable locations
Sea level rise	Global sea levels are predicted to rise by 0.18 to 0.59 metres by 2095	Beach events, and coastal event venues and infrastructure
Storm surge	The frequency and intensity of storms and storm surges are predicted to increase	Outdoor events – sporting, festivals, etc. Particularly problematic for tropical areas
Wildfire/bushfire	Climate conditions are likely to become hotter and drier, creating perfect conditions for more frequent and intense fire storms	Outdoor events, particularly multi-day festivals taking place in natural settings (e.g. national parks)
Water	Lower rainfalls and higher temperatures may also reduce water quality and accessibility	Many events have traditionally had high water use (drinking water, toilets, catering, and dust settling for outdoor events)
Socio-economic impacts		
Settlements	Impacts may include damage to infrastructure such as roads, lifeline infrastructure such as water and power, and beachside dwellings being destroyed	Damage to venues in addition to travel and accommodation difficulties at the event location

Type of climate change impact		Type of event impact
Destination image	The increased threat of extreme weather events, and bushfires, could negatively impact demand	Events held in areas perceived as 'risky' are likely to see a drop in patronage over time
Consumer behaviour	Increased public awareness and understanding of tourism's link with climate change may bring about significant changes in tourist motivations and behaviour	Those where long-haul, or long-distance travel is required to get to the destination, or where there are few public transport options to reach the venue
Policy response	Changes to national and international policy in regards to a carbon tax, and carbon trading, are likely to impact on the cost of air travel	Mega-events to which the audience travels long distances

sponsors of the event and the available resources for adaptation. In many of the examples above, it is likely that the cost and implementation of any adaptation measures would need to be borne by the event organiser, and where these measures can't be implemented (for financial or other reasons), it is likely that events will simply cease to run. Naturally this is not an attractive option for the event organisers, but in many cases, it is also an untenable position for local, state and national governments who have invested heavily in events to meet a range of policy imperatives (Duffy and Mair, 2017). In some cases, governments may intervene to assist events to adapt, particularly where the events have been classified as being a public good, or where governments hold interventionist ideologies (Getz, 2012). However, the willingness of governments to invest and the levels of government involvement to support the adaptive capacity of events to the impacts of climate change is broadly untested to date.

Smit and Wandel (2006) then recommend proceeding to the third question – *how does adaptation occur?* As noted by Mair (2011), the ability to adapt varies from event to event, based on a number of factors including access to resources and knowledge of how to adapt. However, there are a significant number of events which have already been forced to take measures to adapt to risks posed by the changing climate. Some of these adaptation measures are temporary and are only required during the event itself. For example, in relation to increased temperatures, the Australian Open Tennis Championships has had to develop and implement an extreme heat policy, which states exactly when the roofs on the three main arenas should be closed, allowing play on these inside arenas to continue while play on outside courts is suspended (https://ausopen.com/visit/tournament-info/policies). Additionally, a number of outdoor music festivals have had to design bushfire evacuation policies and procedures, some of which were implemented for the first time in 2019. For example, at the Falls Festival in Lorne, Victoria (Australia), an extreme bushfire risk resulted in the evacuation of 9,000 patrons and the cancellation of the event (ABC News, 2019). Other events taking place in the countryside in many countries, such as mountain biking, orienteering and car rallies, could be equally severely impacted by bushfires and will have to incorporate evacuation plans into their risk management if they haven't already done so.

However, other measures require adaptation to ongoing conditions that affect event infrastructure. By the end of the twenty-first century, global mean sea level is likely to rise at least 0.3 meters above 2000 levels, even if GHG emissions follow a relatively low pathway in coming decades, and could be considerably greater (Church et al., 2013). This will affect events traditionally held at the beach, such as beach volleyball, beach tennis tournaments, triathlons and Iron Man events, as well as any event infrastructure located close to the waterfront.

Adaptation options include building new infrastructure on higher ground further away from the beach, or moving events to locations less vulnerable to sea level rise, and even potentially the cancellation of some events, where the conditions make them simply unfeasible. Another biophysical impact that is likely to prove to be a long-term issue is water quality and accessibility. Events have traditionally had high water use (drinking water, toilets, catering and dust settling for outdoor events). Adaptation to reduced water quality and availability is likely to focus on a corresponding reduction in the water needs of events – for example the use of compostable toilets, water recycling and grey water use (Jones, 2017), but whether these will be sufficient to allow events to continue in some locations that are particularly prone to drought remains to be seen.

In tandem with the aforementioned biophysical impacts, climate change has socio-economic impacts for tourism and event destinations, and these will require local authorities and destination management and marketing organisations to take adaptation measures. For example, events in areas that suffer from a decrease in attractiveness and declining destination image as a result of changing climatic conditions may see reduced demand from event tourists (and other visitors, too). Attendees may perceive such destinations to represent a risk – perhaps a financial risk in terms of lost ticket money, or indeed a personal safety risk to the attendee – and this may result in a drop in patronage over time (Mair, 2011). Other socio-economic impacts of climate change relate to potential policy responses – for example, where governments decide to implement carbon taxes or carbon emissions trading mechanisms, this would likely have a corresponding effect on travel prices and event admissions tickets, again potentially resulting in reduced demand for events.

Responding to the final question posed by Smit and Wandel (2006) – *how good is adaptation?* – brings us to the nub of this chapter. We actually don't appear to have any systematic evidence of efforts to evaluate any of the climate change adaptation measures that have been implemented in the events context, or indeed any evidence of strategic efforts to implement adaptation measures to adapt to future climate risks. Thus, it is pertinent to consider what research questions or areas for study appear most important to allow us to address this gap.

Research directions

In the first instance, more and better risk management is likely to be key. Naturally, event organisers already carry out risk management planning as a routine element of event operations (Silvers, 2009). However, undertaking a full climate-related risk management evaluation allows researchers, local authorities and event organisers to itemise a range of potential impacts, and assess how an event can adapt to changing circumstances. The adaptation options available for any given event will depend on the potential climate change impacts identified and the adaptive capacity of the event. Mair (2011) identified a continuum of adaptive capacity for events, suggesting that mega- and major events have the highest levels of adaptive capacity thanks to a combination of available knowledge and resources, and their ability to move to different host destinations as required. This continuum also highlighted the lack of adaptive capacity of smaller events, given that they have fewer resources to call upon in terms of adaptation. Interestingly, Mair (2011) also proposed that hallmark events (where the event and the destination are inextricably linked in the minds of the target audience) have low levels of adaptive capacity, given their close links with specific locations which render them as vulnerable to climate change impacts as the destination themselves. However, in this continuum, those with the greatest levels of adaptive capacity were identified to be event attendees, who can simply choose which events to go to and which to reject on price, risk, attractiveness or indeed any other grounds (Mair, 2011). This is a dilemma for event organisers that certainly warrants further research.

As mentioned previously, adaptation is not the only thing required to address the challenges of climate change. In order to remain competitive, many events have turned to climate change mitigation actions, and have focused on sustainability as a key part of their marketing efforts (Mair and Laing, 2013). Transport is the largest GHG contributor of events, and so many events have introduced biodiesel trucks and tractors, shuttle buses for attendees and car pooling (Jones, 2017). Other pro-environmental carbon mitigation options include the introduction of compostable toilets, biofuel generators and solar and wind power generation. Other events have focused on offsetting their carbon emissions, by introducing voluntary carbon offsetting schemes, zero-carbon events and a range of carbon-neutral events (Jones, 2017). However, research on the efficacy of these carbon mitigation efforts appears to be limited to case study investigations, and larger-scale and longitudinal research is largely absent from the event management literature.

Finally, although some events have invested significant time and resources into sustainable practices and infrastructure which demonstrate understanding of both adaptation to and mitigation of the impacts of climate change (good examples include the Glastonbury Festival in the United Kingdom, the Woodford Folk Festival in Australia and the Burning Man Festival in Nevada, United States), there is still a lack of research into how to encourage other event organisers to be cognisant of climate-related risks in their long-term strategic plans. Despite having some great leaders in this field, as yet, we have little rigorous research into how we can convince other event organisers to follow in their footsteps. Further research into behaviour change, knowledge transfer and leadership specific to the events industry is needed in order to encourage a paradigm shift in how event organisers understand and plan for the future of their industry.

Concerning policy and stakeholder implications, a key implication for policy-makers is recognition of the lack of current legislative or regulatory drivers for many of the climate change mitigation and adaptation options discussed in this chapter. At present, although there is information provision, there is less financial assistance and very few incentives of any kind for event organisers to think strategically about climate change. The Covid-19 pandemic has wrought havoc in the events industry and potentially means that long-term climate-related risks and impacts may seem very far away compared with dealing with the present health and economic crisis. However, even once the pandemic has been brought under control, as it surely will sooner or later, climate change will remain a huge issue for event organisers and funders. Policymakers need to remember their role as facilitators of sustainable economies and livelihoods as well as guardians of the environment by providing a range of incentive mechanisms to encourage and assist event organisers to mitigate, adapt and survive the challenges of climate change.

References

ABC News (2019), Falls Festival in Lorne cancelled due to forecast extreme bushfire risk. Accessed 21 September 2020 at www.abc.net.au/news/2019-12-29/falls-festival-at-lorne-cancelled-due-to-extreme-weather/11831120

Adger, N.W. (2006), Vulnerability, *Global Environmental Change*, 16(3), 268–281.

Adger, N.W., and Vincent, K. (2005), Uncertainty in adaptive capacity, *Comptes Rendus Geoscience*, 337(4), 399–410.

Church, J.A., Clark, P.U., Cazenave, A., et al. (2013), Sea level change. In: *Climate Change 2013: The Physical Science Basis. Contribution of Working Group I to the Fifth*

Assessment Report of the Intergovernmental Panel on Climate Change, Cambridge, Cambridge University Press.

Collins, A., and Potoglou, D. (2019), Factors influencing visitor travel to festivals: Challenges in encouraging sustainable travel, *Journal of Sustainable Tourism*, 27(5), 668–688.

Duffy, M., and Mair, J. (2017), *Festival Encounters: Theoretical Perspectives on Festival Events*, Abingdon, Routledge.

Folke, C. (2006), Resilience: The emergence of a perspective for social-ecological systems analyses, *Global Environmental Change*, 16(3), 253–267.

Gallopín, G.C. (2006), Linkages between vulnerability, resilience, and adaptive capacity, *Global Environmental Change*, 16(3), 293–303.

Getz, D. (2012), Event studies: Discourses and future directions, *Event Management*, 16(2), 171–187.

IPCC (2007), *Climate Change 2007: Impacts, Adaptation and Vulnerability: Working Group II Contribution to the Fourth Assessment Report of the IPCC*, Cambridge, Cambridge University Press.

IPCC (2014), *Climate Change 2014: Impacts, Adaptation, and Vulnerability: Summary for Policymakers*, Cambridge, Cambridge University Press.

Jones, B., Scott, D., and Khaled, H.A. (2006), Implications of climate change for outdoor event planning: A case study of three special events in Canada's National Capital region, *Event Management*, 10(1), 63–76.

Jones, M. (2017), *Sustainable Event Management: A Practical Guide*, Third Edition, Abingdon, Routledge.

Mair, J. (2011), Events and climate change: An Australian perspective, *International Journal of Event and Festival Management*, 2(3), 245–253.

Mair, J. (2014), Events as proenvironmental learning spaces, *Event Management*, 18(4), 421–429.

Mair, J., and Laing, J.H. (2013), Encouraging pro-environmental behaviour: The role of sustainability-focused events, *Journal of Sustainable Tourism*, 21(8), 1113–1128.

Sakurai, R., Jacobson, S.K., Kobori, H., et al. (2011), Culture and climate change: Japanese cherry blossom festivals and stakeholders' knowledge and attitudes about global climate change, *Biological Conservation*, 144(1), 654–658.

Sanderson, C., and Islam, S.M.N. (2007), *Climate Change and Economic Development: SEA Regional Modelling and Analysis*, Palgrave Macmillan, Basingstoke.

Silvers, J.R. (2009), *Risk Management for Meetings and Events*, Abingdon, Routledge.

Smit, B., and Wandel, J. (2006), Adaptation, adaptive capacity and vulnerability, *Global Environmental Change*, 16(3), 282–292.

Sparks, T.H. (2014), Local-scale adaptation to climate change: The village flower festival, *Climate Research*, 60(1), 87–89.

Stern, N.H. and Great Britain Treasury (2007), *The Economics of Climate Change: The Stern Review*, Cambridge, Cambridge University Press.

United Nations Environmental Programme (2019), Human Development Report 2019: Beyond income, beyond averages, beyond today: Inequalities in human development in the 21st century. Accessed 21 September 2020 at http://hdr.undp.org/sites/default/files/hdr2019.pdf

PART III

Going forward

17. Evaluating cultural legacy: From policy to engaged research

Rafaela Neiva Ganga

Introduction

Cultural events evaluation is a central topic for academic research, policy-making and civil society as it emerges from the need to justify the public value of public spend on culture (Scott, 2010). Countless evaluation reports, research journal articles and other outputs have been produced, prompting narratives of success and/or questioning the event impact and the public spending (Belfiore, 2009; Garcia et al., 2010; O'Callaghan, 2012; Ooi et al., 2014; Steiner et al., 2015; Campbell et al., 2017; Baker et al., 2018). The Economic and Social Research Council (2020, n.p.) defines impact as 'the demonstrable contribution that excellent research makes to society and the economy', detailing that it can be instrumental in influencing policy and practice, reframing debates and building capacity. According to this perspective, the most significant impact is the measurable change arising from research and how the research users subsequently interpret that change. In contrast, the definition of 'success' tends to be a more fluid term, escaping academic constraints and placing political advocacy over science.

Most of the contemporary debates concerning cultural events evaluation is led by those who advocate for cultural policy. What must be noted is that much emphasis is placed on contributions from economics and sociology (Throsby, 2001; Holden, 2004; Hennion, 2004; O'Brien, 2010; Lamont, 2012; Crossick and Kaszynska, 2016). Given that interdisciplinary perspectives and ways of analysis differ, these scholars offer methodological instruments to measure the value of cultural policy and event legacy, which adds value and theoretical insights that help problematise the social context of cultural events. In the United Kingdom (UK) and Europe, research has been methodologically-oriented (based on how to evaluate, the ethical implications of using certain methodologies) and epistemologically-oriented (why evaluate at all, whose knowledge is being perpetuated, how the knowledge is been used) (see Holden, 2004; Walmsley, 2018). The methodological and epistemological decisions of cultural events evaluation provide evidence (or not) of its impact on a city's cultural field, local residents' cultural practices, urban public spaces development, and levels of funding and investment. Each of these points is crucial in an engaged civic debate on *what a society is* or *has been*, and above all *what a society might yet be* (Kalleberg, 2005). The impact of the COVID-19 pandemic, Brexit, the financial crisis and the resurgence of the far right raises the need to rethink the plurality of cultural value, beyond marketised perspectives, stressing intrinsic values (Holden, 2004). This requires an engaged scientific public debate, facing an 'epistemological turn' and bottom-up approach to cultural events evaluation.

This chapter aims to offer an analysis of the cultural value debate and the social life of methods that have been used to capture the public value of hosting a cultural event. It does not present a discussion of empirical data, but it draws on my prior and ongoing experience as a sociologist who has focused extensively on the evaluation of culture and cultural events, for example Impact 18 (an evaluation of the 2008 Liverpool European Capital of Culture ten years on) and the Liverpool Borough of Culture (Institute of Cultural Capital, 2019). The chapter discusses events evaluation as a social phenomenon embedded within particular contexts. It offers a contribution to the field by (1) addressing the narratives of success of Liverpool as European Capital of Culture 2008 and how that narrative became a legacy on its own for events' evaluation and urban policy; and (2) reflecting on the methodological design of the evaluation of Liverpool Borough of Culture and the legacy the research might have on the city region's cultural policy. I argue that, by building on expanded dialogical relationships (science, policy, industry and society), policy and public-relevant sociological research can critically co-design policy that accounts for a pluralistic perception of cultural value (Burawoy, 2005; Bergvall-Kåreborn and Ståhlbröst, 2010; Nichols, 2015). While conceptually contributing to contemporary cultural and policy debates, this chapter navigates the challenges of pragmatic research and aims to outline routes for future research.

A theoretical and methodological framework for researching cultural events legacy

Why evaluate cultural events legacy?

Culture has been an essential element of public policy around the world, and this is especially true when we consider the legacy of hosting events. Being awarded a 'City of Culture' has become a brand recognised globally. This helps cities leverage their cultural attractions and promote them to international audiences, which helps with regenerating city images (Wise and Harris, 2017; Richards, 2020). For instance, in 2017, there were 30 similar titles around the world (Green, 2017). Some of these events have adopted a continent-wide approach such as the European Capital of Culture (known as the European City of Culture from 1985 to 2001), while others have focused on a more targeted scale, or a borough-wide reach, such as the London Borough of Culture. While the scale of the event will relate to the amount of funding received, the impact, intended outcomes and legacy directions of each event are maximised so that change is embraced before, during and after the event.

Cities in Europe have recognised the importance of a title awarded externally as an opportunity to grow a new tourism base and service economy (Spirou, 2011), enhance destination competitiveness (Aquilino et al., 2019) and reinvent a city's economy (Smith, 2012; Cudny et al., 2020; Liu, 2019). The recognition of externally awarded titles has been magnified over the past few decades. The rhetoric that supports the European Capital of Culture assumes that this prestige attracts investment and will build a future tourism economy, which translates into a host of new opportunities (Getz and Page, 2016). This means that the most visible and long-lasting event that showcases European cultural policy is seen as an instrument of economic conversion. However, when this conversion occurs, it tends to be short-lived and centred on the year that the city hosts an event. In reverse, it leads to spatial and social fragmentation, disaggregating the real city from the city staged for the European Capital of Culture. Scholars who have evaluated event impacts address how this poses problems of segmentation and social exclusion (Richards et al., 2013; Wise, 2019; Wallstam et al., 2020).

The cultural value debate

The value of culture is a political matter, which cannot be dissociated from the optics one uses to consider them. In Europe, culture is a strategic asset for several reasons. First, culture is a resource for social cohesion across the continent. Second, European heritage and cultural expression are the foundation of the culture and creative industries, providing a significant employment volume (European Commission, 2019). The current political climate and public discourse emphasises the creative economy, prioritising culture's economic value to the detriment of its plurality (O'Brien, 2010). In comparison, the cultural policy has fallen short of providing alternative valuation systems that could be opposed to this approach (Matarasso, 1996; Walmsley, 2012). Currently, this is a fundamental challenge for Europe and other latitudes.

In the UK, the cultural policy field has been prolific in a debate on the instrumentalism of cultural events and the use of an 'evidence base' for making a case for art investment (Belfiore and Bennett, 2008; Belfiore, 2012; Gilmore, 2014). Heir of the New Labour (1997–2010) cultural policy evaluation frameworks intended to capture the impact of the cultural events – its 'legacy' or the added value that that culture bears (economic, social and individual). Furthermore, in the consultancy fertile terrain of evidence-based policy-making, a trending tone of success emerged, one that filtered down the plurality of narratives, epistemologies and methods in favour of a specific aesthetic of research presentation (glossy publications with incisive graphs sprinkled with punch lines aimed to make a media-worthy impact or as a catchy headline) that make visible the preferred policy narratives (Stevens, 2011). In this sense, policy-oriented research dedicated to measure and demonstrate the value of cultural events in regenerating cities has fuelled the academic debate over the selectiveness of research methods in impact evidence (Belfiore, 2012), and the epistemological implication of evaluating cultural value (Walmsley, 2012; Crossick and Kaszynska, 2016).

From a theoretical perspective, the value of culture has been addressed mainly by economists and sociologists (see Throsby, 2001; Lamont, 2012). The economic approach seems to fail to provide a route to overcome the conventional mercantile approach (Throsby, 2001). Thus, to respond to this tendency, it is necessary to define the social value associated with culture from the participatory practice field (Walmsley, 2018; Wallstam et al., 2020). The sociology of valuation and the sociology of culture, along with other interdisciplinary and applied perspectives, have been demonstrating the value of capturing social actors' valuation practices. Such considerations are based upon what counts as a public good, or the significance of arts and culture for those that practise cultural interventions (Hennion, 2004; Lamont, 2012; Boltanski and Thévenot, 2006). This is not an easy task. Different actors in the cultural field (i.e. citizens, art and culture field professionals, public administrators, academics) construct and measure culture value differently. The challenge is to understand and standardise, and from there, to manage and capture the plurality of cultural value.

The methodological and epistemological debates

Social science (or any science) methods are not neutral. Social science researchers have increasingly asked questions about the social status of social science, raising concerns as to how methods shape our knowledge of the social world (Giddens, 1984; Bourdieu, 1996; Bauman, 2013). The search for objectivity is not done by excluding social relations, daily life or power relations, but by reducing ethnocentric analysis, which implies permanent self-surveillance, or better, a critical epistemological vigilance (Bachelard, 1990; Santos, 2002). While detailing this line of thought is complex and does not fit in the scope of this chapter, it is advantageous to understand how methods have a 'social life' in impacts evaluation. This also relates to general preconceptions of the neutrality of social science used to validate a particular policy narrative concerning the value of cultural events. On this debate, it is helpful to consider which methods have been privileged by policy stakeholders for measuring impact and value of culture (Belfiore and Bennett, 2007).

Law et al. (2011) argue that methods have a *double social life*. First, they are closely related and theoretically permeated with the social world from which they emerge. Second, they shape the social world, based on what questions are asked, what type of data are privileged (qualitative, quantitative), thus raising this *double social life* is central to analysing the impact evaluation of large-scale events. Gilmore (2014) argues that the resulting legacy narratives also have their own *double social life*. If the post-event policy narratives are drawn from selective data, the event's profile is also significant because the expectation of success pre-exists the research.

Another key contribution can be drawn from public sociology, which, in Burawoy's (2005) definition, aims to support the institutions of civil society (see also, Kalleberg, 2005). An events evaluation researcher is inherently engaged, as well as situated, between public sociology and policy sociology (Nichols, 2015). Moreover, an events evaluation researcher will leverage empirical methods and theoretical insights from the social sciences while engaging with 'extra-academic publics' on contemporary issues aiming to foster public good (Burawoy, 2005; Scott, 2010). Concerning (critical) sociological imaginations (Mills, 2000; Burawoy, 2005), there is a need to discuss the gap of *what is* (captured through empirical methods) and *what could be* (informed through theory, reflexive knowledge and public dialogue). This reinforces the importance of public sociology to events impact and evaluation research. Potentially, advancing the cultural value debate beyond the definition of cultural value and how to capture the meaning of measuring (Belfiore and Bennett, 2008; Crossick and Kaszynska, 2016) can be found in the gap between *what an event is* and *what it could be* in a critical collective imagination.

Public sociology has been met with criticism questioning both its rationale and its aims, while reclaiming the moral latitudes that make a healthy academic debate – this is based on hindsight that public good has to be perceived as plural (Charles, 2004; Nielsen, 2004). While events evaluation has undergone intense examination for placing policy advocacy above academic integrity (Belfiore, 2009), critical and epistemological vigilance are crucial to revitalising the relationship between academia, policy and events evaluation. After all, what could be the alternative? Both the divorce of the social sciences from its object and its neutrality are illusions long gone (Santos, 2002); still the debates on scholarship, public engagement and advocacy are to be resolved, and the democratic mandate for culture fulfilled (Holden, 2004).

From the capital to the borough of culture: The 'Liverpool model'

For 35 years, the European Capital of Culture has been a laboratory for creative cities, network societies and knowledge-based economies (Castells, 1996; Schneider and Jacobson, 2019). Extensive work has been dedicated to analysing the multiple impacts of the policy locally. However, it tends to fall into two conflicting narratives: either a negative response of critical scholars or the positive conclusions of evaluations (Belfiore, 2016). These evaluations are perceived as agents harbouring 'positive illusions' (Bennett, 2011) and feeding skewed notions of 'evidence-based policy' that eventually act as agents of implicit cultural policy (Ahearne and Bennett, 2009). With exacerbating economic impacts (Bowitz and Ibenholt, 2009), economic incentives consequently lead to recurrent bids that focus solely on potential economic gains and financial legacies. This has also resulted in an explosion of a similar type of event at several scales, such as the organisation of the UK City of Culture, the London Borough of Culture and the Liverpool Borough of Culture. As Boland et al. (2019, p. 249) argue, this 'leads to a disconnect between the "myth/rhetoric" of success and "ambivalent legacies" and "authentic lived realities" revealed in concentrations of unemployment, poverty and multiple deprivations'. The narratives of success by the evaluation were created to justify the 'discrepancy between early promises and actual effects' (Ooi et al., 2014, p. 423). The claims of long-term socio-economic transformation addressed by Garcia and Cox (2013) require further enquiry.

The double social life of Impacts 08 and Impacts 18

When Liverpool was European City of Culture in 2008, this was regarded as the ideal type of culture-led regeneration event that overly emphasises the economic value of culture, 'representing the apogee of a New Labour informed "cultural planning" framework for urban development' (Connolly, 2013, p. 162). Liverpool 2008 was, in fact, not a cultural event but a culture-led urban regeneration strategy designed to airbrush the city's image, attract infrastructural development capital and foster the visitor economy (Liu, 2019). The 'Liverpool model' according to Garcia (2009) and Connolly (2013) became one of the most celebrated ways of transforming cities (see also Sykes et al., 2013). To inspire future culture-led regeneration agendas, the UK Government decided to introduce its City of Culture Programme, and later the London and Liverpool Borough of Culture (Liverpool City Region, 2015).

To evaluate Liverpool 2008, Impacts 08 was initiated as a five-year holistic evaluation framework (2005–2010), commissioned by Liverpool City Council to capture the 'multiple impacts' of the European City of Culture in 2008 (Sykes et al., 2013). Designed in five clusters – (1) cultural access and participation; (2) economy and tourism; (3) cultural vibrancy and sustainability; (4) image and perceptions; and (5) governance and delivery process – this longitudinal and mixed-methods model became the second 'Liverpool model' influencing future events evaluation methodologies in the UK and Europe (see Cox and O'Brien, 2012). Liverpool's 2008 iconic economic impact of £753.8 million (the highest for any European Capital of Culture to date) is the cornerstone to Liverpool's success narrative (Garcia et al., 2010). This grand narrative of local cultural programming legacies focuses on culture's economic value and the importance of the event's attractors (to aid the tourism economy). In this sense, 'both methods, and their findings, in this work have a social life' (Campbell et al., 2017, p. 50).

Delivering the European City of Culture was costly to the city and its citizens (*Liverpool Echo*, 2008). Demonstrating evidence of the impact of culture-led regeneration was essential in the context of Liverpool, as its claims of success were so widely trumpeted by policy and cultural stakeholders even before there was any evidence to sustain those assertions. As Cox and O'Brien (2012, p. 97) put it, 'Liverpool's success at culture-led regeneration owes much to circumstances in which European Capital of Culture was a catalyst, but not the deciding factor'. Yet, even after the publication of the Impacts 08 final report (Garcia et al., 2010), there was little to no evidence of the economic, cultural and social long-term impact.

Revisiting the research ten years on, with Impacts 18, the aim was to address this evidence gap and overcome the social context that led to the intense criticism of the Impacts 08 double social life (Boland et al., 2019), even from its research team. Members of the Impact 08 research team developed a breadth of critical work that has contributed to advance the cultural policy debate (O'Brien, 2010; Campbell, 2011; O'Brien, 2013; Cox and O'Brien, 2012; Campbell et al., 2017), joining other critical voices (Belfiore, 2009; O'Callaghan, 2012). Impacts 18 (*Legacies of Liverpool as European Capital of Culture 10 Years On*) was a four-year programme (2016–2019) of academic research dedicated to capturing the long-term effects of hosting the European Capital of Culture title on the city of Liverpool, led by the Institute of Cultural Capital. However, with history repeating itself, the same narratives of success were replicated around Impact 18 even before the research was concluded. 'Mr. Joseph Anderson (who served as the leader of Liverpool City Council from 2010 to 2012, when he was elected Mayor of Liverpool) said, the 'Capital of Culture marked the start of something special, the last ten years have been an amazing success story' (BBC News, 2018, n.p.).

The final report was well anticipated, and a high-profile seminar was organised with the Liverpool City Council in October 2018 to disseminate the results of the impacts of the European Capital of Culture 10 years on (Culture Liverpool, 2018). Yet, the Impact 18 final report is still to be published due to its own social and ethical context. Impact 18 had the potential to reconcile the policy research and evaluation of cultural events agendas. On the one hand, Impact 18 was, as the original research programme, the first research programme of its kind in scale and scope to collect and analyse unparalleled qualitative and quantitative data of the long-term impact of a single cultural mega-event. Without a doubt, Impact 18 was expected to contribute to the cultural value debate, and address understandings of the short- and long-term changes leveraged in a hosting city. On the other hand, the breadth of the critical mass of the research agenda on the cultural events available has grown significantly in the past decade. Moreover, the Impact 18 evaluation could have actioned the critiques of evidence-gathering practice (Campbell et al., 2017), moving beyond the toolkit approach (Belfiore and Bennett, 2010) and the logic chain approach for articulating 'impact' and 'outcomes' stems (Gilmore, 2014). However,

Liverpool's 'success story' retold repeatedly by the media, policy-makers and private consultants left little to no space to debate the multiple, and often contradictory, narratives of the event's legacies experienced over the past ten years across the whole city of Liverpool. One of the legacies of Liverpool 2008 is how its success story became a recognised post-truth (Keane, 2018), limiting the public debate, critical research and potentially damaging the local urban and cultural policy.

The Liverpool Borough of Culture as legacy

A broader causality of Liverpool's 2008 success story rhetoric was the belief that the 'Liverpool model' could and should be replicated in the Liverpool City Region and across the UK, irrespective of those contexts' specificities. Cox and O'Brien (2012), focusing on Liverpool's influence on the UK City of Culture, have questioned the transferability of culture-led regeneration policies from one site to another, while Bianchini et al. (2018) questioned the 'impossibility of failure' that is inscribed in this policy from the bidding stage.

In a more local context, the Liverpool City Region Combined Authority, the first in the country with devolved power over culture, launched the Liverpool Borough of Culture in March 2018. The title, which formed part of a broader culture and creativity strategy, is awarded annually on a rotational basis to one of the six local authorities that make up the city region, as part of the 1 Per Cent for Culture Programme with a dedicated budget of £200,000. The Liverpool City Region Devolution Agreement addresses the legacy of Liverpool 2008 as 'transformational', stating the intention to place culture 'in the heart of its strategy to accelerate economic growth, improve skills and further develop its distinctive visitor offer' (Liverpool City Region, 2015, p. 14), which set the overall tone for which the value of culture is a fundamental priority in the region. The social context from which the Borough of Culture emerged was, as such, heavily saturated with success narratives from Liverpool 2008.

When I was commissioned by the Liverpool Combined Authority to develop a research programme to evaluate the Borough of Culture, I was faced with a multiplicity of challenges to manage and reconcile a complex set of logics that add to the success story rhetoric. First, the Liverpool Combined Authority is an overarching governmental regional body, however, each individual borough constitutes a political body in itself, with heterogenic cultural policies and strategies on how cultural events are instrumentalised to deliver wider agendas (e.g. urban regeneration, health and wellbeing, tourism economy). In essence, each borough puts its own spin on the event, and the research programme would have to be flexible enough to capture the latitude of interpretations. Second, the research budget would be significantly less than the overall dedicated Culture Programme budget, which meant that reduced resources could be made available for data collection and analysis. Finally, how could I advance the debate on cultural value and methodological innovation, while maintaining a practice of socially engaged science? How can I as a sociologist enter into a public dialogue that deals with questions of cultural policy evaluation, while maintaining research integrity? For full disclosure and practising what I preach concerning epistemological surveillance and criticism (Bachelard, 1990), I am too affected by different logics, and one of those is my professional identity – since I am a sociologist who evaluates culture with a particular interest in social justice. I started the evaluation of the Liverpool Borough of Culture, with the intent and interest of embedding a critical research model to events evaluation relevant to local cultural policy. My goal was to infer a new vision of the plurality of the value of culture and new evaluation methodologies that support effective and inclusive cultural policies.

By engaging with and drawing inspiration from the theoretical and methodological heritage discussed previously, the research that emerged from the evaluation of the Liverpool Borough of Culture aims to reposition the debate of value of culture in the Liverpool City Region. A policy analysis (Bacchi, 2009) was developed of the documents that frame the Liverpool Borough of Culture, namely the Liverpool City Region Devolution Agreement and the Culture and Creativity Strategy, followed by each borough's culture policy. From this exercise, it was possible to reframe the event with the cultural value of the policy and the conceptual logics of policy-makers.

Throughout 2019, a dedicated steering group of representatives from the Liverpool City Region, each borough and colleagues from the Liverpool John Moores University was formed to develop an evaluation framework for the Liverpool City Region Borough of Culture programme. The final product of this co-design exercise, shown in Table 17.1, is a holistic evaluation framework that embraces concurring objectives (O'Callaghan, 2012), which includes market-led outcomes linked to the visitor economy and socially-orientated outcomes including health and wellbeing, while emphasising the economic nature of the event (Belfiore, 2009) and the contribution of the event to the visitor economy and growth of the Liverpool City Region's cultural and creative industries. Furthermore, the methodological strategy and instruments were co-designed and delivered with each Borough of Culture programme and delivery teams to capture the plurality of specialisms.

Table 17.1   Policy and research framework for the evaluation of the Borough of Culture

Devolution objectives						
Recognising Liverpool City Region's plans to place culture and creativity at the heart of its strategy to (1) *accelerate economic growth*, (2) *improve skills* and (3) *further develop its distinctive visitor offer*, the government will work with Liverpool City Region to (4) *support a place-based strategy* and the city region's plans for a local cultural partnership.						

Culture and creativity strategy objectives						
Expand and promote our existing *culture and creative offer* as a core part of a growing *visitor economy* (including retention and growth in numbers of students and residents) alongside more targeted *creative social intervention*		Develop a supply chain for talent and harness what the region has always done – acted as a *pool of talent* with *pathways into the creative sectors*			Sustain and enhance economic growth through culture and creativity; recognising and investing in culture and creativity as major drivers in the *visitor economy* and creative industries, and as catalysts to achieve *positive outcomes in wellbeing, health, education, cohesion and the future world of work*	

Borough of Culture themes						
Economy (added to evaluation model)	Cultural sustainability (infrastructure)	Placemaking (distinctiveness of place)	Engagement (communities)	Creative skills (children and young people)	Wellbeing (positive outcomes)	Visitors (added to evaluation model)

Underpinning operational objectives						
Accelerate economic growth and generate greater economic impact for the Liverpool City Region	Leaving a legacy through better infrastructure ensuring the future sustainability of the sector	Foster creative social interventions to support placemaking	Increase communities' engagement in culture	Improve youth employability and facilitate pathways into the creative sector	Achieve positive outcomes in wellbeing, health, education and social cohesion	Attract a diverse profile of visitors to the city region and improve satisfaction levels

Indicators of impact						
Increased economic impact of the Borough of Culture	Strengthened and new partnerships amongst local and regional organisations	Civic-sector reference bodies working with the cultural sector – numbers, types of relationships, target audiences, etc.	Increased number of events and activities encouraging active engagement and giving opportunities for different levels of participation.	Increased take-up of creative qualifications/ degrees	Increased levels of happiness/ subjective wellbeing	Increased attendance at Borough of Culture events compared to regular attendance
Increased commercial income from cultural activities	Increase the availability of affordable space (short-term and long-term use) for cultural and creative industries/ professionals	Number of cultural ambassadors/ champions	Number of Borough of Culture events hosted in areas of deprivation and inequality	Number of local artists involved in the projects	Increased depth of participation resulting in positive outcomes	Improved visitor satisfaction

Increase in-kind and match funding contributions	Number and quality of local grassroots initiatives	Number and quality of co-produced or collaborative sustainable projects	Increased number and diverse profile of volunteers at Borough of Culture events	Number and quality of new cultural and creative jobs created	Increase levels of residents and visitors stating that they learnt something (e.g. local history) from attending Borough of Culture events	More diverse profiles of visitors recorded – ethnicities, disabilities, religion, etc.
Increase the success rate of external funding	Total Borough of Culture budget spent in local cultural organisations versus total budget allocated	Increased residents' sense of belonging/ civic pride	Facilitate accessible opportunities to engage in the Borough of Culture programme	Quality, quantity and sustainability of schemes and programmes designed to promote access to creative professions	Reduce social isolation, particularly among older people	Increase tourist visits (day visits, overnight stays – regional, national and international)
Increase income through external grant applications	Borough strategy for long-term cultural development, pre-, during and post-Borough of Culture year	Improve resident and visitor perceptions of the borough	Number of residents and local organisations involved in the development of the Borough of Culture programme	Quality, quantity and sustainability of schemes and programmes designed to support professional development of artists and art-sector professionals	Greater ownership of communities' own cultural activities, e.g. crowdfunding	Increase tourism revenue associated with the Borough of Culture programme
Increased GDP and employment in the boroughs' cultural and creative sector	Increase the value of investment in cultural infrastructures and facilities	Increased number of new art installations and public art	Number of community events facilitated and supported through the Borough of Culture programme	Increase gender, class and ethnic diversity of the cultural and creative-sector workforce		
Increase social return on investment	New public spaces development, e.g. urban regeneration	Increased awareness of the boroughs' cultural offer.	Number of local schools and school children engaged in the Borough of Culture programme			
			Increased positive engagement on Borough of Culture social media			

It can be argued that the co-designed evaluation framework in Table 17.1 allows enough scope to develop the appropriate methodologies to perform comparative qualitative and quantitative analyses at the local and regional levels. In addition, this framework allows me to evaluate and map the various forms of cultural engagement, assess the role of cultural participation as a source of wellbeing and identify the economic returns of cultural events. The methodology includes, but is not limited to, the meta-analysis of visitors' surveys (as commissioned by each borough to private external partners); content analysis of audiences' feedback and case studies (each borough had qualitative instruments to capture audiences' feedback on the day, and case studies from participants, partners and those who engaged in the programme); content analysis of focus groups conducted by me with each of the Borough of Culture programme and delivery teams; secondary data analysis of local and regional-level statistical information (e.g. Index of Multiple Deprivation, from the Office for National Statistics, and borough residents' survey); and social media analytics (to show virtual engagement and reach of the accounts and posts of the dedicated programme).

The research framework and methodology for the evaluation of the Borough of Culture constitutes a negotiated pragmatic advance. Its most significant contribution is methodological research co-designed with policy-makers (Bergvall-Kåreborn and Ståhlbröst, 2010) and the real-world valuation of mechanisms and dynamics that operate in the institutional field of local government-led cultural events. Addressing event evaluation and legacy at an organisational and local government level is another contribution of this work. Each borough's cultural policy and cultural team organisational structure, as well as funding streams, were developed while co-designing the evaluation framework. This helped with shaping the research objective and methodologies along with the internal organisation. Each borough travels a different journey and experiences the Borough of Culture momentum and evaluation as a process-focused practice of developing cultural policies, event practices and producing cultural value.

This approach is determined by the limited opportunities for first-hand data collection, which has several implications. The majority of first-hand data is collected by 'extra-academic publics' (Burawoy, 2005), and it can be collected for non-academic purposes. This type of real-world data can be time- and cost-effective because it is generated by the event and the producers and audiences that make an event possible. However, this involves a heavy investment in data curation, validation and standardisation to ensure that the data are fit for purpose. Another significant limitation is the absence of artists and citizens on the research framework and methodology co-design. When addressing methodological innovation, it can help to incorporate the principles of innovation co-design, including the Quadruple Helix Model of innovation, where four major social actors are brought together: science, policy, industry and society (Schütz et al., 2019). The absence of artists (industry) and citizens (society) limits the discussion, scope of understanding of cultural value and potentially narrows the methodological complexity. However, the Liverpool Combined Authority recently created a Policy Living Lab. A Living Lab 'is a user-centric innovation milieu built on every-day practice and research, with an approach that facilitates user influence in open and distributed innovation processes engaging all relevant partners in real-life contexts, aiming to create sustainable values' (Bergvall-Kåreborn and Ståhlbröst, 2010, p. 191). This approach was designed to foster public involvement in the policy innovation processes, which we aim to explore so as to overcome this limitation. The established principles here are not new in public and policy sociology (Burawoy, 2005). As such, the same methodological and epistemological concerns, particularly regarding the cross-contamination between both cultural policy research and its research object (cultural events), and critical and impactful research remain the primary focus (Burawoy, 2005; Martin, 2011).

Finally, while asking what processes can sustain these dynamics of events at a local scale, this research framework aims to develop tools and systematic guidelines for reorienting cultural policy in a pluralistic sense. The ambition is to foster equitable and sustainable legacies of culture in the broad sense through engaged, while objective, scientific evaluations, research co-creation and bottom-up solutions (Burawoy, 2005). The processes are participatory in nature, and thus require ongoing iterative development that is reshaped within each iteration of the Liverpool Borough of Culture.

Lessons learned and to be learned

The debate on the public value of public spending on culture is not new nor is it resolved. The proliferation of cultural events, from continent-wide to borough-wide, fuelled academic research, policy-making and civil society interest on the intrinsic, instrumental and institutional value of culture. This chapter has reframed events impact evaluation as a social phenomenon embedded within particular contexts offering a path to advance the debate beyond the previously prevailing issues on evidencing cultural value. The focus on the sociological practice of evaluation as publicly engaged science gives an opportunity to embrace an 'epistemological turn' that does not shy away from engagement, while remaining vigilant and critical through the research.

The discussion of the methodological options and challenges of evaluating Liverpool Borough of Culture offers possible strategies to navigate pragmatic cultural events evaluation. All the while, however, such evaluation research remains bounded by traditional sociological methods attempting to capture processes and measure cultural value (Scott, 2010). Framing events evaluation as a public sociological practice offers new theoretical and empirical instruments to break from the circular debate on cultural events legacy. Advancing the debate can only be done by the real-world practice of reflexive and collaborative evaluation that recognises cultural policy in interaction with other policy spheres and is bound by budgets, organisational practices and political agendas.

Another consideration is to address cultural policy and events legacy at an organisational level. Attention has been placed on the legacy of events at the macro and micro levels, but there is a lack of research that addresses the process and even the outcomes of events to organisations, nonetheless that refer to their internal cultural policies. Organisational change can and should be considered as key considerations in impact and legacy evaluations. The institutional value of the evaluation of the Liverpool Borough of Culture is demonstrated on the growing process that came from programming, evaluating and delivering the event. Brokering dialogue between different levels of policy-making (regional and local) can be interpreted as one of the roles of the evaluation.

Value co-creation, collaboration and knowledge exchange between academia, policy, industry and society are strategies known to the social sciences, with the intention of generating societal change. An important outcome here is that this leads to meaning making among different stakeholders. The intellectual heritage of social science can steer toward transparency on events' evaluation and legacy by critically illuminating and interrogating contradictory discourses and instigating reflexive practices that eventually lead to lasting impacts and creative futures that are more inclusive.

References

Ahearne, J. and Bennett, O. (2009). Implicit cultural policies. *International Journal of Cultural Policy*, 15(2), 139–244.

Aquilino, L., Armenski, T. and Wise, N. (2019). Assessing the competitiveness of Matera and the Basilicata region (Italy) ahead of the 2019 European Capital of Culture. *Tourism and Hospitality Research*, 19(4), 503–517.

Bacchi, C. (2009). *Analysing policy*. Sydney: Pearson Higher Education.

Bachelard, G. (1990). *A Epistemologia*. Lisbon: Edições 70.

Baker, G., Bull, A. and Taylor, M. (2018). Who watches the watchmen? Evaluating evaluations of El Sistema. *British Journal of Music Education*, 1–15.

Bauman, Z. (2013). *Liquid modernity*. Hoboken, NJ: Wiley.

BBC News, (2018). Liverpool to mark Capital of Culture 'milestone' with year of events. *BBC News*, 11 January.

Belfiore, E. (2009). On bullshit in cultural policy practice and research: Notes from the British case. *International Journal of Cultural Policy*, 15(3), 343–359.

Belfiore, E. (2012). 'Defensive instrumentalism' and the legacy of New Labour's cultural policies. *Cultural Trends*, 21(2), 103–111.

Belfiore, E. (2016). Cultural policy research in the real world: Curating 'impact', facilitating 'enlightenment'. *Cultural Trends*, 25(3), 205–216.

Belfiore, E. and Bennett, O. (2007). Rethinking the social impacts of the arts. *International Journal of Cultural Policy*, 13(2), 135–151.

Belfiore, E. and Bennett, O. (2008). *The social impact of the arts*. Basingstoke: Palgrave Macmillan.

Belfiore, E. and Bennett, O. (2010). Beyond the 'toolkit approach': Arts impact evaluation research and the realities of cultural policy-making. *Journal for Cultural Research*, 14(2), 121–142.

Bennett, O. (2011). Cultures of optimism. *Cultural Sociology*, 5(2), 301–320.

Bergvall-Kåreborn, B. and Ståhlbröst, A. (2010). Living Lab: An open and user-centric design approach. In D.M. Haftor (ed.), *Information and communication technologies, society and human beings: Theory and framework* (pp. 190–207). London: IGI Global.

Bianchini, F., Alexander, C., Borchi, A., Byrne, J. and Morpeth, N.D. (2018). *Cultural transformations: The impacts of Hull UK City of Culture 2017*. Hull: Culture, Place and Policy Institute, University of Hull.

Boland, P., Murtagh, B. and Shirlow, P. (2019). Fashioning a City of Culture: 'Life and place changing' or '12 month party'? *International Journal of Cultural Policy*, 25(2), 246–265.

Boltanski, L. and Thévenot, L. (2006). *On justification: Economies of worth*. Princeton, NJ: Princeton University Press.

Bourdieu, P. (1996). *Lição Sobre a Lição*. Porto: Estratégias Criativas.

Bowitz, E. and Ibenholt, K. (2009). Economic impacts of cultural heritage: Research and perspectives. *Journal of Cultural Heritage*, 10(1), 1–8.

Burawoy, M. (2005). For public sociology. *American Sociological Review*, 70(1), 4–28.

Campbell, P. (2011). Creative industries in a European Capital of Culture, I. *International Journal of Cultural Policy*, 17(5), 510–522.

Campbell, P., Cox, T. and O'Brien, D. (2017). The social life of measurement: How methods have shaped the idea of culture in urban regeneration. *Journal of Cultural Economy*, 10(1), 49–62.

Castells, M. (1996). *The rise of the network society, the information age: Economy, society and culture*, Vol. 1. Oxford: Blackwell.

Charles, R. (2004). The arrogance of public sociology. *Social Forces*, 82(4), 1639–1643.

Connolly, M.G. (2013). The 'Liverpool model(s)': Cultural planning, Liverpool and Capital of Culture 2008. *International Journal of Cultural Policy*, 19(2), 162–181.

Cox, T. and O'Brien, D. (2012). The 'scouse wedding' and other myths: Reflections on the evolution of a 'Liverpool model' for culture-led urban regeneration. *Cultural Trends*, 21(2), 93–101.

Crossick, G. and Kaszynska, P. (2016). *Understanding the value of arts and culture: The AHRC cultural value project*. London: AHRC.

Cudny, W., Comunian, R. and Wolaniukc, A. (2020). Arts and creativity: A business and branding strategy for Lodz as a neoliberal city. *Cities*, 100, 102659.

Culture Liverpool, (2018). Impacts 18: A cultural legacy. Culture Liverpool, 18 October. Retrieved from: www.cultureliverpool.co.uk/news/impacts-18-a-cultural-legacy/

Economic and Social Research Council, (2020). What is impact? Economic and Social Research Council, 30 September. Retrieved from: https://esrc.ukri.org/research/impact-toolkit/what-is-impact/

European Commission, (2019). Creative Europe: European Capitals of Culture. Retrieved from: https://ec.europa.eu/programmes/creative-europe/actions/capitals-culture_en

Garcia, B. (2009). *Impacts 08 – The Liverpool model: Understanding the impact of culture-led regeneration in Liverpool, 2008 European Capital of Culture*. Liverpool: Institute of Cultural Capital. Retrieved from: http://iccliverpool.ac.uk/wp-content/uploads/2013/04/Impacts082008BURAMAgazine-FINAL.pdf

Garcia, B. and Cox, T. (2013). *European Capitals of Culture: Success strategies and long-term effects*. Luxembourg: Office of the European Union.

Garcia, B., Cox, T. and Melville, R. (2010). *Creating an impact: Liverpool's experience as European Capital of Culture*. Liverpool: University of Liverpool.

Getz, D. and Page, S. (2016). Progress and prospects for event tourism research. *Tourism Management*, 52, 593–631.

Giddens, A. (1984). *The constitution of society: Outline of the theory of structuration*. Berkeley, CA: University of California Press.

Gilmore, A. (2014). Evaluating legacies: Research, evidence and the regional impact of the Cultural Olympiad. *Cultural Trends*, 23(1), 29–41.

Green, S. (2017). Capitals of Culture: An introductory survey of a worldwide activity. Retrieved from: http://prasino.eu/wp-content/uploads/2017/10/Capitals-of-Culture-An-introductory-survey-Steve-Green-October-2017.pdf

Hennion, A. (2004). Pragmatics of taste. In M.D. Jacobs and N. Weiss Hanrahan (eds), *The Blackwell companion to the sociology of culture* (pp. 131–144). Malden, MA: Blackwell.

Holden, J. (2004). *Capturing cultural value: How culture has become a tool of government policy*. London: Demos.

Institute of Cultural Capital, (2019). *Evaluation of the Liverpool City Region Borough of Culture programme*. Institute of Cultural Capital, 1 March. Retrieved from: http://iccliverpool.ac.uk/?research=evaluation-of-the-liverpool-city-region-boroughs-of-culture-programme

Kalleberg, R. (2005). What is 'public sociology'? Why and how should it be made stronger? *British Journal of Sociology*, 56(3), 387–393.

Keane, J. (2018). Post-truth politics and why the antidote isn't simply 'fact-checking' and truth. *The Conversation*, 23 March. doi:https://theconversation.com/post-truth-politics-and-why-the-antidote-isnt-simply-fact-checking-and-truth-87364

Lamont, M. (2012). Toward a comparative sociology of valuation and evaluation. *Annual Review of Sociology*, 38, 201–221.

Law, J., Ruppert, E. and Savage, M. (2011). The double social life of methods. CRESC Working Paper Series, Working Paper No. 95, 1–18.

Liu, Y.D. (2019). Event and sustainable culture-led regeneration: Lessons from the 2008 European Capital of Culture, Liverpool. *Sustainability*, 11(7), 1869.

Liverpool City Region, (2015). *Liverpool City Region devolution agreement*. Liverpool: HM Treasury.

Liverpool Echo, (2008). Council tax shock: Pay more and get less. *Liverpool Echo*, 27 February.

Martin, B.R. (2011). The research excellence framework and the 'impact agenda': Are we creating a Frankenstein monster? *Research Evaluation*, 20(3), 247–254.

Matarasso, F. (1996). *Defining values: Evaluating arts programmes*. Stroud: Comedia.

Mills, C.W. (2000). *The sociological imagination*. Oxford: Oxford University Press.

Nichols, L.T. (2015). Sociology, evaluation and dialogue. *American Sociologist*, 46(4), 435–436.

Nielsen, F. (2004). The vacant 'we': Remarks on public sociology. *Social Forces*, 82(4), 1619–1627.

O'Brien, D. (2010). *Measuring the value of culture*. London: Department for Culture, Media and Sport.

O'Brien, D. (2013). *Cultural policy: Management, value and modernity in the creative industries*. New York: Routledge.

O'Callaghan, C. (2012). Urban anxieties and creative tensions in the European Capital of Culture 2005: 'It couldn't just be about Cork, like'. *International Journal of Cultural Policy*, 18(2), 185–204.

Ooi, C.S., Håkanson, L. and LaCava, L. (2014). Poetics and politics of the European Capital of Culture Project. *Procedia: Social and Behavioral Sciences*, 148, 420–427.

Richards, G. (2020). Deigning creative places: The role of creative tourism. *Annals of Tourism Research*, 85, 102922.

Richards, G., de Brito, M. and Wilks, L. (eds) (2013). *Exploring the social impacts of events*. London: Routledge.

Santos, B.S. (2002). *Toward a new legal common sense: Law, globalization and emancipation*. Cambridge: Cambridge University Press.

Schneider, W. and Jacobson, K. (2019), *Transforming cities: Paradigms and potentials of urban development within the 'European Capital of Culture'*. Hildesheim: Olms Verlag.

Schütz, F., Heidingsfelder, M.L. and Schraudner, M. (2019). Co-shaping the future in quadruple helix innovation systems: Uncovering public preferences toward participatory research and innovation. *She Ji: Journal of Design, Economics, and Innovation*, 5(2), 128–146.

Scott, C. (2010). Searching for the 'public' in public value: Arts and cultural heritage in Australia. *Cultural Trends*, 19(4), 273–289.

Smith, A. (2012). *Events and urban regeneration: The strategic use of events to revitalise cities*. London: Routledge.

Spirou, C. (2011). *Urban Tourism and Urban Change*. London: Routledge.

Steiner, L., Frey, B. and Hotz, S. (2015). European Capitals of Culture and life satisfaction. *Urban Studies*, 52(2), 374–394.

Stevens, A. (2011). Telling policy stories: An ethnographic study of the use of evidence in policy-making in the UK. *Journal of Social Policy*, 40(2), 237–256.

Sykes, O., Brown, J., Cocks, M., Shaw, D. and Couch, C. (2013). A city profile of Liverpool. *Cities*, 35, 299–318.

Throsby, D. (2001). *Economics and culture*. Cambridge: Cambridge University Press.

Wallstam, M., Ioannides, D. and Pettersson, R. (2020). Evaluating the social impacts of events: In search of unified indicators for effective policymaking. *Journal of Policy Research in Tourism, Leisure and Events*, 12(2), 122–141.

Walmsley, B. (2012). Towards a balanced scorecard: A critical analysis of the culture and sport evidence (CASE) programme. *Cultural Trends*, 21(4), 325–334.

Walmsley, B. (2018). Deep hanging out in the arts: An anthropological approach to capturing cultural value. *International Journal of Cultural Policy*, 24(2), 272–291.

Wise, N. (2019). Towards a more enabling representation: Framing an emergent conceptual approach to measure social conditions following mega-event transformation in Manaus, Brazil. *Bulletin of Latin American Research*, 38(3), 300–316.

Wise, N. and Harris, J. (2017). *Sport, events, tourism and regeneration*. London: Taylor and Francis.

18. A research synthesis of organizational forms for events legacy delivery

Kylie Wasser, Landy Di Lu, and Laura Misener

Introduction

The legacy, or the lasting impacts that remain after the hosting of major events, has become a central focus of event planning and management (Misener et al., 2013; Thomson et al., 2013, 2019). Creating and delivering an enduring legacy has become an important way to guarantee the "sustainability of events" (Liu, 2018, p. 1). This ongoing shift towards sustainability is also reflected in the bidding and planning documents of major sport events. For instance, the International Olympic Committee (IOC) Charter was amended in 2003 to include the "promot[ion of] a positive legacy from the Olympic Games to the host city and the host country" (IOC, 2003, p. 12). Since 2004, organizing committees (OCs) for Olympic Games have also included specific mandates in the bidding documents dedicated to legacy planning for sustainable outcomes. The inclusion of legacy in the bidding and planning process of major sport events contributes to positioning the event to potential host regions as a community-wide, broad-serving spectrum of positive impacts (Kohe and Bowen-Jones, 2016; Sant and Mason, 2015) in areas of health (e.g., Thomas et al., 2016), culture (e.g., Cashman, 2006), environment (e.g., Chappelet, 2008), economy (e.g., Gratton et al., 2005), tourism (e.g., Sant et al., 2013), and politics (e.g., Grix, 2012), amongst others.

In order to better achieve sustainable legacies from hosting sports events, scholars (e.g., Chalip, 2014, 2017; Chen and Misener, 2019; Schulenkorf et al., 2019) have argued for the use of a leveraging approach, as it implies an active, ex ante focus. Sustainable strategies through leveraging are in stark contrast to the typical sports event organizational strategy, which is purposefully short term in design (Phillips and Barnes, 2015). Leveraging focuses on employing tactics and strategies before, during and after the hosting of the event itself, rather than expecting that planning efforts alone will carry legacies after the event is complete. While this may appear to further convolute the rhetoric surrounding legacies, it is important to note that regardless of strategy the event will have various impacts on its host residents and communities, but an active, leveraging process contributes to strategically obtaining sustainable legacies and outcomes ascertained from an event (Misener et al., 2020; Sant et al., 2019; Smith, 2014).

While this continued focus on sustainability and lasting outcomes has been noted extensively in recent scholarship on event management (Chalip, 2017; Fairley et al., 2016; Leopkey and Parent, 2012, 2017; Misener et al., 2020; Preuss, 2015) and throughout IOC documentation, less is known about the organizational forms for the legacy delivery of major sports events. The term organizational form describes a combination of organizational structure and organizational strategy (Ingram, 1998). Understanding such organizational forms contributes to providing direction for best practice of how to pursue intended event benefits. Thus, the aim of this chapter is to examine the scholarly literature regarding past legacy delivery organizational forms, with a specific focus on the locus of responsibility of legacy. In particular, we sought to synthesize outcomes from previous events in order to enhance understanding of how to better organize and execute sustainable legacy strategies, and offer new directions for research on the managerial aspects of delivering legacy or executing leveraging in the host community.

Systematically reviewing the evidence

In order to consider the different types of organizational forms used for legacy delivery, we turned our attention to the scholarly literature in this space. Performing a systematic research synthesis helped us understand how previous scholars have articulated organizational forms of legacy delivery. As empirically based data are recognized as the golden standard for superior evidence quality to assist in demonstrating the "best evidence" (Weed, 2005, p. 79) we focus on empirical studies only herein emphasizing the importance of primary data collection and analysis. We want to offer a robust perspective of organizational forms, so we followed Cooper and Hedges' (2009) six-step process for conducting research syntheses. The process enabled us to identify key variables: event legacy, legacy organization, responsibility for legacy, and interorganizational relationships. We focused on eight different academic databases (Annual Review of Sociology, EBSCO SportDiscus, SCOPUS, Kinesiology Publications, Physical Education Index, PubMed, and Google Scholar). Our key search terms included "events", "sport events", "special events", "Olympics", "FIFA", "Games", "mega events", "sport mega events" all with "governance", "policy", "responsibility", and "legacy", "leverage", and/or "strategic leveraging". A total of 3,437 papers were retrieved, demonstrating the popularity and salience of sports event legacy within the literature. The search results and titles were then examined and sorted based upon preliminary inclusion criteria (n = 687). The abstracts of these papers were then read and separated to confirm secondary inclusion criteria of examining the planning, organization, and/or execution of event legacies, and as a result a total of 142 articles were downloaded and organized in a reference manager for textual analysis. The articles themselves were then read carefully to match the inclusion criteria of investigating the planning, organization, or execution of event legacy, as well as excluding studies that were purely theoretical or conceptual.

While initially we were optimistic about the large number of results, a vast amount of literature had to be excluded as they did not actually consider the conceptualization or responsibility within the context of legacy delivery. A total of 38 articles were analyzed that matched our interest in event outcomes and organizational responsibility. This is a telling result that begs further consideration for our future research discussions. It is unsurprising that none of the articles examined were published prior to 2004, since legacy was only added to the IOC Charter in 2003. There are a number of areas that became apparent in reviewing the papers that should be considered when examining event outcomes: government involvement; modes of governance; actors involved in legacy governance; use of leveraging; intended versus actual outcomes; constraints on legacy delivery; factors supporting success; control of legacy (resources); recipients of legacy outcomes; and responsibility. We also emphasize the importance of power and responsibility within the individual legacy objectives, resulting in distinct classifications of organizational forms that have been responsible for event-related outcomes.

Organizational forms and responsibilities

In most of the studies that we analyzed, legacy delivery was centralized with the host OC as a hybrid organizational form. However, the OCs were not the only groups responsible for delivering specific event-related outcomes. Five distinct variations in organizational forms responsible for delivering legacy have been observed, with varying degrees of "success" in their strategic delivery of legacy objectives: (1) hybrid OC (i.e., hybrid multi-agency OC, hybrid localized OC); (2) government-directed OC; (3) national governing organization; (4) individual tactics/entrepreneurial organizational form; and (5) non-profit organizational collaboration (see Table 18.1). The following section describes the different organizational forms taking shape to execute and deliver legacy strategies; some existing and some created by circumstance in order to execute the task/legacy at hand.

Hybrid organizing committees

Hybrid organizational forms appear to be the most commonly reported form (see Table 18.1). We further categorize these into two specific subcategories: hybrid multi-agency OC and hybrid localized OC. These subcategories were created based on the increased power to more localized individuals and organizations, versus the standard multi-agency OC, wherein power over legacy delivery was centralized in a government agency.

Hybrid multi-agency organizing committee

The most common form utilized by legacy organizers was the traditional multi-agency OC, a version of the private–public partnerships (PPPs) that characterize the event execution. Previous researchers (Andranovich et al., 2001; Burbank et al., 2001) have demonstrated that PPPs are central to event bidding and hosting. These interrelated, multi-level organizational forms enable unprecedented access to resources, policy, and power (Andranovich et al., 2001). Several authors (e.g., Bloyce and Lovett, 2012; Bretherton et al., 2016; Samuel and Stubbs 2013) have examined the multi-agency OC that conceptualized and executed some of the legacy strategies for the 2012 London Olympic Games. For the 2012 Games, the national Department of Culture, Media and Sport (DCMS) defined and published legacy objectives, including the promise of getting 2 million people in the United Kingdom (UK) more physically active by the time of the Games (Bloyce and Lovett, 2012). In examining policies and documents leading up to the Games, Bloyce and Lovett (2012) found that the increasing number of actors involved combined with numerous programs created made the network surrounding legacy more complex, leading to a diminished control of communication, resources, and the execution of legacy

Table 18.1   Research synthesis of empirical evidence surrounding legacy delivery

Organizational form	General outcomes of organizational form	Authors
Hybrid organizing committees	Very few legacy partners openly prepared to claim responsibility or accountability for achieving objectives pre-Games. Many stakeholders legitimized and authenticated legacy without critically evaluating it beyond the aesthetic surface. Abandonment of pre-Games targets and accompanying policies. Regional legacy definition contested amongst stakeholders. Increased intraregional collaboration, but weakened capacity with lack of direction and resources. Legacy policy not designed to enable local strategies (vague policy mandates), resulting in many unfulfilled legacies. Formal legacy strategy not conceptualized with no post-event legacy plan. Discrepancy between external requirements and local/national realities. Olympic endorsement bestowed legitimacy, but also hindered access to other networks (through IOC sanctions). Increased success with legacy embedded throughout planning processes. Positive benefits delivered to local communities (social, economic) through event-themed program.	Bell and Gallimore, 2015
		Bellas and Oliver, 2016
		Bloyce and Lovett, 2012
		Bretherton et al., 2016
		Chen and Henry, 2016
		Chen and Misener, 2019
		Christie and Gibb, 2015
		Gilmore, 2014
		Kellett et al., 2008
		Leopkey and Parent, 2017*
		Misener et al., 2015
		O'Brien, 2006
		Pereira et al., 2015
		Rogerson, 2016
		Samuel and Stubbs, 2013
		Sant et al., 2013
		Smith and Fox, 2007
		Werner et al., 2016

Organizational form	General outcomes of organizational form	Authors
Government-directed organizing committees	Questionable commitment to legacy objectives with some evidence of other positive outcomes. Loss of legitimacy, weakened internal capacity, and external support post-event to carry-out further (re)development. Sport infrastructure and education improved, but questionable access for local population. Event assumed as a catalyst for business and networking for long-term economic legacy. Lack of evaluative mechanisms.	Deng et al., 2016
		Jung et al., 2016
		Kaplanidou et al., 2016
		Kristiansen et al., 2016
		Tichaawa and Bob, 2015
		Wang and Theodoraki, 2007
National governing organizations	Disjunction between national agenda and local realities. Modest increase in rugby participation, although quoted by organizers as "not the sole reason" for increased registration. Increases (albeit inconsistent) in sport participation following event, however, local realities suggest that discrepancies exist.	Brown and Pappous, 2018
		Frawley and Cush, 2011
		Hayday et al., 2017
		Pappous and Hayday, 2015
Individual tactics	Mixed positive visitor spending during the event, not sustained. Unintended positive sport development and participation outcomes. Collaboration has the potential for increasing leveraging capacity.	Bek et al., 2019
		Chalip and Leyns, 2002
		Hoskyn et al., 2018
		Schulenkorf et al., 2019
		Taks et al., 2013
		Wood et al., 2018
Non-profit collaborations	Extensive post-event plans put into place with clear responsibilities. Legacies are planned and executed external to OC, while utilizing associated power and networks.	Kaplanidou and Karadakis, 2010
		Leopkey and Parent, 2017*
		Misener et al., 2020
		Williams and Elkhashab, 2012

Note: *Leopkey and Parent (2017) examined two separate events and are featured separately twice itself. As a result, very few legacy partners were openly prepared to claim responsibility for achieving specific legacy objectives. Along this line, Bretherton and colleagues (2016) further found that although multiple agencies within the 2012 OC were attempting to define and plan for the sport and physical activity legacy, how the legacy was to be executed and measured was strongly disputed across stakeholders. Consequently, the pre-Games targets were abandoned and organizers shifted their focus to a young demographic, versus the nationwide benefits originally promised within the bid (Bretherton et al., 2016). In contrast to the unfulfilled physical activity legacy, Samuel and Stubbs (2013) noted that a less popular legacy objective of environmental sustainability was quietly implanted within the planning process for London 2012, resulting in a deeply embedded commitment to the environmental legacy promise. While no specific department or organization was responsible for enacting the legacy, strategies to embed the legacy included full environmental impact assessments within the bid document, as well as the development of compliance policies with key environmental indicators, to ensure minimal carbon footprint surrounding Olympic construction (Samuel and Stubbs, 2013).

In the case of the 2000 Olympic Games, Leopkey and Parent (2017) found that although the multi-agency OC both conceptualized and delivered legacy, there was no formalized legacy strategy, including nothing for crucial post-event legacy plans. This is not surprising given the timing of these Games precedes the IOC's formal adoption of legacy as an outcome. What is interesting about this case is that a government agency, the Olympic Coordination Authority (OCA), took on responsibility for the development and management of the Sydney Olympic Park and Sydney Harbour during the Games. Post-Games, the Sydney Olympic Park Authority (SOPA), which was not clearly linked to the OCA, was created by the state government to develop and manage the former Olympic site for future sports and event use. Leopkey and Parent (2017) demonstrated that without post-event legacy plans formed prior to the Games, the SOPA took almost a decade to develop into its full potential and finally settle on a strategic plan for future use versus the original design of "trying to be everything to everyone" (p. 9). Leopkey and Parent (2017) showed the need for coordinated early planning with such a multi-agency approach if the host region wants a sporting legacy.

At the 2006 Victoria Commonwealth Games (CWG), Kellett et al. (2008) revealed a much different relationship between those conceptualizing legacy and those delivering outcomes. The state government, within the multi-agency OC, set the legacy objectives and parameters for municipalities to design their own strategies involving hosting and welcoming international teams during the Games. However, without sufficient direction and resources supporting the desires of the OC, many local organizers were overwhelmed with the creation and steering of legacy outcomes. As a result, outcomes varied across municipalities, including many that experienced unfulfilled legacies where nothing was done, and no opportunities were created. Kellett et al. (2008) determined that while several municipalities were able to capitalize on the Games, the overall legacy of the 2006 CWG was a spectrum of outcomes inconsistent with the original policy design, resulting in many unfulfilled legacies. Thus, in this case the multi-agency approach did not really work.

Several authors (e.g., Christie and Gibb, 2015; Werner et al., 2016) also discussed a collaborative process surrounding legacy governance. For instance, in the lead up to the 2014 CWG, Christie and Gibb (2015) described the Glasgow Legacy Board as a typical multi-level/agency/actor collaborative created to coordinate the delivery of legacy objectives alongside the OC. While no evaluation of legacy or responsibility of legacy delivery was included, Christie and Gibb (2015) noted that the cross-agency synergies created by the new collaborative processes and mechanisms will serve as a valuable legacy in itself. In another study of legacy delivery of the 2014 CWG, Misener and colleagues (2015) argued the multi-layered policy environment surrounding the 2014 CWG also brought challenges for legacy delivery, with the responsibility of objectives difficult to pinpoint. More specifically, in their examination of disability and inclusion, Misener and colleagues (2015) noted that the integrated OC (including both able-bodied and parasport at CWG) was intended to positively affect planning processes in order to create opportunities for community participation, and positively influence attitudes towards disability. In reality, the lack of clear and precise projects relating to the legacy objectives, particularly those pertaining to accessibility and inclusion, demonstrated the discrepancies existing between the bid requirements at the state level and the social realities of local recipients of legacy outcomes (Misener et al., 2015). Thus, the cases above demonstrate that while a multi-agency approach is most common in terms of the organizational form of event legacy, the research examining these strategies suggests that they may not be particularly successful due to a lack of strategic oversight and intersecting policy priorities.

Hybrid localized organizing committees

Apart from the traditional multi-agency OC, a more localized multi-agency OC has been reported as a common organizational form in legacy delivery, wherein regional or local organizers worked with the OC to play a more prominent role in delivering legacy outcomes (Bell and Gallimore, 2015; Chen and Henry, 2016; Chen and Misener, 2019; Gilmore, 2014; Pereira et al., 2015; Sant et al., 2013; Smith and Fox, 2007). While the OC still conformed to the above hybrid organizational form, legacy initiatives and organizers in this category were more locally involved than the standard OC. For instance, Smith and Fox (2007) analyzed the unique event-themed legacy programming for the 2002 Manchester CWG, where projects were funded across a wide range of community objectives. A more localized, regional multi-agency OC implemented a state-funded competition for legacy projects with extensive monitoring to ensure communities and organizations were delivering the intended outcomes. Smith and Fox (2007) noted that the roles and responsibilities within each project were described in detail in order to receive funding, as well as the appropriate procedures for measurement and evaluation. As a result, numerous benefits were delivered to local communities through documented evidence: jobs created, volunteer organizations supported, disadvantaged populations engaged, etc. (Smith and Fox, 2007).

Also in London, several studies (e.g., Bell and Gallimore, 2015; Chen and Henry, 2016; Chen and Misener, 2019) analyzed regional steering groups from the 2012 Games and their respective policies aimed at increasing physical activity. For instance, Chen and Misener (2019) examined the leveraging strategies of Leicestershire (a non-host region during the 2012 Games), where local authorities and stakeholders had formulated a leveraging group and strategy that spanned across seven objectives of business (i.e., sport and physical activity, health and well-being, children and young people, culture, volunteering, and touristic economy). The dedicated leveraging group was perceived "as being significant in terms of how the quantity and quality of London 2012 related activities delivered in the subregion compared with other subregions" (Chen and Misener, 2019, p. 285). The authors further stated that non-host region event leverage is possible with a dedicated local leveraging group, even in areas with resource or financial scarcity (Chen and Misener, 2019).

Numerous authors (e.g., Bloyce and Lovett, 2012; Bretherton et al., 2016; Gilmore, 2014; Samuel and Stubbs, 2013) further noted how the UK government conceptualized legacy as providing "benefits to communities across the UK" (Bell and Gallimore, 2015, p. 721), while encouraging local communities and/or boroughs to implement localized legacy processes. In the case of the London 2012 Olympic and Paralympic Games, although the process of legacy conceptualization has been top down from the national government from the outset, the London 2012 OC enabled communities to participate in the conceptualization of localized legacy plans, albeit within the parameters of the objectives of the DCMS. The 2012 Games also utilized non-host OCs in the delivery of both cultural and physical activity outcomes to communities. For instance, Gilmore (2014) examined the regional agency that was developed in the north west of London to deliver "cultural programming" (p. 33), as mandated by the state government. The cultural development program was seen as being able to capitalize on social and regenerative outcomes, however, the regional legacy definition was strongly contested amongst stakeholders. As a result, localized legacy plans were "pragmatically hazy" (Gilmore, 2014, p. 37) and did not strategically approach the objectives in question, rendering its direct impact unknown. Thus, the outcomes of planning varied between regions based on their own investment of resources.

Based on the above review, both organizational forms of the hybrid OC demonstrated various mechanisms previously utilized in the delivery of legacy. The increased tension amongst organizers, as well as the unclear definition of legacy and/or objectives, represent the vast number of interests involved in these types of organizations. Within hybrid organizing, these are referred to as competing logics, or the core drivers of the collaboration (Battilana and Lee, 2014). It appears that without localized engagement, there is a distinct lack of responsibility or accountability for legacy delivery within hybrid OCs.

Government-directed organizing committees

Our analysis shows that specific legacy strategies can also be directly controlled by the government, in contrast to prior categories where the state government played a much lesser role in legacy delivery and a greater role in shaping overall sports event delivery. In the form of government-directed OC, private industry also had a much lesser role in the legacy processes, both in conceptualization and delivery. A number of authors (Deng et al., 2016; Jung et al., 2016; Kaplanidou et al., 2016; Kristiansen et al., 2016; Tichaawa and Bob, 2015; Wang and Theodoraki, 2007) have found that government-led or directed OCs have taken responsibility for legacy strategies associated with major games. The planning in this category is described as strict and controlling in undemocratic nations (China, Qatar), and as a tactical strategy for resources in democratic countries (UK, Austria, and Liechtenstein).

In preparation for the 2022 Qatar World Cup, Kaplanidou et al. (2016) examined legacy preparations and objectives designed by the Qatari state government. The 2022 World Cup was the first World Cup awarded to an Arab nation. Hosting the 2022 World Cup provided a great opportunity to demonstrate Qatar's post-oil transformation into a rapidly developing country. The Qatari government thus intended to use the event as a catalyst for business and networking to leave a long-term economic legacy for the country of Qatar and its hosting communities (Kaplanidou et al., 2016). The multi-agency OC, the Supreme Committee for Delivery and Legacy, was created and directed by the Qatari monarchy, alongside various sport, business, and tourism stakeholders (Kaplanidou et al., 2016). Qatar 2022 epitomizes a top-down planning process for legacy, as the national government has conceptualized legacy within the bid document and has the absolute power to execute it as per its own design. While Qatar's legacy is yet to be realized for the upcoming 2022 FIFA World Cup, Kaplanidou et al. (2016) have assumed the event will act as a catalyst for many of the widespread impacts depicted in the bid document, yet there remains a gap in understanding how these will be delivered.

In their examination of the 2008 Beijing Olympics, Wang and Theodoraki (2007) analyzed how the Chinese national government defined and led legacy commitments. Within the bidding document, the centerpiece of the legacy objectives was to increase mass sports participation throughout the Chinese hosting cities (Wang and Theodoraki, 2007). The authors noted that in Quingdao (the city that hosted the Olympic sailing event), the Chinese national government designed the legacy objectives and then mandated local government to further plan and execute various sports participation initiatives. The increased influence of the Chinese Communist Party is further illustrated in the hosting of the 2010 Shanghai Expo, where Deng et al. (2016) described how the Chinese government created the overarching legacy goal of "Better City, Better Life" (p. 167) to revitalize a former industrial area of Shanghai. The bid promised a legacy of urban renewal, and the Chinese government quickly began creating organizations to pursue related legacy outcomes. However, a strong government-led approach of legacy delivery also has its limitations. As noted by Deng and colleagues (2016), once the 2010 Expo was complete, the post-event strategy lost legitimacy due to a lack of continued government support and association.

In another study of the 2010 FIFA World Cup in South Africa, Tichaawa and Bob (2015) examined the African Legacy Programme initiated by organizers, designed to leave a lasting pan-African legacy. This program was the joint responsibility of the South African federal government and the local multi-agency OC, and was conceptualized as a catalyst to spur socio-economic growth and development not just in South Africa but the African continent as a whole (Tichaawa and Bob, 2015). Their findings indicated that the definition of legacy was not well communicated outside of South Africa, and program intentions may have been lost in the many layers of personnel between the OC and local communities, leaving the final legacy unknown (Tichaawa and Bob, 2015).

Our analysis shows that the government-led form may also be adopted in democratic countries as a strategic approach to leverage resources. For instance, in the case of the 2012 London Olympics, it has already been described how the UK governments conceptualized legacy outcomes relating to sport and physical activity early in the planning process. Jung et al. (2016) further examined how the British government implemented physical education (PE) policies to complement legacy objectives. While schools and instructors were ultimately responsible for delivering increased time spent in PE, Jung et al. (2016) asserted that the schools "were [also] urged to take responsibility" (p. 14) in providing increased competitive sporting opportunities for students. After the 2010 election, the Coalition government ceased the increased attention and funding to PE programs, and the resultant legacy from the PE policies remains unknown.

Based on the above review, government-directed OCs demonstrated cohesive attempts at event legacy strategies. The lack of hybridity within these organizational forms decreased the amount of internal conflict and provided ample resources dedicated to legacy strategies. Unfortunately, the opportunities and benefits garnered from these organizational forms faded with the conclusion of the event, changes in government, or a lack of prioritization. Also, researchers identified that benefits to local populations were questionable with a lack of cooperative effort and few evaluative mechanisms within event strategies. Without definitive evaluative or sustainable mechanisms in place, impacts will be unrealized or unequally distributed amongst community members.

National governing organizations

Our findings show that national governing bodies (NGBs) for sport were also held responsible for delivering legacy outcomes. Several studies revealed the important role of national sport organizations (NSOs) in executing legacy strategies (Frawley and Cush, 2011; Hayday et al., 2017; Pappous and Hayday, 2015). For instance, in the case of the 2003 Australian Rugby World Cup, Frawley and Cush (2011) reported that the rugby NSO articulated a sport participation legacy, but assumed a trickle-down flow of players. While the authors observed a modest increase in junior men rugby participation post-event, it was quoted by organizers as not the sole reason for increased registration. No leveraging strategies were utilized, but educational rugby programs in place since the 1990s were suspected to have played a role in increasing participation (Frawley and Cush, 2011). Senior managers referred to the continued investment into their rugby development programming and highlighted its importance in increasing long-term participation (Frawley and Cush, 2011).

More recently at the 2012 London Olympics, the DCMS set mechanisms for NSOs to receive funding based on models of increasing sport participation (Hayday et al., 2017; Pappous and Hayday, 2015). These NSOs, or NGBs, were delegated with the responsibility of creating participatory strategies (Hayday et al., 2017). However, these strategies were not aligned with those of the local clubs that were responsible for executing the national strategies to their communities. This further resulted in increased competition between clubs and sports organizations. No evidence of increased participation was noted (Hayday et al., 2017). In another study, Brown and Pappous (2018) furthered that the unfulfilled participation legacy, particularly for those with a physical disability, was due to the NGB's previously mentioned lack of knowledge and capacity, and a temporal conflict with the OC. As the OC and DCMS administered legacy from the top down, organizers focused increasingly on participatory numbers versus creating sustainable structures for participation (Brown and Pappous, 2018).

In contrast, under the same NGB model, Pappous and Hayday (2015) found small increases in grassroots sports participation, albeit inconsistent across sports. Further, the authors asserted that discrepancies were noted between qualitative and quantitative data at the local and national levels, and one sport experienced much lower participation numbers in the years preceding the Games (Pappous and Hayday, 2015). These studies, as well as the work of Frawley and Cush (2011) suggested that there is a detachment between the NGB's funding strategy and the local realities of clubs and communities. This, in turn, prevented these local clubs from effectively delivering legacy strategies.

NSOs/NGBs are a critical component of Australian, Canadian, and UK sport infrastructure delivering both grassroots and high performance sports programming (Hayday et al., 2017). The reliance on NSOs to deliver event legacy objectives is further complicated by the top-down creation of objectives, wherein those targets may not be compatible with both the NSO and its member organizations. Also, the lack of organizational mechanisms for local sports organizations to collaborate with either NSO or OC contributed to increased confusion and conflict. While internal conflict was lessened due to the lack of hybridity, the logics of localized sport organizations was in direct conflict with the NSO and the OC. These competing logics were also prevalent between local sports organizers and the OC, as the OC was focused on the temporal, event-hosting timeline, whereas sports organizers were concerned about sustaining or growing participation in the long term.

Individual tactics/entrepreneurial organizational form

Scholars have also discussed legacy outcomes as realized or delivered through individual tactics (Bek et al., 2019; Chalip and Leyns, 2002; Hoskyn et al., 2018; Schulenkorf et al., 2019; Taks et al., 2013; Wood et al., 2018). While these outcomes may be regarded as a legacy of the event by organizers, it is problematic to assume that the function of event leveraging is to produce a legacy. Leveraging strategies must be created and produced separately on a distinct timeline from the event. In this way, this organizational form is regarded as more of individual entrepreneurial efforts to leverage the events for various outcomes.

In a study of the 1999 Gold Coast Honda Indy, Chalip and Leyns (2002) examined how local businesses attempted to leverage the event for economic stimulation. Unfortunately, the authors reported that the businesses were poorly coordinated in their attempt to produce sustainable outcomes, visitor spending was not sustained post-event, and many potentials for leveraging were left largely unrealized (Chalip and Leyns, 2002). While the responsibility of executing strategies was left to inexperienced business owners, local organizations did not establish an external coordinating body to focus on leveraging strategies, and preferred to execute individual tactics (Chalip and Leyns, 2002).

In another study of a sports facility legacy project during the 2010 FIFA World Cup, Bek and colleagues (2019) investigated how a local organizer and business owner in Gansbaai (a disadvantaged, remote non-host region in the Western Cape) developed a multi-purpose sports facility for the residents in the Gansbaai region, using the 2010 World Cup to garner attention and traction with locals. International funding and government alignment were possible through the individual organizer's strong business ties, "strong management, good governance and effective networking" (Bek et al., 2019, p. 450). The project has ensured long-term viability through funding linked to broader sport non-governmental organizations, and municipal responsibility for facility maintenance (Bek et al., 2019).

In addition to larger-scale events, individual entrepreneurial efforts were seen in several cases of event leverage of medium- to smaller-scale events. For instance, Wood and colleagues (2018) examined the leveraging tactics utilized by 16 local restaurants during three medium-sized multi-sport events over the course of two summers. The authors found that the majority of restaurants did not engage in leveraging opportunities due to a lack of belief in leverageable benefits, inconvenient event proximity, and a lack of preparedness (Wood et al., 2018). In particular, the majority of restaurant owners said that a lack of belief in benefits from leveraging was largely shaped by the lack of trust in city officials' claims of promised impacts. The local tourism organization was also constrained in its actions and ability to assist local businesses due to limited local engagement and insufficient resources (Wood et al., 2018). Wood and colleagues (2018) concluded that if leveraging local benefits from events hosting is important for local organizers, leadership from a supporting agency is necessary, and local businesses need "prioritized attention ... shared financial and human resources and information" (p. 47). Local businesses, including touristic organizations and municipal offices, require additional knowledge and resources to understand leveraging strategies and tactics to accrue beneficial event impacts.

Similarly, Hoskyn et al. (2018) looked at the sport participation leveraging strategy by local clubs from two medium-sized events from the World Tennis Association tour. Organizers offered free lessons to event attendees, in the hope of converting spectators into club members. Although less than 10 percent of spectators showed interest in the potential opportunity, and at most four clubs "recruited at least one new member from the initiative ... [t]here was optimism that others would join for the following season" (Hoskyn et al., 2018, p. 207). The authors demonstrated that the collaborative capacity of the local clubs has the potential to overcome the aforementioned "capacity or resource-related challenges" (Hoskyn et al., 2018, p. 210), and may contribute to assisting local sports organizers with leveraging strategies.

Schulenkorf and colleagues (2019) further examined a smaller-sized event in Greece, the Spetses Mini Marathon (SMM), where a private communication and public relations company staged an annual, non-elite, mass participation event in conjunction with the local community. The authors determined that the participatory community model surrounding the SMM's strategy enabled for successful leverage of social, cultural, economic, and sports participation outcomes for the local community. While local organizers do not always have the capacity for successful leverage of events, the smaller-scale nature of events such as the SMM offers opportunities and possibilities that a large-scale event cannot afford. The authors argued that "the small-scale nature of the event was an important factor for the successful generation of community benefits ... as the close engagement between the change agent and the local community resulted in a common vision, trustworthy networks, and reciprocal support" (Schulenkorf et al., 2019, p. 515). The smaller-scale nature of this event was found to be beneficial for delivering more localized impacts and meaningful community engagement.

The evidence offered by this organizational form (or lack thereof) echoes previous research that event impacts do not occur by mere happenstance (Misener et al., 2015; O'Brien, 2007; O'Brien and Chalip, 2007). Local organizers lack the knowledge and resources to be able to successfully leverage positive impacts from an event. Without hybridity within the local organizations, there is a distinct lack of expertise with regards to leveraging strategies. Hybrid structures enable collaboration and a sharing of expertise, knowledge, structure, and programs (Babiak and Thibault, 2009), which would assist local organizers in better leveraging events.

Non-profit organizational collaboration

The last organizational form describes the not-for-profit collaborations created apart from the OC to deliver legacy. This applies to several cases, including the Vancouver 2010 organization LegaciesNow (formerly 2010 LegaciesNow) (Kaplanidou and Karadakis, 2010; Leopkey and Parent, 2017), the collaborative body the 2010 Tourism Consortium (Williams and Elkhashab, 2012), and the Ontario Parasport Collective Group (OPLG) for the 2015 Pan/Parapan American Games (Misener et al., 2020). These not-for-profit collaborative groups were developed external to the OC, while utilizing their associated power and networks, in order to develop legacy strategies and deliver localized objectives. For instance, as noted by Leopkey and Parent (2017), while the Vancouver OC would be responsible for the main planning and staging of the Games, legacies now focused specifically on delivering outcomes to a myriad of groups, organizations, and communities across British Columbia.

In the case of the 2010 Vancouver Olympics, Williams and Elkashab (2012) examined another non-profit collaboration between local tourism organizations, the 2010 Tourism Consortium. Within their case study, the authors found that the Consortium was positioned amongst members as an intervention amongst "the traditional Games planning and delivery process" (Williams and Elkhashab, 2012, p. 328). The collaborators shared resources, personnel, and strategies to cross-leverage the Games in a more meaningful way than any individual organization could. As a result, the Consortium leveraged a range of benefits, particularly social capital, afforded using the "once-in-a-lifetime -opportunity" of Vancouver 2010.

In a more recent study of the 2015 Pan American Games, Misener et al. (2020) provided an in-depth analysis of collaborative formation and dynamics of an event leverage collective group, the OPLG, composed of a group of individuals and organizations representing diverse interests (e.g., high performance, grassroots programming, coaching) and across different sectors (e.g., sport, parasport, communities, university, government). In particular, their studies revealed how a combination of broader institutional environmental conditions (e.g., changes in cultural norms around collaboration, resource deficiency, and window of collaborative opportunities) and essential drivers (e.g., strategic leadership, consequential incentives) together influenced the formation of this broad-based cross-sector collaborative group. In the process of collaboration, Misener and colleagues (2020) further illustrated how the continued development of the OPLG and its effectiveness in leveraging efforts were shaped by "key domains of collaborative dynamics (i.e., principled engagement, shared motivation, and joint capacity)" (p. 447).

The non-profit collaborative organizational form demonstrated several opportunities within event leveraging strategies. First, the hybridity of the organizations allowed for the sharing of knowledge, expertise, and resources. Second, the long-term focus of the leveraging groups allowed for a sustainable strategy to be developed apart from the Games timeline. As a result, the temporal logic of the organizational form was not in conflict, and organizers could focus on the leveraging strategy and not the competing logic of hosting a successful event.

Directions for future research

From the research synthesis conducted, it is evident that there are many academic discussions occurring regarding event legacy and why it is so important within the event hosting space. And yet among this research, there is a distinct lack of focus on the responsibility for legacy delivery, as well as a lack of exploration into organizational forms and specific mechanisms. Understanding organizational forms/mechanisms by which the outcomes are delivered is essential to understand the resulting strategy (and goal-driven approach). This requires an examination of the level of responsibility and accountability in order to understand who will "take hold" of the outcomes after the event.

This chapter provides insights into what previous scholars have found with regards to organizational forms and event legacies. Specifically, the chapter elucidates the organizational forms used in event legacy delivery and/or leveraging strategies. While all previous organizations utilized a form of hybrid organizing, those using a localized structure or distinct non-profit collaboration had an increased number of event impacts reported as delivered and/or realized. Localized OCs, particularly non-host OCs, may be united by a long-term process view, versus a short-term event-hosting timeline. As a result, the lack of competing logics within the hybrid localized OC provides the opportunity for less conflict and increased goal achievement (Battilana and Lee, 2014). An increasing number of communities are attempting individual tactics to lever event benefits, but without extensive prior planning and collaboration, it is unlikely the impacts will be sustainable. Further, the chapter provides insight into how host communities can consider event leveraging even if they are not attached to or considered part of the event.

This chapter also reveals that the distinction from the OC allowed some collaborative forms to focus increasingly on delivering localized outcomes, while using the network and legitimacy to execute strategies. As per the evidence provided, this is the only organizational form presenting evidence of clear responsibilities, long-term planning, with a commitment to local sustainability within legacy delivery. Without the connection to the OC, the organizational forms were able to focus beyond the hosting of the event and devise strategies embedded within the local context. Future research can further examine the level of responsibility within these forms, and how they are able to both deliver and be held accountable to event outcomes.

References

Andranovich, G., Burbank, M.J., and Heying, C.H. (2001). Olympic cities: Lessons learned from mega-event politics. *Journal of Urban Affairs*, 23(2), 113–131.

Babiak, K., and Thibault, L. (2009). Challenges in multiple cross-sector partnerships. *Nonprofit and Voluntary Sector Quarterly*, 38(1), 117–143.

Battilana, J., and Lee, M. (2014). Advancing research on hybrid organizing: Insights from the study of social enterprises. *Academy of Management Annals*, 8(1), 397–441.

Bek, D., Merendino, A., Swart, K., and Timms, J. (2019). Creating an enduring developmental legacy from FIFA2010: The Football Foundation of South Africa (FFSA). *European Sport Management Quarterly*, 19(4), 437–455.

Bell, B., and Gallimore, K. (2015). Embracing the games? Leverage and legacy of London 2012 Olympics at the sub-regional level by means of strategic partnerships. *Leisure Studies*, 34(6), 720–741.

Bellas, L., and Oliver, R. (2016). Rescaling ambitions: Waterfront governance and Toronto's 2015 Pan American Games. *Journal of Urban Affairs*, 38(5), 676–691.

Bloyce, D., and Lovett, E. (2012). Planning for the London 2012 Olympic and Paralympic legacy: A figurational analysis. *International Journal of Sport Policy and Politics*, 4(3), 361–377.

Bretherton, P., Piggin, J., and Bodet, G. (2016). Olympic sport and physical activity promotion: The rise and fall of the London 2012 pre-event mass participation "legacy". *International Journal of Sport Policy and Politics*, 8(4), 609–624.

Brown, C., and Pappous A. (2018), "The legacy element … It just felt more woolly": Exploring the reasons for the decline in people with disabilities' sport participation in England 5 years after the London 2012 Paralympic Games, *Journal of Sport and Social Issues*, 42(5), 343–368.

Burbank, M., Andranovich, G., and Heying, C.H. (2001). *Olympic dreams: The impact of mega-events on local politics*. Boulder, CO: Lynne Rienner.

Cashman, R. (2006). *The bitter-sweet awakening: The legacy of the Sydney 2000 Olympic Games*. Petersham: Walla Walla Press.

Chalip, L. (2014). From legacy to leverage. In J. Grix (Ed.), *Leveraging legacies from sports mega-events: Concepts and cases* (pp. 1–12). New York: Palgrave Macmillan.

Chalip, L. (2017). Event bidding, legacy, and leverage. In R. Hoye and M.M. Parent (Eds), *The SAGE handbook of sport management* (pp. 401–421). London: SAGE.

Chalip, L., and Leyns, A. (2002). Local business leveraging of a sport event: Managing an event for economic benefit. *Journal of Sport Management*, 16(2), 132–158.

Chappelet, J.L. (2008). Olympic environmental concerns as a legacy of the Winter Games. *International Journal of the History of Sport*, 25(14), 1884–1902.

Chen, S., and Henry, I. (2016). Evaluating the London 2012 Games' impact on sport participation in a non-hosting region: A practical application of realist evaluation. *Leisure Studies*, 35(5), 685–707.

Chen, S., and Misener, L. (2019). Event leveraging in a nonhost region: Challenges and opportunities. *Journal of Sport Management*, 33(4).

Christie, L., and Gibb, K. (2015). A collaborative approach to event-led regeneration: The governance of legacy from the 2014 Commonwealth Games. *Local Economy*, 30(8), 871–887.

Cooper, H. and Hedges, L.V. (2009). Research synthesis as a scientific process. In H. Cooper, L.V. Hedges, and J.C. Valentine (Eds), *The handbook of research synthesis and meta-analysis* (pp. 3–16). New York: Russell Sage Foundation.

Deng, Y., Poon, S.W., and Chan, E.H.W. (2016). Planning mega-event built legacies: A case of Expo 2010. *Habitat International*, 53, 163–177.

Fairley, S., Lovegrove, H., and Brown, M. (2016). Leveraging events to ensure enduring benefits: The legacy strategy of the 2015 AFC Asian Cup. *Sport Management Review*, 19(4), 466–474.

Frawley, S., and Cush, A. (2011). Major sport events and participation legacy: The case of the 2003 Rugby World Cup. *Managing Leisure*, 16(1), 65–76.

Gilmore, A. (2014). Evaluating legacies: Research, evidence and the regional impact of the Cultural Olympiad. *Cultural Trends*, 23(1), 29–41.

Gratton, C., Shibli, S., and Coleman, R. (2005). Sport and economic regeneration in cities. *Urban Studies*, 42(5–6), 985–999.

Grix, J. (2012). The politics of sports mega-events. *Political Insight*, 3(1), 4–7.

Hayday, E.J., Pappous, A., and Koutrou, N. (2017). Leveraging the sport participation legacy of the London 2012 Olympics: Senior managers' perceptions. *International Journal of Sport Policy and Politics*, 9(2), 349–369.

Hoskyn, K., Dickson, G., and Sotiriadou, P. (2018). Leveraging medium-sized sport events to attract club participants. *Marketing Intelligence and Planning*, 36(2), 199–212.

Ingram, P. (1998). Changing the rules: Interests, organizations, and institutional change in the US hospitality industry. In M.C. Brinton and V. Nee (Eds), *The new institutionalism in sociology* (pp. 258–276). Stanford, CA: Stanford University Press.

International Olympic Committee (IOC) (2003). *Olympic charter*. Retrieved from: https://stillmed.olympic.org/Documents/Olympic%20Charter/Olympic_Charter_through_time/2003-Olympic_Charter.pdf

Jung, H., Pope, S., and Kirk, D. (2016). Policy for physical education and school sport in England, 2003–2010: Vested interests and dominant discourses. *Physical Education and Sport Pedagogy, 21*(5), 501–516.

Kaplanidou, K.K., and Karadakis, K. (2010). Understanding the legacies of a host Olympic city: The case of the 2010 Vancouver Olympic Games. *Sport Marketing Quarterly, 19*(2), 110–117.

Kaplanidou, K.K., Al Emadi, A., Sagas, M., Diop, A., and Fritz, G. (2016). Business legacy planning for mega events: The case of the 2022 World Cup in Qatar. *Journal of Business Research, 69*(10), 4103–4111.

Kellett, P., Hede, A.M., and Chalip, L. (2008). Social policy for sport events: Leveraging (relationships with) teams from other nations for community benefit. *European Sport Management Quarterly, 8*(2), 101–121.

Kohe, G.Z., and Bowen-Jones, W. (2016). Rhetoric and realities of London 2012 Olympic education and participation "legacies": Voices from the core and periphery. *Sport, Education and Society, 21*(8), 1213–1229.

Kristiansen, E., Strittmatter, A.M., and Skirstad, B. (2016). Stakeholders, challenges and issues at a co-hosted youth Olympic event: Lessons learned from the European Youth Olympic Festival in 2015. *International Journal of the History of Sport, 33*(10), 1152–1168.

Leopkey, B., and Parent, M.M. (2012). Olympic Games legacy: From general benefits to sustainable long-term legacy. *International Journal of the History of Sport, 29*(6), 924–943.

Leopkey, B., and Parent, M.M. (2017). The governance of Olympic legacy: Process, actors and mechanisms. *Leisure Studies, 36*(3), 438–451.

Liu, Y.D. (2018). Legacy planning and event sustainability: Helsinki as the 2012 World Design Capital. *Sustainability, 10*(7), 2453.

Misener, L., Darcy, S., Legg, D., and Gilbert, K. (2013). Beyond Olympic legacy: Understanding Paralympic legacy through a thematic analysis. *Journal of Sport Management, 27*(4), 329–341.

Misener, L., McGillivray, D., McPherson, G., and Legg, D. (2015). Leveraging parasport events for sustainable community participation: The Glasgow 2014 Commonwealth Games. *Annals of Leisure Research, 18*(4), 450–469.

Misener, L., Lu, L.D., and Carlisi, R. (2020). Leveraging events to develop collaborative partnerships: Examining the formation and collaborative dynamics of the Ontario Parasport Legacy Group. *Journal of Sport Management, 34*(5), 447–461.

O'Brien, D. (2006). Event business leveraging the Sydney 2000 Olympic games. *Annals of Tourism Research, 33*(1), 240–261.

O'Brien, D. (2007). Points of leverage: Maximizing host community benefit from a regional surfing festival. *European Sport Management Quarterly, 7*(2), 141–165.

O'Brien, D., and Chalip, L. (2007). Sport events and strategic leveraging: Pushing towards the triple bottom line. In A.G. Woodside and D. Martin (Eds), *Tourism management: Analysis, behaviour, and strategy* (pp. 318–338). Cambridge, MA: CABI International.

Pappous, A., and Hayday, E. (2015). A case study investigating the impact of the London 2012 Olympic and Paralympic Games on participation in two non-traditional English sports, judo and fencing. *Leisure Studies*, 1–17.

Pereira, E.C., Mascarenhas, M.V., Flores, A.J., and Pires, G.M. (2015). Nautical small-scale sports events portfolio: A strategic leveraging approach. *European Sport Management Quarterly*, 15(1), 27–47.

Phillips, C., and Barnes, M. (2015). Whose legacy is it, anyway? A tale of conflicting agendas in the building of the Hamilton Pan Am Soccer Stadium. *Annals of Leisure Research*, 18(4), 549–568.

Preuss, H. (2015). A framework for identifying the legacies of a mega sport event. *Leisure Studies*, 34(6), 643–664.

Rogerson, R.J. (2016). Re-defining temporal notions of event legacy: Lessons from Glasgow's Commonwealth Games. *Annals of Leisure Research*, 19(4), 497–518.

Samuel, S., and Stubbs, W. (2013). Green Olympics, green legacies? An exploration of the environmental legacies of the Olympic Games. *International Review for the Sociology of Sport*, 48(4), 485–504.

Sant, S.L., and Mason, D.S. (2015). Framing event legacy in a prospective host city: Managing Vancouver's Olympic bid. *Journal of Sport Management*, 29(1), 42–56.

Sant, S.L., Mason, D.S., and Hinch, T.D. (2013). Conceptualising Olympic tourism legacy: Destination marketing organisations and Vancouver 2010. *Journal of Sport and Tourism*, 18(4), 287–312.

Sant, S.L., Misener, L., and Mason, D.S. (2019). Leveraging sport events for tourism gain in host cities: A regime perspective. *Journal of Sport and Tourism*, 23(4), 203–223.

Schulenkorf, N., Giannoulakis, C., and Blom, L. (2019). Sustaining commercial viability and community benefits: Management and leverage of a sport-for-development event. *European Sport Management Quarterly*, 19(4), 502–519.

Smith, A. (2014). "De-risking" East London: Olympic regeneration planning 2000–2012. *European Planning Studies*, 22(9), 1919–1939.

Smith, A., and Fox, T. (2007). From "event-led" to "event-themed" regeneration: The 2002 Commonwealth Games legacy programme. *Urban Studies*, 44(5–6), 1125–1143.

Taks, M., Misener, L., Chalip, L., and Green, B.C. (2013). Leveraging sport events for sport development. *Canadian Journal for Social Research*, 3(1), 12–23.

Thomas, J., Walker, T.W., Miller, S., Cobb, A., and Thomas, S.J. (2016). The Olympic legacy: Journal metrics in sports medicine and dentistry. *Journal of International Society of Preventive and Community Dentistry*, 6(6), 501.

Thomson, A., Schlenker, K., and Schulenkorf, N. (2013). Conceptualizing sport event legacy. *Event Management*, 17(2), 111–122.

Thomson, A., Cuskelly, G., Toohey, K., Kennelly, M., Burton, P., and Fredline, L. (2019). Sport event legacy: A systematic quantitative review of literature. *Sport Management Review*, 22(3), 295–321.

Tichaawa, T.M., and Bob, U. (2015). Leveraging mega-events beyond the host nation: A case study of the 2010 FIFA World Cup African Legacy Programme in Cameroon and Nigeria. *Leisure Studies*, 34(6), 742–757.

Wang, W., and Theodoraki, E. (2007). Mass sport policy development in the Olympic City: The case of Qingdao – host to the 2008 sailing regatta. *Journal of the Royal Society for the Promotion of Health*, 127(3), 125–132.

Weed, M. (2005). Research synthesis in sport management: Dealing with "chaos in the brickyard". *European Sport Management Quarterly*, 5(1), 77–90.

Werner, K., Dickson, G., and Hyde, K.F. (2016). Mega-events and increased collaborative capacity of tourism destinations: The case of the 2011 Rugby World Cup. *Journal of Destination Marketing and Management*, 5(3), 227–238.

Williams, P.W., and Elkhashab, A. (2012). Leveraging tourism social capital: The case of the 2010 Olympic tourism consortium. *International Journal of Event and Festival Management*, 3(3), 317–334.

Wood, L., Snelgrove, R., Legg, J., Taks, M., and Potwarka, L.R. (2018). Perspectives of event leveraging by restaurants and city officials. *International Journal of Event and Festival Management*, 9(1), 34–50.

19. Concluding remarks and event impacts going forward

Kelly Maguire

The purpose of this book was to showcase avenues for event management, event studies and event impacts research. Given the complexity and range of event impacts, this book is directed at students, practitioners and scholars who are interested in events research and concerned with the wide range of contemporary issues facing the events industry (see also Van Niekerk, 2017). This book was inspired by the proliferation of research focusing on evaluating the diverse and complex range of impacts that events have the potential to create and cause in places and on societies around the world (Evans, 2020; Wise and Harris, 2019). The previous 18 chapters present a number of examples and research approaches. This is further exemplified by the case study representations presented in this edited collection, each highlighting the fundamental importance of progressing *A Research Agenda for Event Impacts*.

This book challenges and emphasises the need to rethink future directions for event research. This means drawing on expanding perspectives, in theory and in practice, to show these interlinkages which can help inform policy, planning, development and decision-making across diverse stakeholder groups who contribute to the growth and success of the events industry (Whitford, 2009; Ziakas, 2019). Now, when we think about event impacts, in light of the ever changing and dynamic nature of the industry, events more than ever have the ability to impact significantly on the economic, social and environmental resource bases of host destinations. In recognising the volatile nature of the industry and its capacity to be disrupted significantly by situations both within and beyond the control of organisations, this edited collection has pointed to the importance of understanding, monitoring, measuring and managing event impacts moving forward.

All chapter contributors were encouraged to present event impact-based research across a number of key themes, including, but not limited to, economic impacts, environmental impacts and socio-cultural impacts. The emphasis was to recognise, following their insights, some directions for future research in each respective area discussed in this book. The chapters comprised in this book focus on diverse case studies which draw on wide-ranging perspectives and offer valuable insights and examples from various geographical regions from around the world. All of the contributors involved in this book teach and research in the areas of events, and therefore recognise the importance of contributing to and advancing this research agenda. This edited collection has permitted us to explore how events are utilised by destinations, organisations and communities and offers insights into the impacts often created by different events hosted in various destinations and staged in different geographical settings. We hope that this collection provides readers with different viewpoints towards the evaluation and understanding of event impacts research and, as mentioned previously, we believe that this book can be used as both a key or supplemental reading source in a range of event management or event studies classes, but it is not limited to these programmes as the insights also relate to a range of tourism, social science and management disciplines.

It is evident from this collection that events of various types, sizes and scales are and will continue to be increasingly crucial components to the tourism offering of destinations and communities throughout the world (see also Robertson et al., 2018; Smith, 2012; Spirou, 2011; Wise and Harris, 2017), as people want to feel empowered and embrace the impacts that events create (Rojek, 2013). Within several chapters, the powerful role of events has been confirmed and their reputation as valuable components of tourism industries worldwide is renowned (see also Maguire, 2019). Authors throughout this collection have noted the crucial role of events in place-making, image-branding and as catalysts and drivers of economic and social change and development (see also Richards, 2017). Insights and evidence from a wide range of festivals and events have been discussed in this collection, with each example presented having unique characteristics, benefits and drawbacks for host destinations. As destinations begin to emerge and navigate in the era of Covid-19, the events industry will begin to experience new creativity. Moreover, the need to assess and evaluate technological innovations will continue to be at the forefront of event planning and operations. It is also anticipated that the industry will experience greater impacts – both positive and negative – and as such, the need for event practitioners and policy makers to better prepare for, plan for and manage events is essential. More specifically, a focus on creating event legacies and transitioning towards greater levels of event sustainability and continuously monitoring, measuring and benchmarking impacts moving forward is critical and cannot be underestimated (see Grix et al., 2017).

The structure of this book has been divided into three parts to ensure an ease of understanding as contributors address impacts from broader insights to more narrowed and focused examples. Following the introduction by Nicholas Wise, Part I, *Assessing event impacts*, includes three chapters focusing on the theory and concepts that relate to the triple bottom line of sustainability, with a chapter dedicated to the economic (Larry Dwyer), the environmental (Kelly Maguire) and the social (Nicholas Wise et al.) impacts of events. Part II, *Research themes and case examples*, includes 12 chapters, each showcasing a diverse range of research themes, topics and issues. Each chapter presents examples of different events in different settings in different geographical locations, to show more holistically how event impacts are evaluated across economic, environmental and social impacts. Part III, *Going forward*, presents three chapters (including this Conclusion) to provide food for thought as we move forward with event impacts research. The purpose of this final section is to point to directions concerning policy, legacy and sustainability, stipulating the need for continued assessment and benchmarking so that event impacts are not descriptively overviewed, but instead are critically evaluated and understood by different stakeholders.

Looking back at *Research themes and case examples*, for consistency we asked contributors to structure their chapters in a way that begins by introducing a research area by reviewing existing work and conceptual directions concerning the specific area of research. Authors then presented a case example to show and discuss their work, and to end each chapter each contributor includes a brief discussion of directions for future research. This emphasis on future work in each chapter allows the authors to frame and position both theoretical and practical avenues that need consideration moving forward. A review of the content of each contribution is now presented according to some key themes that appeared throughout this co-edited collection. Each of the key themes that have emerged in the chapters is closely related to the economic, environmental and social impacts of events and offer beneficial perspectives on various different types of events. By painting a picture of this collection and by understanding the content of each chapter and its key themes, valuable insights can be drawn and useful examples highlighted with regard to broad-based event impacts research.

Larry Dwyer (Chapter 2) confirms the value of special events to host destinations and has provided critical theoretical insights into the first pillar of the triple bottom line – the economic impacts of events. Building on his recent work (see Dwyer, 2019), Dwyer touches on the use of events by governments and has presented approaches to the economic evaluation of special events including economic impact analysis, computable general equilibrium modelling and cost–benefit analysis. Dwyer advocates the need to measure and manage economic event impacts and has drawn on the Melbourne Grand Prix as an example within his chapter. Building on the insights from Chapter 2, the link between the use of events by governments is also carried through in Kelly Maguire's chapter (Chapter 3). Maguire notes the economic and social value of events but provides a critical insight into the environmental impacts of events and the need to transition towards greater levels of environmental event sustainability. Maguire draws attention to five adaptable approaches that may potentially aid the transition towards greater levels of sustainability in the process of planning for environmental impacts of events, something advocated for in previous research (Maguire, 2019, 2020). The link to the third pillar of the triple bottom line is evident in Chapter 4 where authors Nicholas Wise, Susanne Gellweiler and Enqing Tian offer insight into the social value and social impacts of events to host destinations and communities. This chapter has provided valued perspectives in relation to the social conditions in social impact research previously put forward by Wise (2019), and builds on this as a guiding framework for exploring, evaluating and assessing social impacts in communities.

The research themes begin with a focus on places and conventions as highlighted by Jeeyeon Jeannie Hahm in Chapter 5. Here, Hahm has identified the benefits of hosting conventions and outlined how periods of crisis have impacted the sector. To provide context, Hahm provides insight from Orlando and discusses specifically the Orange County Convention Center. Drawing upon theory and concepts in relation to sports tourism and event impacts, Marko Perić, Jelena Đurkin Badurina and Nicholas Wise (Chapter 6) explore the Risnjak Trail running events in Gorski kotar, Croatia as an example of how sports tourism can be developed to expand event opportunities and experiences. In this chapter Perić et al. expand on existing research to outline how the use of events by destinations and communities can extend the impact of tourism and create new sporting activities in a destination.

Flávia Ulian and Angela Fileno (Chapter 7) offer insights on religious events and commercialisation. Ulian and Fileno focus on the Lavagem do Bonfim, a religious festival, which is an event that has been deeply embedded in culture since the nineteenth century in Salvador, the capital city of Bahia, Brazil. The authors have provided a number of critical directions on aspects of culture, heritage and pilgrimage and have explored how religious events have the capacity to create wider social and cultural impacts to host destinations using this case focus to demonstrate such impacts. Takamitsu Jimura's research (Chapter 8) signifies how events can be based on intangible cultural heritage. Jimura considers both social and economic impacts, and points to the need to focus on environmental sustainability as well while identifying research directions on the impact of heritage. Jimura utilises the UNESCO principles to guide the importance of research, by first focusing on the intangible cultural heritage convention before moving to present his case focus of fireworks (*hanabi*) and fireworks displays (*hanabi-taikai*) in Japan which have been a tradition and form of cultural entertainment in the country since the seventeenth century.

Jada Lindblom (Chapter 9) offers conceptual directions and perspectives on transformational atmospheres in the context of an international sporting event. Lindblom presents findings from the Red Bull Cliff Diving World Series, a popular event hosted in the city of Mostar, Bosnia and Herzegovina. In this research, the emphasis is placed on co-production which Lindblom notes can enhance the experiences of those attending and participating in events. Lindblom has considered a range of community impacts here and has put forward insights from a resident survey and interviews with those attending the event to paint a rather comprehensive insight into the topic. Lucia Aquilino (Chapter 10) focuses on events in remote areas and considers how such events contribute to social development to provide perspective on how events contribute to new community identities, which are embraced and contested. Aquilino focuses on the case of the World Alternative Games, an event that takes place in Britain's smallest town, Llanwrtyd Wells, Wales. Aquilino provides a critical overview of how events as human experiences and social practices boost social development in rural communities. Kelly Maguire's case study focus (Chapter 11) highlights how Local Authorities play an important role when it comes to planning and implementing events. Maguire outlines the need for Local Authorities to work closely with host communities to ensure that events are socially, economically and environmentally sustainable. Insights from Ireland are offered here and directions that aim to shape future national and local planning procedures and policies are outlined so as to ensure that positive impacts are maximised and negative impacts minimised. Through advocating for greater efforts being made towards event sustainability, Maguire believes that progress can be made to secure future long-term sustainable and competitive event industries.

Geographical insights building on theoretical perspectives of space and place are put forward by Waldemar Cudny (Chapter 12), assessing the role that events play in creating place brands of specific locations and focusing on the case of Euro 2012 in the city of Gdańsk, Poland. Cudny considers the impact of events on place branding and has presented insight into media messages (focusing on image spaces) and event experiences and how such dimensions may contribute to an impression of a place. An emphasis on event hosting in emerging economy nations, with specific emphasis on the BRICS (Brazil, Russia, India, China and South Africa) countries, is presented by Tara Fitzgerald and Brij Maharaj (Chapter 13). Fitzgerald and Maharaj provide an overview and insight into mega-event hosts in BRICS nations and offer some critical perspectives around different political structures while looking at issues that often emerge during the bidding process and at the time of hosting events.

Drawing on the recent impacts of Covid-19 in the events industry, Alexander Bond, Daniel Parnell and Jan Andre Lee Ludvigsen (Chapter 14) reflect on the current state of events directly impacted by the Covid-19 pandemic. In light of the significant impacts created by Covid-19 to the events industry in terms of event cancellations, postponements and adaptations, Bond et al. highlight the need for flexibility in light of challenges and issues organisations face when it comes to financial commitments, securing investments and logistical issues surrounding planning and organising. To explore these insights, Bond et al. look at the impacts of the postponement of UEFA Euro 2020. Erin Pearson and Laura Misener (Chapter 15) focus on disability, access and inclusion and focus on the example of parasport events and the growth of these events, where there are a number of tensions surrounding access and inclusion. Pearson and Misener view these concepts in the context of social legacies. The example referred to in this chapter is the Ontario Parasport Legacy Group and the 2015 Pan/Parapan American Games. Pearson and Misener address the approaches, strategies and challenges that emerged, and point to a number of informed recommendations going forward. Judith Mair (Chapter 16) discusses climate change which is an increased cause for concern in both the tourism and events industries. Mair presents different types of events most affected by different climate change impacts, which is having negative implications on economies and societies. Mair offers critical insights into this contemporary topic and highlights the need for resilience, mitigation and adaptation. Moreover, Mair points to a number of critical research directions and addresses links across policy and practice by pointing to important policy and stakeholder implications.

In the final three chapters illustrated in the book (which includes this Conclusion), some critical directions moving forward with event impact research are presented. Chapters 17 and 18 place attention on legacy and policy. Rafaela Neiva Ganga (Chapter 17) focuses on event policy and evaluations by providing insights on how legacy is maximised through event evaluation. Ganga's arguments in this chapter highlight the need to address a wide range of event impacts like many other contributors. Ganga presents insights from evaluations of cultural events and the impact of hosting these events in Liverpool. Next, Kylie Wasser, Landy Di Lu and Laura Misener (Chapter 18) present concepts of legacy and long-lasting impacts through the topic of sports event development and governance perspectives. Directions for moving forward have been written with stakeholders in mind so as to maximise future long-term impacts and opportunities for collaboration.

To conclude, a number of perspectives and examples across different types of events have been presented. A number of key themes have emerged in this edited collection illustrating the relationship between events and the economic, social and environmental resource base of host destinations and communities. The benefits and disadvantages of events have also come to the forefront of this research agenda for event impacts. This collection testifies events as a valuable driver for tourism development, place change and economic and social development worldwide, which is evident through many of the chapters presented in this collection. The strategic use of events by policy makers and industry organisations and the research focus placed on events by academics and scholars is immense, making it a valuable sector of concentration and an important sector in which to advance research and knowledge. As such, it is vital for us to continuously monitor, measure, evaluate and manage event impacts so that policy makers and practitioners can work to ensure events serve as a catalyst for long-term improvement in the economic, physical, social and environmental state of an area where people live, work, invest and visit. This has been well discussed in this collection and the need to transition towards greater levels of sustainability and work towards creating event legacies is evident. The safeguarding of positive event outcomes and the mitigation or minimisation of negative outputs of events has been placed centre stage. Authors have reflected upon the points being made within their chapters and have identified new ideas with which to take such research forward given the holistic research avenues in events management and event impact studies.

Future research must continue to compare and contrast the opinions of local residents, practitioners, policy makers and event attendees towards event impacts in order to identify any important gaps amongst them, as insight on different impacts from multi-stakeholder perspectives is important if a holistic understanding of event impacts is to be achieved. It is suggested that research by way of longitudinal analysis that looks across economic, environmental and social impacts of events in various destinations over prolonged periods of time enables planners, developers and hosting organisations to benchmark success and improve procedures as a result of lessons learned. Research studies that examine the planning mechanisms and procedures in place to facilitate and implement events permit researchers to seek the views of various stakeholder groups and examine how possible perceptions may have changed over time. The continuation of such research also allows us to expand and advance on the already broad and diverse perspectives and examples of event impacts research which is essential to enhancing future knowledge and understanding of the complex and changing phenomenon that is events.

References

Dwyer, L. (2019), Economic assessment of special events: A perspective article, *Tourism Review* 75(1), 191–193.

Evans, G. (ed.) (2020), *Mega-Events: Placemaking, Regeneration and City-Regional Development*, Routledge, London.

Grix, J., Brannagan, P.M., Wood, H. and Wynne, C. (2017), State strategies for leveraging sports mega-events: Unpacking the concept of 'legacy', *International Journal of Sport Policy and Politics* 9(2), 203–218.

Maguire, K. (2019), Examining the power role of Local Authorities in planning for socio-economic event impacts, *Local Economy* 34(7), 657–679.

Maguire, K. (2020), An examination of the level of local authority sustainable planning for event management: A case study of Ireland, *Journal of Sustainable Tourism*, https://doi.org/10.1080/09669582.2020.1828431.

Richards, G. (2017), From place branding to placemaking: The role of events, *International Journal of Event and Festival Management* 8(1), 8–23.

Robertson, M., Ong, F., Lockstone-Binney, L. and Ali-Knight, J. (2018), Critical event studies: Issues and perspectives, *Event Management* 22, 865–874.

Rojek, C. (2013), *Event Power: How Global Events Manage and Manipulate*, SAGE, London.

Smith, A. (2012), *Events and Urban Regeneration: The Strategic Use of Events to Revitalise Cities*, Routledge, London.

Spirou, C. (2011), *Urban Tourism and Urban Change*, Routledge, London.

Van Niekerk, M. (2017), Contemporary issues in events, festivals and destination management, *International Journal of Contemporary Hospitality Management* 29(3), 842–847.

Whitford, M. (2009), A framework for the development of event public policy: Facilitating regional development, *Tourism Management* 30(5), 674–682.

Wise, N. (2019), Towards a more enabling representation: Framing an emergent conceptual approach to measure social conditions following mega-event transformation in Manaus, Brazil, *Bulletin of Latin American Research* 38(3), 300–316.

Wise, N. and Harris, J. (eds) (2017), *Sport, Events, Tourism and Regeneration*, Routledge, London.

Wise, N. and Harris, J. (eds) (2019), *Events, Places and Societies*, Routledge, London.

Ziakas, V. (2019), Issues, patterns and strategies in the development of event portfolios: Configuring models, design and policy, *Journal of Policy Research in Tourism, Leisure and Events* 11(9), 121–158.

Index